1

Creative Writing in the Real World:
A Reader for Writers

By Shawn Kerivan

Published by: Summerfield Publishing
New Plains Press
PO Box 1946
Auburn, AL 36831-1946
Newplainspress.com

The text of this book is composed in Helvetica.

Much of this volume is fiction and so must be accepted as such, meaning
any mention of places, peoples, things, or ideas that seem related to real
life places, peoples, things, or ideas are actually fictional in nature, and
coincidental to the writing of the stories.

I dedicate this
To the Roundtable Writers
For love and support

Acknowledgements

Excerpt from THE COMPLETE STORIES by Flannery O'Connor, Copyright © 1971 by the Estate of Mary Flannery O'Connor. Reprinted by permission of Farrar, Strauss and Giroux, LLC.

Excerpt from "The Nature and Aim of Fiction" from MYSTERY AND MANNERS by Flannery O'Connor, edited by Sally and Robert Fitzgerald. Copyright © 1969 by the Estate of Mary Flannery O'Connor. Reprinted by per- mission of Farrar, Strauss and Giroux, LLC.

Excerpts from THE FOURTH HAND by John Irving, Copyright © 1992, and THE DEEP AND OTHER STORIES by Mary Swan, Copyright © 2003, used by permission of Random House, Inc.

Excerpts from THE RIGHT TO WRITE by Julie Cameron, Copyright © 1998 by Jeremy P. Tarcher, and THE PORTABLE CHEKHOV edited by Avrahm Yrmolinsky, Copyright © 1977 by Penguin, used by permission of Penguin Group (USA), Inc.

Excerpt from BLOOD LINES by David Quammen, Copyright © 1988 by Graywolf Press, used by permission of Graywolf Press. Excerpt from FATHERS AND SONS BY IVAN TURGENEV edited and translated by Ralph E. Matlaw, Copyright © 1989 by W.W. Norton and Company, used by permission of W.W. Norton and Company.

Lines from "Bless Me, Father," "The Captain," and "A Father's Story" from THE TIMES ARE NEVER SO BAD by Andre Dubus reprinted by permission of David R. Godine, Publisher, Inc. Copyright © 1983 by Andre Dubus.

Excerpt from JOHN IRVING: A CRITICAL COMPANION by Josie P. Campbell Copyright © 1998 by Greenwood Press. Reproduced with permission of ABC-CLIO, Santa Barbara, CA.

Creative Writing in the Real World:
A Reader for Writers

Table of Contents

Part Two: Critical Writing

Part Three: Creative Nonfiction

Writing and Innkeeping and Business and Blogs

Foreword

Often writers are described by the genre in which they write or the vocation they choose to make ends meet: a fiction writer, a poet, a journalist, a writing professor. But what of us who are all of these and more, who find pleasure in various ways of expressing ourselves, in the process of expression itself?

Shawn Kerivan's collection *Creative Writing in the Real World* offers a glimpse into the world of a writer who refuses to be defined, but rather considers the role of "writer" to be definition enough. Kerivan's collection explores not just the end products of creativity but also the process of it. He boldly shows the rough corners of his works-in-progress, his eventual understanding of different genres, and formation into what we can, indeed, consider a true creative writer: a person who writes, no matter what situation presents itself.

From his short stories to thoughtful literary criticism, Shawn offers here a glimpse of the true creative process—the formation of under-standing, the consideration of communicating in several forms, and the practical life he leads alongside his creative self. Shawn challenges us to reconsider what is truly creative.

Danita Berg

MFA, Goddard College, 2007
Ph.D in Composition and Rhetoric, University of South Florida, 2010
Director of the Red Earth MFA in Creative Writing Program, Assistant Professor of Writing, Oklahoma City University

An Introduction to the Reality of Writing

I thought to myself, "What next?"

It's that moment of terror every writer dreads. One project is finished, and it's time to decide what to write next: An award-winning screenplay? A short story for a national magazine? The Great American Novel? So many choices. But then I realized that I'm never really between projects. I've always got something going on: blogs, short stories, columns, even novels. That diversity helps keep things fresh, if only in my mind.

The product of that industry is collected here, and it happened the way most things happen: by accident. In the spring of 2008, my friend Max gave me a book to read called *Slumgullion Stew: An Edward Abbey Reader*. The book is a collection of Cactus Ed's writings, and after I read the first paragraph of his introduction to the book, I knew what my next book would look like. Over the years I'd accumulated a staggering amount of writing across almost every discipline. Why not collect it into a cohesive and comprehensive volume that can be used both recreationally and professionally?

This isn't a book of musings on writing, such as Stephen King's *On Writing*, or Ray Bradbury's *Zen and the Art of Writing*. It's actually closer to John Irving's *Trying to Save Piggy Sneed*, which has been erroneously categorized as a memoir. That book could actually be called a *John Irving Reader*, because it's full of fiction (all the short stories he ever wrote) and essays, as well as memoir. But it also contains the author's reflections on the writing and the circumstances surrounding the creation of the pieces. That's what makes it different.

I've taken a similar approach in this book. And I've tried to keep the reader—or potential readers—in mind when assembling the pieces. One of the techniques I teach students for beginning an essay is to start with a story: Relate a short, relevant anecdote that introduces the reader to the subject of the writing. From there the discussion quickly moves to the reader, and his or her needs. That there exists a reader, and that the reader has needs, is usually a touchstone moment in the teaching of composition. Most writers are horrified to discover that there is actually someone out there who will eventually read what they are writing. Moreover, they're repulsed by the knowledge that these unknown readers have needs. When it's suggested that the needs of these readers be kept in mind, many writers go over the edge, twitching and drooling into the loony bin.

What's so shocking about the relationship between reader and writer? I think it comes down to the thinking that most people who write would hold something back if they thought their words would ever make it into print. There's some kind of mechanism in humans that arrests the truth in creativity if such a situation occurs. There's a feeling in us that we'll upset the natural or man-made order of things if our true feelings are allowed into the public domain. Yet it's that truth that makes writing good. It's the honesty within the writing that elevates the craft into a memorable and important place.

The quest for this honesty—this truth—characterizes much of the writing in this volume. No matter what the format—newspaper columns, short stories, blogs—I've been trying to render the world into accessible, true form. The closest I've come to hearing this goal articulated was by Ernest Hemingway, from an interview in The New York Times in 1954:

I was trying to write then and I found the greatest difficulty, aside from knowing truly what you really felt rather than what you were supposed to feel, was to put down what really happened in action, what the actual things were which produced the emotion that you experienced. The real thing, the sequence of motion and fact which made the emotion and which would be as valid in a year or in ten years or, with luck and if you stated it purely enough, always, was beyond me and I was working very hard to try to get it.[1]

When I read that, I understood why he wrote about bullfighting and shooting rhinos and fishing and the complex relationships of the people who did those things. Hemingway is talking about the senses, which is how humans interpret the world. Think about it: everything you have, everything you know, is based on your interpretation of one or a combination of your senses. You see things, you hear things, you smell things, you taste things, you touch things—that's the way you live and grow and learn. All the thoughts and feelings inside you, all the intangible stuff, it all came through your senses. Even instinct is learned behavior.

Describing the things that come through the senses sounds like it should be easy. If you were asked to describe the smell of a lilac bush, what would you say? It smells like…what? Whatever you say, whatever words you use to describe the lilac bush will come with their own context, and that context will vary from reader to reader. You might say that the lilac bush smells "light and sweet, and it tickles the edge of the nose, but not in an unpleasant way." Or you might say, "it smells like lavender." Both are right. Both display the diversity of interpretation, and that's just on the writer's side. Throw the reader into the equation and things begin to multiply. Flannery O'Connor, in her excellent and inspirational book *Mystery and Manners*, said "[t]he beginning of human knowledge is through the senses, and the fiction writer begins where human perception begins."[2]

Whether I'm trying to render my experience as an innkeeper, or explore corners of human emotion through fiction, the goal remains the same: find a way to allow the reader into something true. The examples of that effort in this book are replete with reflective moments that can be enjoyed as simple reading pieces, or used as teaching tools. Dig into them and discover the writing you need, not just the writing you think you want.

Shawn Kerivan
Stowe, Vermont

Part One:
Fiction

Introduction to Stories from *You're Entitled to the Meat*

Preface: You're entitled to the truth

You're Entitled to the Meat is a collection of short stories from the early part of my writing career. It's no mistake that I call *You're Entitled to the Meat* a collection of short stories, and not a short story collection. There's a difference.

Many short story collections are nothing more than samplers, the collected published works of the author. The way you can tell is by opening the inside cover of the book, turning to the title page, and looking at the bottom for a list of the stories that appeared first in periodicals. Most of the best-known short fiction writers of the 20th and 21st century produce volumes of work collected together like this. This may come as a surprise for the reader who gazed thoughtfully at the title of a volume of short stories and imagined a theme running through them. Often there is nothing more unifying in the collection than the author's tone, or the fact that the stories feature an endless supply of characters brooding in New York City apartments about whether their feelings have changed or not. I loathe this kind of writing. While I respect the level of craft dis-played by the authors, collections of this ilk feel pre-masticated to me. Everybody on the planet has had a chance to read the stories by the time they're placed in an exoskeleton volume, and they feel tired and used, cobbled together with scraps of leather and bent nails.

There's another level of short story collections, and that's the collection featuring previously published stories that do display a unifying theme. Two examples of this are *Heart Songs*, by Annie Proulx, and *The Times Are Never So Bad*, by Andre Dubus. Proulx's stories—besides being featured previously in paragons of modern short fiction publishing such as Esquire, The Atlantic, and Ploughshares—all deal with the hard-scrabble lives of dirt poor New Englanders. I've never had the chance to ask Ms. Proulx if she planned this. I suspect the stories were the result of a period in her life, and they coalesced as she published them in various periodicals. This is borne out by two later collections of stories from her set in Wyoming: *Close Range* and *Bad Dirt*.

The theme running through Andre Dubus's *The Times Are Never So Bad* is perhaps more subtle. Its stories deal with familial relationships in all their glorious and grotesque forms. Specifically, Dubus centers his writing around the point of view of fathers, and he does something the authors of other collections don't do: he places his stories in an order that is orchestral in arrangement, arranging the stories for maximum effect, so that the collection builds to a crescendo, with the final note fading away like the last piano chord in The Beatles' "A Day in the Life."

Which brings us back to *You're Entitled to the Meat*. Most of the stories in this collection (which can be found in its entirety on my website, www.shawnkerivan.com) were written when I lived in the Alsace region of France. It was a time of exploration and development for me, of days spent cycling through the vineyards at the foot of the Vosges Mountains, and of intense amounts of writing. Like other artists, I believe that the early twenties to the early thirties are an artist's most productive years. You may write better later in life, but you'll never write as much.

And so many of the stories in the collection appeared in magazines and literary journals, the fruits of my first essay at becoming a published writer. I decided to include none of the previously published stories in this sample of *You're Entitled to the Meat*. Those stories have had their shot, and now it's time for a few others to see the light of the page. I've started out by including the Introduction from the collection, and I've bracketed the stories here with the final story that appeared in the collection, "You're Entitled to the Meat." The Introduction and the last story are essentially the same in that they deal with the same theme: you get what's coming to you.

As for the other stories, I felt they represented the formation of what I was after as a writer: the truth. Like Hemingway, I'm always looking for the truest moment to render into words, the thing that will convey to the reader the absolute pure essence of the story. It's an impossible task, but I love trying. "The Way It Went" is a love/lust quadrangle set in Maine, among students at the University of Maine, where I attended college. It features some of the early themes I experimented with, such as hunting and alcohol. "Frank the Pigeon" is a sad story about a man dying. It was inspired by the death of my wife's godfather, Marcel Rochotte. We visited him in his hospital bed one afternoon while the cancer consumed him, and I found it too painful to look directly at him for too long. While my wife and her godmother held Marcel's hand, I looked out the window. There, a few feet away from a dying man, were pigeons—rats with wings—copulating. The multiple layers of irony weren't lost on me. "The Stern Man" comes from my experience in the fishing industry. My father was a lobster fisherman, and after college I worked at a friend's wholesale/retail business. Each day the lobster fishermen would bring in their catch to be weighed. One of the stern men (a stern man is sort of a helper who fills bait bags and stacks traps) was a dead-looking character that I never forgot. This story owes a lot to Melville's "Bartleby the Scrivener."

So here are a few stories from *You're Entitled to the Meat*. I hope they sound like nothing you've ever read before.

Introduction from *You're Entitled to the Meat*

Though it may sound somewhat agnostic, it has been my experience that fate—defined as "what happens"—is the quotient of dreams divided by hard work. In the end, what happens happens, and you do your best along the way, and you're entitled to the meat.

When I was senior at the University of Maine, I lived off campus in Orono with two other roommates. Our neighbors were typical Mainers: sweet, honest, forthright, and a little quirky. They immediately adopted us, taking an interest in our activities. Soon they were bringing us food, and soon that food became a little too exotic for our urban palates. The moose lasagna and venison gumbo was not that much of a stretch, but beaver stew and shepherd's pie made with raccoon and squirrel...well, um.

We always gratefully accepted what they made for us, and they were pleasant people to have as neighbors. When we asked if Ted, the father, had shot the raccoon for the shepherd's pie, he just laughed.

"I ran him over," said Ted lustily.

"And I cooked him up," said his wife.

"You know," said Ted, on the sly, "when you kill an animal with your car in the state of Maine, you're entitled to the meat. By law."

As disturbing as the revelation of that particular statute was, more disturbing was Ted's use of the word "when." Not "if" you kill an animal with your car, "when."

You're entitled to the meat.

I immediately wondered if this law also applied to pedestrians.

Our neighbors had a big mutt named Dumdum that they kept tied up outside, and the pooch was always barking. Yapping day and night. Occasionally Ted would go out and kick it, resulting in a few minutes of peace. His wife would go out and take her turn, cussing at the hound, sometimes braining him with a cast iron skillet and threatening to cook him alive.

One Sunday evening Ted and his wife came over with their weekly casserole for us. We accepted it and wondered what species gave its life beneath Ted's tires for us this week. Ted and his wife seemed a little down that evening, and for conversation's sake, I inquired what was the matter.

"It's Dumdum," said Ted's wife. "Ted ran him over this morning. Crushed his neck under a steel belted radial."

They left us alone in the kitchen with ghastly looks smeared across our faces. We carefully peered under the tin foil, looking for a bit of cloth collar, or the glint of a rabies vaccination tag, but there was nothing except noodles and mystery meat and gravy.

Later that night, after fortifying ourselves with dozens of beers, we took the casserole and snuck across the street to the state liquor store. We threw the casserole--the remains of Dumdum--into the dumpster and resolved never again to be home on a Sunday night.

We were entitled to the meat, and we got it.

"The Way It Went"

I

We were all four walking down the road when it happened and we didn't know it then but the thing that we had began to change. The road was wide and a solid double yellow line was painted down the middle. There were deep ditches just off the verge. It was pitch dark out and our breath came out white and dreamy. We were walking down the middle of the road. There was really no verge, just deep, wide ditches. That's the way it went in the great state of Maine.

Lou was walking beside me and I saw the dull gleam of the flask bouncing in the dark as she drank. She had been at it pretty hard and I had an idea what it would be like later. I liked her well enough, especially because she was short. Not petite, but compact: a full-sized woman pushed down into a manageable package.

"Let's have some," I said.

She looked up at me and smiled and handed over the flask. It was tequila and it tasted smooth but different from the other liquor we had already drunk. It went down easy and I liked it. We were pretty gone already but five minutes in that air and you feel like nothing, nothing at all, and I was certainly glad Lou brought her flask. Good old Lou. I started to think about getting back when Jimmy fell down.

"Oh, Jimmy," said Lou. She went over to help him and Kate went over with her.

"Jimmy," said Kate. "Jimmy, I knew you shouldn't have had that stuff. What was that stuff? He can't drink that stuff."

They were kneeling next to Jimmy and I couldn't see him getting sick but I could hear him all right. The air was cold and everything was loud. There was nothing else around, no sounds at all.

"Here," Lou was saying. "Here, it's all right now. Just sit down and have some of this."

"Don't give him any more. He's sick."

"He's not sick, he's just dizzy, right Jimmy?" Lou gave him the flask and he took it. Jimmy was really gone, worse than I had ever seen him, but he was a trouper. He was the Tex Cobb of drinking. You just couldn't knock that guy down, and no matter how bad it got he was usually the last one around.

"Jimmy, don't, honey, please."

Jimmy wasn't listening to Kate. He wasn't looking at her. He looked at Lou and he drank most of the flask until Lou took it away.

"I'm all right," he said. "All right. Somebody gave me a bad beer, that's all."

He was gone and he didn't even know it. Someday I was going to get my Ph.D. and do my dissertation on Jimmy. He was something else. He got up and put his arm around Kate and started kissing her ear. I started back walking down the middle of the road.

"Did you see the goldfish?" Lou asked.

"A goldfish? Really?"

"Right on the road. Jimmy's crazy."

"He's OK. He just can't stop."

"He drives Kate nuts."

I'll bet. I didn't say it but Jimmy told me everything so I knew. Kate didn't need anybody to drive her nuts. Lou was wearing a jean jacket and a T-shirt and I could see that she was cold. Lou had the body of one of those supermodels pushed down into a five-foot frame and so far I hadn't been able to find an ounce of fat on her. If you just looked at her you couldn't tell because she always wore dumpy clothes. Jimmy told me how lucky I was but I wasn't sure. I liked Lou an awful lot. She gave me the last of the tequila and I almost put my arm around her but I wouldn't have been able to walk very well.

Tequila was a funny liquor. We were all wrapped pretty tightly from the long day but after I drank the tequila my eyes felt funny. Jimmy would have said it was a bad beer. I felt like I had super vision but at the same time I couldn't see anything. And then I saw them.

I thought it was some low ground fog at first. Friar's lantern. But then they kept moving, slowly and deliberately, crossing the road like a column of ghosts. The does went first because the buck was a bastard. He had spent all of his sweat getting them together and there was no way he was going to go across first. If something was on the other side they could find out. I held up my hand and behind me they stopped.

"I think Jimmy is going to get sick again," I heard Kate say. Even in the dark when I couldn't see her and didn't want to hear her. She had a lovely voice.

"Just ahead," I said in a whisper.

"What? What's just ahead?"

Lou was hanging on tight to me. She was from the city and the only darkness she wanted to be in was the kind you got at the end of the night between the sheets.

"Deer."

Nobody said anything. Then they saw them, everyone but Jimmy. I could see that he was trying to fix a point on the road in front of him. His world was moving considerably faster and he needed it to stop. Kate came up on my other side and touched my arm. I wanted to lean into her and feel her weight lean against me but Lou would have caught on. Besides, the deer were putting on a good show.

Some of the does stopped and looked in our direction. Their huge ears rotated independently, triangulating our position. They couldn't see us but they knew we were there. It wasn't the first of November yet so they knew they would be all right. I've listened to people tell me how much bunk that was but I knew deer pretty well.

Somehow Jimmy had pulled himself away from Kate. He went next to Lou and leaned against her.

"The buck is going to come up next," I whispered to Kate. I knew she didn't care but her smell was nice and I wanted to get a little closer to her.

"The buck?"

"The male."

Seven, then eight went across the road, and then there was nothing.

"Did the buck go by?"

In the dark and the quiet Kate's delicate fingers found mine. My throat felt funny and I couldn't answer her. I was afraid that if I opened my mouth a squeal would come out and Lou would punch me. She was trying to keep Jimmy up and that was a job for her. The big buck stepped out onto the road.

It was all gone then, all the whiskey and the beer and the tequila and it was just me and the buck. Even Kate went away and I could feel him looking at me, sensing my presence, content in the knowledge that though he didn't know what we were all about, he was all right. He was right in the middle of the road, his head low, his big rack pulling it down, just skulking across the smooth pavement, great flanks moving like a dancer, the shoulders taking the weight then releasing it back to his haunches. He was taking his time and his flag was pinned down and I thought I could count twelve points on his rack.

I was just going to whisper to Kate about the rack and the points, I was just going to tell her that she was seeing a god out there in the night, a deistic creation, that men spent their lives going to bed wishing that they could see one like him just once, not even to shoot him but just to see him and tell their friends about him and go to their graves secure in the knowledge that he existed. I just wanted to tell Kate that one thing. Then his flag went up.

The car almost clipped Jimmy. We all dove into the ditch, me taking

Kate and Lou, but Jimmy was a lump and he was fixed on a crack in the pavement and he wasn't moving anywhere. I felt the dirt ground into my face, then my feet up in the air and then I stopped. Lou and Kate were lying next to me and for a second we didn't move.

They were all right and I climbed up out of the ditch, which was steep, and onto the verge. Jimmy was just standing there, staring at the pavement, a long line of saliva coming out of his mouth. He was asleep. I looked and saw the taillights of the car go around a corner and then it was gone and there was no sound again. Except for Jimmy asleep on his feet as if nothing had happened.

There wasn't much left of the big buck. There probably wasn't much left of the car, either, but it must have been a big one because the buck was all twisted up with his head bent back impossibly to his rear quarter. His rack was gone, shattered all over the road. I found a couple of pieces and put them in my pocket. He was a beauty and I felt like crying. That was something. Just standing there in the dark with that big deer all twisted up at my feet and no sound and I just felt like crying.

Later when the Old Town cop showed up he looked at the deer and said, "Well, do you want the meat?" The girls made faces. Jimmy was awake now and making a lot of sick noises. "By law someone is entitled to the meat," the cop was saying.

II

The Indian was sitting at the bar. There was a big mirror against the wall, thirty or forty bottles of liquor in front of the mirror, the bar, three tables and a television set. The television didn't hang above the bar as in most bar rooms; rather, it sat atop a table as in someone's living room. The place had the feel of a living room because that's what it was.

The Welcome Inn belonged to Miles and Linda Lachine. The rest of their house was on the other side of the bar: a kitchen and a bedroom. The bathroom, down the end of the hall, was used by the patrons of the Welcome Inn. Linda and her two children sat out at the tables while

27

Miles stood behind the bar, pouring drinks and smoking Luckys.

From where I sat at one of the tables close to the door, I couldn't see the Indian's face. The table closest to the door was the best for two reasons. One, you got fresh air whenever somebody walked in or out (the cigarette smoke hung blue and thick in the place). And two, when the fights started you could get out the door fast. The Welcome Inn was on French Island.

If you drove over it, you wouldn't know French Island was an island. It sat in the middle of the Penobscot River, an island of land with about a hundred houses and the Welcome Inn planted on it. I lived on French Island. So did the Indian.

He had big, round shoulders and his elbows splayed out so that his head hung low and his shoulders hunched higher and his back looked bigger than it really was. The blue atmosphere of the Welcome Inn made everything look dead. I did a lot of blinking in there.

The Indian's name was Larry Dubois and if you didn't know anything about the local people you wouldn't be able to tell that he was a Micmac Indian. He didn't have long, straight black hair. He was going bald and he wore thick glasses that his bulbous nose had grown around; the flesh had literally grown over the rims, and it didn't look like Larry could take the glasses off if he wanted to. On his head he wore a cheap plastic and Styrofoam baseball cap that had "Fleury's Gun Shop" emblazoned across its crest.

In the morning when I got up to get the Bangor Daily News I would see Larry. He was usually sleeping in his car, an old Chevy Malibu. When the weather turned cold that first year, I went out and woke him up.

"Did you sleep out here all night?" I had asked.

"What's it look like?" He rolled over and turned his back to me.

"Why?"

"Because my old lady won't let me in the house when I get all liquored up."

He didn't talk like an Indian, either. His accent was that of the locals. He was a local. He was of the Penobscot tribe.

"Do you want the sports page?" I had asked him.

He took it and I cursed myself for having offered. The weekend baseball scores were in there. The pennant race was wild that year. Larry slept in his car five or six nights a week.

"Hey, prof," Larry said from the bar. I got up and pushed through the smoke across the sticky carpet to the bar. By accident I kicked one of the Lachine children as I was walking. Linda spanked the child and told him to go get her glass refilled. I sat next to Larry.

"Hey, prof," Larry said again. "How come you ain't kickin some kid outta UMO?"

I shrugged.

"Whatta you teach down dere, in Orono?"

"English," I said.

Larry laughed and his laugh was more like a squawk. "Fuckin English. Ain't no fuckin English, 'cept in England. Christ."

Larry Drained his drink and took a good pull from the next one before he continued talking.

"I had a dream last night, prof."

I looked at Larry but he wasn't looking at me. He wasn't looking at me but I could feel his eyes burning into me and I turned my head and I could see that he was staring at me through the big mirror that hung behind the bar. Sitting next to him, I couldn't see his eyes. But they were clear and bright in the mirror. I hated it when Larry did this.

"You know what I saw in my dream, prof? I saw you. And I saw the deer. And you were together and now he is in you because your heart cried when that deer died. The spirit of the deer was impressed that you felt that way when that car ran it over, and to pay you back he has come into you."

He turned and looked at me.

"What you got in your pocket, that's important."

Without realizing it, my fist had closed around the pieces of the deer's antlers in my pocket. "Anyway," Larry continued, "you and that deer got some unfinished business." I couldn't get Larry to talk any more. I left and went home.

III

The weather up in central Maine was always nice in the early part of the
fall. That was when they took all the pictures of the University of Maine
at Orono campus, the kind of pictures they printed in the brochures sent
to prospective freshman. They never took pictures when the snow was
ten feet deep and nobody's car would start.

It was getting cold fast and even though it was still October, Duffy
said we'd have snow by the first. That was fine with Duffy the Hunter, but
Duffy the Head Groundsman said it with a note of disgust.

"You know what that means, Rourke."

I couldn't tell if it was a question or a statement. But when Duffy said
it he put the emphasis on the word "know." I wanted to laugh because
the way he said it made it sound like we were all going to get laid if there
was snow by the first of November. But I didn't laugh. Duffy only had
three teeth left. He didn't laugh about much.

"It means the football field will be a mess for the last two games.
That's it."

"It means you'll take your buck on opening day," I rejoined. Duffy
bared his three teeth, all muddy brown from decades of tobacco juice
and coffee.

I left Duffy and walked past the field house and onto the mall, wide,
flat and long enough to land a light plane on, lined on each side with majestic oaks leading up to the library. The mall was a pretty place but I
always thought those trees were too even, the spaces between them too
empty. When I walked up the mall I always stayed in the shadows of the
trees.

To the left of the library was the student union building. I walked in
and went downstairs to the Bear's Den, the campus cafe. Kate was sitting at a table in the far corner, partially hidden by the popcorn machine.
The bar was dark and only a few people dotted the rest of the place, sit-

30

ting in twos and threes, drinking coffee over opened books, gossiping. One or two people recognized me and waved. I went over and sat across from Kate.

"How do you feel?" I asked her.

"A little tired."

I got up and got a cup of coffee for me, tea for her.

"I talked to my advisor today," she said.

I didn't think much of advisors.

"He said there are a lot of openings at the Southern Maine Medical Center in Portland and that I should have no problem getting a job."

"A nurse? You're right in the middle of your dissertation."

She shrugged. "For a while--not really a nurse, but I could work in the hospital."

"That would be a good place. Not much philosophy, but plenty of rectal thermometers."

I regretted that the instant it passed my lips. She looked away, and the angle of her face that I saw was just beautiful, just perfect, smooth skin sloping almost translucently in the dim light, her hair falling across her cheek, her brushing it back with long fingers.

"Jimmy's sleeping," I said. Another poor subject choice on my part. Rectal thermometers and Jimmy. I was firing on all cylinders, but I couldn't help it. Not when I was around Kate.

"What else is new?" She was still looking down and I was still look-ing at her.

"Are you going to tell him?"

Now she looked up at me with those brown eyes and I felt like a warm breeze was blowing through me.

"I don't think I should've told you."

"You don't have to, if you don't want."

Sometimes the silence that came between Kate and me was the best part. We sat in it and didn't have to talk. Just being within a couple of feet of her made my throat dry up and my words come with difficulty.

"It might be Jimmy," I said. I hated myself for saying it, but it just

31

came and I couldn't stop it.

"Jimmy's too drunk all the time. Besides, I always made him use something."

"But you didn't make me."

"You're different."

It was what I wanted to hear, just not at that moment.

"You know I can't do it any other way. It just complicated things, that's all."

She sighed. "Besides, telling Jimmy would just kill him. Especially the truth."

"Telling Jimmy would be the best thing in the world. It's better than carrying on with him."

"You carry on with him," she said.

"I live with him. I drink with him. I don't sleep with him."

"We haven't slept together in months."

"That's how you know it's me."

"Yes."

"Look, maybe we could get away. For a few days."

"Just you and me?" She looked past me to the door of the Bear's Den, watching people come in. The bar started serving in twenty minutes. "I couldn't do it to Lou."

"I have to do it to Lou. You have to do it to Jimmy."

"And then we can do it together? Look what that's gotten us so far."

"All right," I said. "All right. We can all four go away for the weekend. I know a cabin. It's where I hunt."

"I don't know."

"The weekend after next. Maybe we could do it then."

"I don't know."

I took her hands and she looked at me again.

"By next semester you'll have to say something. If you're not already in Bed Pan Alley."

"At least the graduation gown will hide it," she laughed. But I could see her eyes getting shiny.

"I have to go."

Before I went home I stopped at Pizza Heaven. Jimmy was already there. It was after midnight when we got back to French Island. Lou was already in bed, and her skin was warm and soft as I slid in beside her.

IV

On Friday mornings neither Lou nor I had any classes. We hadn't talked since the night the deer was hit by the car, not even last night after she rolled off me and curled up with my pillow. I was awake a long time, then I slept in a very blank place that I didn't remember because there was nothing to remember. Lou got up and I watched her stretch, naked and voluptuous, but I didn't love her.

I'd never love Lou and I knew it but I just couldn't tell her. I liked having her around. I liked the sex. I liked holding her against me and feeling the huge swell of her breast, her nipples scraping against my chest, her legs wrapped around me, her lips, big lips for a small mouth, dragging down my belly. But I didn't love her.

Lou liked being naked. She was a big exhibitionist and I liked to joke that she picked the wrong university to teach at. She should have picked some school out in California, where her body could have been discovered by an adult film producer, and she could have led a torrid but short life. Lou loved it when I told her that and told me it excited her.

I watched her stretch. She said she had to be naked to stretch properly. She started by touching her toes and she did it slowly, deliberately. Then she spread her feet apart and reached up with one arm, then another, her breasts swaying, fighting the pull. Finally she clasped her hands behind her back and lifted them up, thrusting her chest out into the cold air of the bedroom.

"Let's all go away for a weekend."

Lou was cooking breakfast at the stove and I was sitting at the kitchen table drinking cranberry juice.

"All?" she said.

33

"You, me, Jimmy and Kate." I was careful to mention Kate last.

"Where would we go?"

"Up to Boyd Lake. To the cabin I stay at when I go hunting."

"Oh, that sounds like fun." She was sarcastic and I could imagine her smirking into the scrambled eggs. She put them on plates and came over to the table.

"Jimmy and I will go hunting for the day and you and Kate can go for a hike."

"We'll get shot."

"Think about it." I ate the eggs.

"You should have taken the deer meat that the cop offered you the other night," she said. "Then you wouldn't have to go hunting."

"It's not the meat. It's something else."

She wasn't listening so I stopped talking.

"Kate says Jimmy's pretty bad these days."

He was, but that wasn't news. He'd arrived on his way and in nearly four years surpassed everyone's expectations. Now we all doubted he'd last the winter.

"Don't you worry about me, paco," he liked to say. "I know a few people around this state."

Jimmy's father was in his second term as governor of the state of Maine; Jimmy's job as assistant athletic director was a sinecure designed to keep him out of his father's politics. Orono was good for that.

Before I met Jimmy I was only a bird hunter, and that only occasionally, usually in the fall for duck. Fishing was my thing. Blues, stripers, tuna, anything that swam in the ocean. Everybody on Cape Cod fished, most for a living. Jimmy took me hunting one fall and I bagged a handsome buck and I hadn't thought much about fishing since then.

"Wait'll we go to Africa and you get a big, nasty cape buffalo right between the nostrils just before he impales you. Then you won't remember what a whitetail deer looks like," Jimmy said.

"Do I look like Francis Macomber?"

Jimmy didn't waste his time teaching me conventional things like tracking deer, looking for sign or scouting country.

"Anybody can shoot a deer," he said. "Sit down where it's filthy with sign, pop a can and wait for some spike buck to stagger by. But if you want to shoot a king you have to think like them. You have to live in the woods. It has to be your home. When you do that, you're like them, and then you have the right to your buck."

A week before opening day Jimmy would vanish. Athletics be damned. He always took a huge buck within two or three hours of sunrise that first day, and twice he had made the Biggest Bucks in Maine record book.

Jimmy had ended last night by retching out the passenger's window while I drove home from Pizza Heaven.

"Jimmy's always pretty bad before deer season," I said to Lou.

"I just don't understand it. Someone like him could do anything. I told Kate she should end it." I tried not to choke on my coffee.

V

I had the dream that night.

It started with Kate. We were all at the Bear's Den and Jimmy was drinking except he wasn't drinking beer or whiskey or tequila. He was drinking spit. It was really the Jones' fault but when it came to sticking fingers in electrical outlets Jimmy needed no encouragement.

The Joneses, twin refrigerators who also happened to be starting linebackers for Maine's football team, had filled an empty popcorn bucket with tobacco juice spat from their mouths. Some of Jimmy's own spit was in there, too, but none of mine. Jimmy loved fraternizing with the boys, especially the football players. I told him he was on spongy ground, but he just laughed. The more trouble, the better for Jimmy.

On the table in front of the Jones twins were twenty or thirty empty plastic cups in various states of disuse. The cups had begun life as draft beer holders soon to be drained by the Jones twins, then they metamorphosed into spittoons that were subsequently poured into the empty

35

popcorn bucket and given to Jimmy to drink.

Jimmy drank it.

If pressed for an estimate, I would have said that there was about a pint of tobacco juice in that popcorn bucket. None of it was mine. I had been cutting back recently, and now I only dipped when I was outdoors, helping Duffy work on the baseball diamond or the football field or when I was hunting.

Lou was philosophical about the whole thing. "Jimmy," she said, "is a sociopath."

Kate was less impressed and she left. When he was physically ejected by Harry, the Bear's Den bouncer, Jimmy unintentionally followed Kate out. Kate never knew it, however, because Jimmy was ejected into the back alley.

That's what really happened. The dream started when I got home.

Kate was there. When I walked into the living room she was sitting on the couch. The television was on and she was looking at it but I could tell she wasn't watching it. It flickered and popped, strobing her face with a preternatural irregularity. She looked weak and beaten and I didn't feel sorry for her but it was then, right there as I stood watching her cower before the television, that I fell in love with Kate.

It was a deep purple thing, that love I felt, a liquid thing pushing on my entire body from every direction, as if I had been chained to the bottom of a deep, warm swimming pool. The warmth and the dark light, ultraviolet, infused me, pushing through my pores and stroking me somewhere around the pit of my stomach. I thought that Jimmy was behind me so I didn't move. There would be time for moving later.

"Where's Jimmy?" Kate asked as she looked up to me from the television. The question snapped me from my trance and I turned to find Jimmy not standing behind me. Out the living room window I could see Jimmy slumped over in the front seat of my car. I went over and sat next to Kate.

What I felt first was her cold. She was glacial, cold enough to generate a chilling breeze, and I felt her shiver. She folded against me.

36

"It's over," she said. "It has to be over and it has to be now."

"It's been over for a long time," I reminded her.

"Then why am I here?"

Welling and red, her eyes were far away, seeing movies I had only heard about.

"Do you want me to tell you?"

She sniffled once and shook her head. Then she kissed me.

I knew she loved me then because she didn't kiss me fiercely. She began slowly, kissing my cheek and working around to my chin and finally my lips. It had been a long time and I had forgotten the things, her smell, her feel, the way she pressed into me. There was a smooth hum in the back of my head and I just closed my eyes.

When I opened them again I saw the deer in the window. Next to me Kate was asleep. She fit into me comfortably and I saw myself wearing her around like an accessory. Kate didn't have the voluptuousness of Lou; instead she was long and leggy. I reached down and slowly stroked her thigh, feeling the muscle there, firm in relaxation, and I wondered about where those muscles had been, how far they had run to get here.

When I saw the deer in the window I almost cried out. Not because there actually was a deer outside my bedroom window: I had often woken up and seen deer in the fields that ran down behind my house to the Penobscot River. Though I had never seen one so close to the house, it wasn't an unbelievable thing.

What made me want to scream was this: the deer standing outside my bedroom window in the flat steel light before dawn was the same deer I had seen smashed by a car three nights earlier.

Most people might look at one deer or another and see only a deer, a generic representation of the species. But for three years I had devoted myself to the whitetail's temple, studying him, following him, trying to become his equal so that I might one day meet him in a place where only he and I would exist, a sort of Central Maine hunter's nirvana.

I got up from the bed, feeling the cold air stirring around me without really feeling it. It was somewhere else now, replaced by that thing I felt earlier when I came home and saw Kate sitting on the couch. Then I was there, at the window, staring at the dead buck.

He was magnificent.

After staring at him from a distance of three feet for what seemed like ages, I began to wonder if he was dead. Perhaps somebody was playing a twisted joke on me by standing a stuffed deer in front of my window, knowing that I would be drawn to it, knowing that I would awake and mistake it for the deer I saw killed three nights ago.

But just as that began to ease me away from the dream, just as that doubt had begun to creep into the fuzzy borders of my vision, the buck's ear twitched.

I learned very quickly that if you could outlast a deer in the woods, he was yours. If you could survive the standoff, in essence wait for him to blink, twitch, or sniff, you could take him. Deer have a way of stopping whatever they're doing and melting into the woods. But if you stop too, and wait long enough, he'll move. He has to; his brain isn't that big.

The trick isn't in the waiting; it's knowing that there's a deer to wait for.

As I stood there watching him I realized that he had managed to disappear. Somehow this huge buck had accomplished the daunting task of blending into his background, even though that background consisted of a shed, two cars and two empty trash barrels.

But the twitch of his ear betrayed him, and he filled my eyes again. Like all extraordinary bucks it was his rack of antlers that drew all attention. Unlike the other night, they were not mangled and smashed. Instead they were as I had glimpsed them in the dark, thick and knotty, flowing back like the brush strokes of an artist. I counted the tips of each tine, or point, and got twelve. That's a lot.

Then I was out of the bedroom, out of the house. I didn't know it at first, because I was following the buck down the long slope of field that fell away from the house and ended up eventually at the edge of the Penobscot River. When I didn't feel the cold grasses as my feet pushed through them I began to suspect something unusual, but so enthralled with the buck was I that the thought was quickly brushed aside.

I watched him walk into the river. The whole time I was following him he never stopped or acted as if he were being tracked, never looked back to acknowledge me. He just did what he did. Maybe the thought of a naked man following him diffused his fear. I hesitated at the river's edge.

A thick mist hung over the water. The buck was gone now and though I didn't want to lose him, a part of my being still shunted the thought of strolling into the Penobscot completely naked in late October. But once my toes felt the water, it's unnatural warmth, what little reality I had left quickly evaporated. I felt like I had just settled down in a comfortable chair with a good book and somebody just brought me a glass of milk and a tray full of Oreos.

We were back in the woods. Not the woods surrounding French Island and that stretch of the Penobscot River; we were at a place called Boyd Lake. It wasn't the woods I recognized. It was the cabins. Each cabin was named, and even in the dim, pre-dawn light I could make out their eclectic monikers as I walked past them: Dad's Digs, Seldom Inn, U-Needa Rest, A Waze Back.

The buck had stopped but still did not turn to see if I was there. I saw him arch his head back, his huge rack scraping his spine almost all the way to his haunches, his nose flaring. His nose led his head to the left and I followed it with my gaze.

I wasn't surprised to find the buck staring at my camp.

It wasn't my camp. Rather it was the camp I stayed at for one week each fall during hunting season. "Camp" was an adequate term to describe the building, four patchworked walls of sheet metal, wood, plastic, rubber and anything else that Edgar Pelletier, the camp's owner, could find to justify a structure.

By the time I had turned back the buck had moved on, up to the end of the rode that encircled Boyd Lake like a Celtic bracelet, not quite a complete circle. He moved into the woods and I hurried to catch up to him.

By now I realized that this was some kind of funky dream. Dreaming was something I did so prolifically that to become a conscious spectator in the theater of my own subconscious was for me rote. I was used to dreams, though never had I dreamed so texturally and so clearly as now. But following a deer through the woods while completely naked challenges even the most untethered minds with obvious surrealism.

The buck struck a trail I knew well, moving through the thick brush with an ease I would have guessed impossible. There hadn't been a hard freeze yet so the ground was soft underfoot, damp and spongy with the leaves of the trees rotting and coating the forest floor with a noise.

What happened next would take me a week to understand completely.

Finding a covered deadfall, the buck moved about in a fashion that told me he was getting ready to bed down. That's it? I thought. This dream was all about finding a place to bed down? This ghost came back to me to show me where he sleeps. After he had bedded himself, the buck stretched his rack back and looked at me.

I was frightened suddenly, for in the buck's eyes I saw not the inanimation of a hunted animal, but some kind of divine spark that rendered the buck real in human terms. I felt he was trying to say something to me, so I lay down next to him, straining my ears to hear. Instead I fell asleep.

Next weekend was the opening of deer season.

VI

Kate's eyes were open when I awoke. She was leaning up on one elbow looking at me, a small, thin smile on her lips.

"You were talking," she said.

I rubbed my eyes. "Let me guess: a deer."

"No. You were talking about me."

I looked at her sharply but her expression was warming.

"What was I saying?"

"You said you loved me."

"Love, not loved. Present tense. It's true. I do love you."

"I know. I love you, too. But that's not the problem, is it?"

I shook my head and kissed her.

"We better go check on Jimmy."

VII

When I snuck away from the camp there was still no light in the sky, nothing to illuminate the denuded branches of the trees shivering in the pre-dawn cold, nothing to break the monotony of darkness that ran in liquid dimension around me.

They were all still asleep, far away, tumbled under the narcotic of the cold mountain air, momentarily chasing their own demons.

Jimmy had passed out on the couch and after I left Lou, I stole into Kate's room and kissed her for a long time. She kissed me back instantly and passionately and for a minute I thought maybe she confused me with Jimmy. But before she even opened her eyes she hugged me and said, "I love you, Kevin."

"I love you, too."

"When you get back. We have to do it when you get back."

"I know."

"And Kevin?"

"Yeah?"

"Make sure you leave your gun out in the car."

We knew it would be bad, but with Jimmy around you never knew. He was a loose cannon in so many ways, ways that were destroying him, and as I heard the crunch of frozen mud under my boots I wondered if I was one of those destructive ways.

Something was going on, something beyond the hunt, something beyond our plan to come out with it to Lou and Jimmy, something that burned in my gut like hot coal. A fog rolled through my head, a fog that not even the cold, dry air outside could dispel, but its origin remained unknown to me.

Each step I took into the woods had the effect of plunging me deeper into the cloak of consternation that muddled my head. Finally I stopped and looked around.

A burning pink began to rim the crescent of horizon that I could see through the bare tree branches. Now an ethereal glow began to throb gently across the forest floor, giving it its own luminescence. Now the world took on dimension, definition, and I was afraid.

I was suddenly very afraid to be there, alone in the middle of the dark woods. Not afraid of any beast, or afraid of losing my way. Rather I was afraid of myself, who I was, what I was.

Jimmy had always been my focus, I had spent endless hours trying to guide Jimmy, but now I knew that I had no idea what to do with myself. The confusion that had descended on me earlier now manifested itself in images that I began to hallucinate through the tangle of the lightening forest.

There was Lou in repose. A tangled deadfall became her image, her very being, mocking me, laughing at me. My chest physically hurt to see her there, but I knew what I had to do. It was over.

A shadowy swale in the rolling terrain became Kate, an inviting smile urging me on. With Kate I felt things I had never felt before, washes of emotion that ruled my body and mind. I closed my eyes against tears, tears of pain and of joy, for I knew that with Kate I would be getting everything. And that was exactly what I wanted.

When I opened my eyes the buck was there.

Not ten feet in front of me he stood, chest broad and wide, his rack swung back, his head cocked slightly to one side so that his eye might better view me. Automatically I felt my arms bring my rifle up to my shoulder, slide the safety forward and squeeze the trigger--

There was nothing in my hands. My gun was gone. I looked around but only the forest stared me back. That was when I realized that this was the buck that Larry Dubois had spoken about, the buck that was run over by the car that night.

My arms fell to my side, my mouth felt cold and dry. The buck started moving toward me.

Just as I had watched him that night I watched him now, watched his shoulders take the weight and move it back, watched his eyes remain wary and alert, watched his tail stay pinned down.

As he passed me on the narrow path his thick gray coat rubbed me, and through three layers of clothing I felt it, warm and firm, the static electricity catching the hairs and standing them momentarily.

I closed my eyes and tried to disbelieve what I saw, what I felt. When I opened them we were no longer on the narrow path. Now we were standing before the camp, the ramshackle cabin that sat on the edge of Boyd Lake. I saw my car parked in front and I knew that my rifle was in the trunk, locked in its case.

It was almost full morning now, and though the sun had yet to make an appearance, in the gray light the magnificent buck looked even more dignified, sagacious and majestic than I could have ever imagined. He moved over to the side of the cabin and stood behind a window. It took me a minute, but then I understood.

It was the window to the bedroom that Kate slept in. I walked up to it and looked inside. There slept Kate, curled amidst a pile of blankets. She must not have been asleep, for when I appeared in the window, she looked up. Seeing me, she smiled.

My doubts, my fears, my confusion all melted away in that instant. I knew I was doing the right thing, that we were doing the right thing.

When I turned around he was gone. Not even his hooves had left a mark in the rapidly melting mud that covered the ground around the camp. I stood back and wondered for a moment if he had even been there at all. Maybe everything that happened did so because I wanted it to.

After that fall hunting was never the same for me. Maybe it was because I never saw Jimmy again. But a part of me saw the spirit of that buck in every deer out there. Part of me never forgot that morning, the

43

morning the buck brought me home, the morning I drove away from Boyd Lake with Kate.

"Frank the Pigeon"

Uncle Frank was dying. Rather quickly, judging from the proliferation of tubes intruding his failing body. Like amoebae they multiplied overnight in shamanistic mitosis, for each morning when I arrived to visit there were more. None of it seemed to bother Uncle Frank, a remarkably cheerful man considering the better part of him had been consumed by cancer.

There were days when he was alert and able not only to recognize me, but to crack jokes.

"Hey, Billy, do me a favor, will ya? Under the bed is a big jar with a tube running out of my butt. Check it, will ya, and see if I took a crap today?"

Other days he was a gurgling mass of portent death, nothing more than a spiritless organism waiting to punch his card and head for the light. Though almost every day was upsetting to Aunt Marion, the latter variety were especially hard on her.

On the days when Uncle Frank was more a thing than a man, Aunt

Marion got religion. Sometimes Uncle Frank would snap out of his incremental dying suddenly. If I was in the room, I'd feel a tug on my shirt sleeve, and Uncle Frank would whisper:

"What is she today?"

"I don't know," I would answer back. Aunt Marion, unaware that today was not Frank's day, convulsed and called out to Jesus, Allah, and anyone else who might me listening.

"Maybe an Eighth Day Inventist."

My answers always broke Uncle Frank up, which was good and bad. It was nice to see him emerge from a painful semi-coma and laugh, but the strain of it usually knocked him cold. And the whole time Marion, the erstwhile Catholic, would be kneeling and praying and sprinkling the bark of an exotic tree over Uncle Frank.

I usually left the room when Aunt Marion went into her Jerry Falwell meets the witch doctor routine. It was bad enough that my uncle needed a tube to carry away his excrement. Also, I knew it was just the type of thing he despised. He was far too pragmatic to tolerate soul searching. "Get your thumb out of your ass and do something," had been Uncle Frank's motto.

I found it cruelly ironic that Uncle Frank was dying in the very way that mocked his robust existence. Not only did he lack the energy needed to stick his thumb up his own ass, but once in there he would be too weak to remove it. The whole bizarre thought was rendered moot by the plethora of plastic already there.

Further, as if in mean punctuation to his morbidly hopeless situation, Uncle Frank's hospital room had a bogus view. It overlooked the corrugated tin roof of an adjoining annex that had been built with function, not form, in mind. A brick wall rose suddenly, cutting off any view beyond the rippled metal of the roof. As far as Uncle Frank and I could tell, the roof itself served no function save for providing a convenient spot for pigeons to copulate.

"Look at 'em," Uncle Frank said to me one particularly lucid day. "Out there banging each other silly while I lie in here gurgling. Rats with wings getting laid! Don't that beat all?"

His tone was ironically comical, not the bitter vituperation that might be expected from someone dying a few painful cells at a time. Outside an orgy was witnessed, as a dozen or so pigeons with lifeless eyes, highly polished pebbles, climbed atop one another, flapped their wings, gouged one another and performed *coitus uninteruptus* for all to see. It must have been too much excitement for Uncle Frank, for when I turned back, he was snoring. But with all the tubes in him, his snores sounded more like the breathing of Darth Vader than anything human.

"The doctor doesn't think he'll live out the week."

Aunt Marion had come in and taken up her usual bedside seat. A large woman with large moles on her pale, flabby skin, she was more subdued today. Though it saddened me to hear it, I was not surprised. Aunt Marion also looked out the window at the pigeons, who alternated between lustful frenzy and stupid contemplation. Whether or not she actually saw them was debatable, for her look thickened by the day. Though it was Uncle Frank who was dying, the life was being sapped from Marion.

"Hey, sport," Frank said to me. "What are they doing?"

"They're having a conference about whether or not they should disconnect you from these machines." I thought he was referring to his wife and the doctor.

"No, no, not those bozos. The horny pigeons outside."

Uncle Frank could no longer roll his head to one side and look out the window, and the sheet covering his withering body was more con-cave each day. His mouth worked fine.

"The pigeons," he repeated hoarsely.

"They're not doing anything, Uncle Frank. They're all just sit-ting there, looking around."

"Oh, pigeons are useless creatures. We used to kill them in the park when we were kids. Killed them by the truckload, we did. State used to pay us a penny a pigeon. They figured it was cheaper than cleaning up all their crap. Rats with wings."

The end of the week came and Uncle Frank showed no signs of packing it in. I think Aunt Marion was running out of religions, for she was quieter with each passing day. I noticed she was now reading from a bible. I also noticed that she held it upside down.

"I don't talk to her anymore, kid," Frank said unexpectedly when Aunt Marion left the room. His hoarse voice was losing volume and gaining that breathy quality that reminded me of the expiration date on a carton of milk.

"Who?" I asked.

"My wife. Years now. She used to be a doll, real looker. Hotter than those pigeons out there. Then she got polluted. What are they doing today? The pigeons?"

"There aren't any today. I don't know where they went."

"They're gone? The pigeons are gone?"

I interpreted Frank's speech as the beginning of the end. Even Marion didn't seem to be spending as much time at his bedside anymore. Now she would come in, look at Frank, and leave, spending her time in the lounge.

I came in on the last day and I knew it right away. Uncle Frank had been dying for a very long time, piece by minuscule piece, but I knew today was the day. His eyes were wide open, and there was a hollow blackness around them, as if Frank himself had just been told the news.

"Uncle Frank, I'm going to get Aunt Marion," I said, startled. But he made a gurgling noise and his eyes softened. He spoke my name, and I leaned close.

"Pigeons," he said, his voice a dusty whisper. "I'm going to come back a pigeon. Nice and dumb. Don't tell your aunt. It'd really piss her off. Just between me and you. Think of me when you see the pigeons, kid."

Frank's bony hand was on mine, but he didn't squeeze it. His eyes closed and that was it. Outside the window the pigeons returned. They settled down and looked blankly at one another.

"The Stern Man"

The lobsterman watched the stern man through watered, red veined eyes. He squinted his leathery face, dragged on a filterless cigarette, and watched the stern man work: Open trap, empty bait bag, fill bag, re-place, close trap, slide onto transom. Stack 'em up.

When he finished with the ten pot run, the stern man turned and stood silently, his flabby arms hanging like huge slabs of un-butchered meat. I seen a million assholes like you, the lobsterman thought. Seen'em come and seen'em go.

"Definition of a stern man," the lobsterman shouted over the *lub-lub-lub* of the engines, feeling his head swish with sun and beer. "Dumb fuck what stands on a boat and humps bug boxes."

The stern man stood, motionless, expressionless, staring, as if he could read his captain's mind, read beyond the sharp words.

The heat was with them, even a mile offshore. The sun broiled the air around them, and the black water reflected it back. A smooth, ironed surface, the water hardly lapped at the hull. A seagull perched on the bow, it's lifeless expression mirroring the stern man's.

Returning to his logbook, the lobsterman could not shake the contempt he held for his stern man, whose wages cut into his earnings. He tried to drown the feeling with another can of beer. Like all stern men, this one had been hired out of necessity, not choice. Well, at least the sonofabitch shows up, he thought.

He drained the can of beer, throttled up the engine and felt the 37-foot lobster boat slice forward, cutting the black ocean with a small, foamy surge. The engine's chug was creamy and smooth. Thick French cream, the lobsterman thought with some pride.

The blank face of the stern man spoiled his moment of self-indulgence, and the lobsterman watched the stern man pull a pack of cigarettes from his shirt sleeve, selected one, bit the filter off and put the cigarette in his mouth backward. Then, shakily, he lit it and dragged deeply, returning the lobsterman's gaze. "Dumb shit," muttered the lobsterman.

"OK," the lobsterman said finally, after circling around the featureless water for several minutes, "let'em fly."

The stern man leaned into the first trap and it splashed into the boat's wake. Weighted with bricks, it sank quickly. For a second the rope between the first and second pots was pulled taught. Then the second pot followed the first over the edge and into the ocean. The process continued until all ten pots were gone, floating dreamily to their resting spot on the rocky bottom.

The lobsterman had been working on his 12th beer of the day while noting the loran number in his log, and when he looked up, the stern man was standing beside him, staring with sunken eyes that gave his skin a jaundiced hue. Trying not to show his surprise, the lobsterman gritted his teeth and flashed an angry look.

The freaky fuckin' bastard, he thought.

"Box'em up!" he bellowed, trying to scare the stern man. But the stern man showed no reaction. He simply shuffled over to the live tank and began transferring the lobsters into a green plastic fish box.

Suddenly, the stern man reached across a large plastic barrel and snatched the long knife that lay beside it. The motion was so quick, so deft, that the lobsterman flinched with surprise, and he felt that surprise paint itself across his face with a blush. The stern man remained pale and lifeless, but his eyes flashed with delight for a second as he replaced the knife in its sheath on his belt. The lobsterman saw this and redoubled his hate for the stern man.

*

When they had tied up to the mooring in the harbor, the boxes of lobsters were loaded onto the dinghy. The stern man stood in the dinghy while the lobsterman dropped the heavy boxes as awkwardly as possible, trying to injure the stern man, or knock him into the water. What he could not accomplish physically he made up for verbally, abusing the stern man with a torrent of foul language that only a fisherman can produce.

"Don't just stand there, you rat's cunt!" the lobsterman bellowed. "Stack those fuckin' boxes! Get movin', you useless piece of scabby foreskin!"

If the stern man heard the abuse he didn't show it. Inside the lobster pound the dealer invited the lobsterman into his office for a beer. The stern man waited in the front room, staring numbly into the live lobster tanks.

"How's your new stern man working out?" asked the dealer.

"Fucked if I know."

"Does he want a beer?"

"Beats me. You can ask him, but the fucker never talks."

"At least he shows up and works, right?"

The lobsterman grunted and downed half his beer with one gulp.

"He smokes his cigarettes backward."

"Yeah, but he works, right?"

"Stands around and stares at me mostly." He paused for a moment, looking into the foam at the bottom of his cup. "Yeah, he works." The lobsterman rubbed his hand over his bleached white beard. It contrasted sharply with his cracked, deeply tanned and deeply lined skin. Inside his bloodshot and glassy eyes were traces of blue from a time long gone.

"I'm gettin' too old for this shit," he said. "That kid's kind of freaky looking. I can't figure out why he wants to be a stern man on my boat."

"You started out working stern." The dealer was studying his friend now, eyes narrow, head tilted thoughtfully.

"Yeah, I guess I did. But that bastard gives me the creeps. Just stands there sayin' nothin' all day long."

"You're a piece of work, you know that?" The dealer was laughing as he said it. "You ain't so old that I can't remember the wacky shit you used to pull."

Finished with his beer, the lobsterman left the pound, the lifeless stern man falling into in his wake. When his unsteady legs failed him, the lobsterman banged his shoulder into the door. For a moment the stern man hesitated and stared at the door. Then he continued following the lobsterman. The dealer watched them leave and thought they looked more like master and puppy than hater and hated.

*

Though the lobsterman was becoming less agitated about the stern man's behavior, he was still amazed to find his charge waiting for him every morning at six. This was a rare feat among stern men, who were known for their belligerence, their transient nature, and their capricious and resentful attitude toward regular work.

But there he was, standing idly as the lobsterman glided his battered pickup into the dim, empty lot. In the cool gray light of predawn, the stern man's face was puffy and grotesque, his eyes still narrow slits under a mop of matted hair. The lobsterman had stopped asking the stern man if he wanted coffee long ago. In fact, he seemed to want nothing.

As they steamed out of the harbor, the stern man began automatically to work, just as he had the first day, without having to be told. It was as if he had been programmed at birth for this calling. They cleared the breakwater and the lobsterman lit his second cigarette of the day, washing some of the smoke down with the last of his giant coffee. The effect was oozy, he thought, a nice, numb beginning to the day.

"We're gonna haul four hundred today, kid."

The lobsterman had taken to calling the stern man "kid" only because it was less uncomfortable that calling him "you," or "hey." The boat chugged along with a creamy roar as the lobsterman tried to plot out his day. After a few minutes he decided his arteries weren't lubricated enough, so he fished out a bottle of rye whiskey from the forward cabin. When he reemerged, the stern man had moved from his customary wet seat on the transom to a spot just to the left of the cabin door.

"I don't suppose you want any of this?" the lobsterman asked, waiting only a second for the non-reply that always never came. A torn cigarette hung backward from lips which seemed too bloodless and waxy for a living thing.

"Didn't think so." The Styrofoam coffee cup was still muddy with the last cold remnants of sugar and cream and coffee, but that was how he liked it, and he smiled as he splashed the whiskey into the mixture. Whiskey had a funny taste when drunk like this, the lobsterman thought as he squeezed the liquid through his teeth, gargled it once, and swallowed. Almost immediately he felt his head clear and he was able to concentrate on the day's work.

They began the repetitive labor of hauling pots, moving across the surface of the choppy ocean. After finishing a run, a huge, red-hulled dragger steamed across their bow. The stern man gazed after the dragger with a narrow eyed, frightful intensity, the most expression the lobsterman had seen since he hired him two weeks earlier. On board the dragger, men were visible as specs, moving with purpose and precision as they headed out to sea, out to the Bank.

"I was gonna own one of them, too," said the lobsterman, trying to pry a word out of the stern man. A familiar buoy broke the lobsterman's gaze and he slacked the engine, then disengaged and let the boat glide easily forward. With a gaff and an effortless sweep of his arm, he snatched the line under the buoy and lifted it up through the niggerhead and threaded it through the wheel. He engaged the hauler and a second later the first trap appeared below the water's surface, a limp body spiraling up morbidly from the deep. With a sucking gasp it broke the surface.

"You know, I was gonna do a lotta shit a long time ago." The lobsterman let the dripping trap sit on the gunnal.

As he spoke to the saturated lobster pot, a slight ringing began to split his ears. Inside the pot the lobsters listened, and because most of them were shorts, he knew they would take his story back down to the bottom with them when they were thrown back. The stern man's hand appeared and dragged the trap away from him.

"You probably want to know what happened, eh?" said the lobsterman as he jabbed the air with his cigarette. "Well, I can't tell you, because I forgot. All I remember is a bank, a broad, and a bottle. That's it."

They moved to the next set, and to the one after that. The stern man stared and the lobsterman thought about his Styrofoam cup.

"I'll tell you, kid," the lobsterman said as he tried to note the loran numbers in his log book. "Broads." He gave up with the book and looked at the stern man. "It's all broads. Who knows where I'd be if it wasn't for broads. Them and the bank, you see? And a lady banker? Holy Christ, head for the hills, the planet's about to be fucked to a fare thee well!"

The lobsterman wasn't drunk enough to be able to ignore his own yelling, and he felt foolish for it. If the stern man felt embarrassed for him was anybody's guess, for he stood in his classic position, shoulders slumped forward, mouth slightly agape, knuckles out.

"Ahh," he said with disgust as he turned from the stern man. "It don't matter, but I'd probably have a whole fleet of friggin' draggers by now. A bloody armada, that's what I'd have."

The sun rose higher in the sky as they worked in silence, and the lobsterman became more and more drunk as the morning wore on. He poured more rye and noticed that the bottle that had been fresh that morning was now down half. Even he realized that he was on a good one today.

The alcohol made his eyes more sensitive to the light, which out on the water is always twice as bright, and he squinted his face until it fell into its familiar relief map of age and abuse. But the dazzling light never

54

bothered the stern man. He never squinted, never turned away from the glare off the water. It was as if his sunken eye sockets were black holes for light, sucking it in, returning nothing. Even the stinging smoke that drifted up from his backward cigarette did not disturb him.

"Broads," the lobsterman continued to mumble off and on as they worked. "Broads thought I drank too much," he said excitedly at one point, trying to startle the stern man, who had been hunched over a pot. But he was immune to reaction, and the lobsterman looked instead to the shimmering ocean.

"Drink too much. Shit, you don't drink enough."

*

The heat grew and the day melted, its edges spilling outward from the boat's epicenter, into the stabbing atmosphere of the horizon. They pulled traps and moved from spot to spot. My spots, thought the lobsterman. Each time they finished a set he would push the chrome throttle forward and the languid clug-clug of the engine would reassure him, tingling in his loins. Who the hell needs broads? he thought with a smile.

His mouth was moving but now he couldn't hear the words for the ringing in his head. Suddenly nervous, he tried to focus on the stern man, and succeeded only in straining his facial muscles, which demanded more whiskey. The stern man finished baiting the trap, pulled a cigarette from his pack, bit the filter off, and put it in his mouth. Backward. He looked at the lobsterman.

"What is it? What?" the lobsterman barked. "What are you trying to pull?"

Behind the stern man the ten stacked traps that were ready to be dropped came slowly into the focus of the lobsterman. He hung on to the console for support and nodded his head.

"OK," he said, wiping a string of drool that had escaped his lips, "OK, let's go."

He returned to his log book and discovered that he could not focus on the numbers. Shit, he thought, never got the numbers to blur before. Must be a pissa today! He solved the problem by covering one of his eyes and pressing his face close to the book.

The stern man watched silently and smoked his cigarette.

A little more rye, thought the lobsterman, to steady the writing hand. But the bottle was empty, and he staggered back into the middle of the deck laughing at it.

"Ho-lee shit, kid, check that out! Must be a pissa today!"

The lobsterman held the empty bottle by the neck and inverted it. But the stern man was looking at the lobsterman, not the bottle. With his matted hair and apish shoulders, he simply stared silently, without emotion, as he had done from the first day. The lobsterman threw the bottle into the boat's wake with a whoop.

"Into the briny deep with ya! Oh shit! I shoulda put a message in that bottle: 'Help--I am trapped on board my own boat with a crazy fuckin' stern man!' That's what I shoulda said."

With the boat still moving at half throttle, the lobsterman took a step toward port, tripped, and almost fell overboard. He hung over the gunnal and scooped cold seawater up to his face, drinking as much as he could. Then, he vomited the contents of his stomach.

When he had finished, he stood and made his way to the console, where he wiped his face with a rag. He disappeared into the cabin and returned with a can of beer, which he opened and took a sip from. After a deep breath, he spoke.

"I don't even know where I am, kid. Honest to Jesus. You probably think I'm whacked, but I ain't. I just have me days from time to time, and this is one of 'em." His head was clearing and the horizon was stabilizing, making his words easier.

"It was the three b's what got me, kid. Broads, booze and boats. The broads screwed me up, the booze straightened me out, and the boat got me here today. Yup, that's how it works, kid. I'm only tellin' ya 'cause you ain't got the friggin' tongue to ask me. No more broads left, and I got a funny feeling it's gonna come down to the booze or the boat, yes sir. I gotta give one of 'em up, 'cause the other can't stand it. Look at me."

His thinning white hair was still dripping and his eyes pointed in dif-

ferent directions. He was not an old man but his features plead otherwise.

"I'm the biggest bugfisher in this harbor. Keep drinkin' and I won't be.
I'm also the hardest drinkin' bastard around. Keep fishin' and I won't be.
You see my, my problem, my dilemma, kid? I don't know whether to shit
or wind my watch." The lobsterman looked back landward, back where
the majestic cliffs guarded the entrance to the harbor, his harbor. He
looked one more time at the stern man and turned the boat in.

They steamed in early that day, and the lobsterman gave the keys to
his truck to the stern man, telling him to bring the lobsters up to the
pound. When the stern man was gone, the lobsterman walked over to
Pete's Diner and ordered two very large breakfasts and a pot of coffee.

The stern man found him just as he finished eating. He gave the
lobsterman a wad of twenties, four of which were peeled off and given to
the stern man. The stern man took the bills and stuffed them into the
pocket of his grimy jeans. For a moment he paused and looked at the
lobsterman. Then he turned and walked away, melting into the thick tide
of tourists outside.

The lobsterman went back to the dock, crawled into the cabin of his
boat, and slept away the rest of the afternoon.

*

"Just what in the hell happened to you?" It was the dealer's greeting
to the lobsterman upon seeing him walk into the bar room later that
evening. Though the dealer was speaking to the lobsterman, his question could have been directed at any one of the twenty or so patrons of
the Grog Shop. It was a noisy, smoky, dark place with no stools or
chairs, and the men who drank there all looked as if they had been ex-
humed especially for the occasion. The jukebox was broke: foul language riding angry growls and explicit descriptions of the female anato-
my served as background music. The lobsterman's eyes were heavy
and red from his long afternoon sleep, and his gait was shuffling.

"I figured something was wrong when your stern man brought those
bugs up this afternoon," the dealer continued.

"Why? Did the sonofabitch say anything to you?"

"No. Was he supposed to?"

The lobsterman simply grunted and pawed the bottle of beer before him. His hands moved poorly and his fingers refused to close on the brown bottle's worn surface. In one corner of the bar a fight broke out, and despite the bar's smallness, few took notice of the melee, most eyes remaining glued to the television that hung limply from the wall. The dealer was looking through narrow eyes at the lobsterman.

"You plan on fishin' tomorrow?"

"Plan on fishin' every day."

"Why don't you take the day off? It's gonna blow like hell anyway. You could use the rest. You look like shit--even for you."

The lobsterman waved him off. "I gotta fish. I got bills like every-body else--I gotta drink. Besides, my stern man will be waiting for me at six sharp. Couldn't call him if I wanted to, he ain't got no phone, no ad-dress."

"What's going on with this guy? Why's he bother you so much? If you want, I can find another kid to work for you."

The lobsterman shot a wary look at the dealer.

"Nothin', I don't know what you're talkin' about. He's just a friggin' stern man--a stern man that gives me the creeps, that's all."

He studied his beer bottle for a moment, his eyes beginning to clear. A small smile cracked his thin lips. I wonder what he sees each day? the lobsterman thought to himself, the din of the bar room dying in his ears. Maybe if I was the stern man on my boat I'd have the same dead look on my face. Maybe he has never seen a dead man before.

"Listen," the dealer said, leaning close to the lobsterman, "stay in the harbor tomorrow, all right? The fuckin' lobsters ain't going nowhere. Just come up the lobster pound and keep me company, OK? We'll murder a coupla cases." He paid the tab and left the lobsterman smiling at his beer.

*

Much later the lobsterman left the Grog Shop on unsteady legs, weaving his way through the waterfront. It had begun to rain, a sharp, biting rain that tasted of a nor'easter, but the lobsterman didn't notice. He was searching for his truck. Instead of his truck, he found the gas dock where he left his boat tied up. Thoroughly soaked now, he staggered down the gangway and crawled into the front cabin of his boat. Darkness closed swiftly around him.

*

It was the stern man's presence that woke the lobsterman the next morning. He had actually been awake for quite some time, his internal clock functioning despite the damage done to the rest of his body, but his eyes remained stubbornly closed. Cemented shut was a better description. When he finally managed to pry them open, the blurry image he fixed on was the stern man's face.

"What the fuck?" he exclaimed, jumping in his skin. The stern man stood over him, arms dangling. When he tried to sit up, the lobsterman's head spun painfully. But he was more disturbed by the presence of his stern man. Outside, the wind blown rain drummed loudly against the fiberglass hull of the boat.

"What are you lookin' at? Did you get my pogies?"

In reply the stern man disappeared through the hatch and left the lobsterman alone in the stuffy cabin. Too many Budweisers, he thought, taking a nasal inventory. When he emerged from the cabin he found the stern man standing next to a full box of pogies, staring out at the harbor beyond the stern of the boat. Small whitecaps dotted the harbor's most inner reaches, and its green surface was speckled from the blowing rain.

"You really can't talk, can you?" the lobsterman said. "You're a mute or something, ain't you?" The stern man didn't reply. Instead, he fixed his lifeless stare on the lobsterman as he performed his cigarette ritual. The lobsterman stuck his hand out into the rain, then tasted it.

"It won't get bad 'till tonight," he announced. From a drawer in the console he produced a bottle of aspirin, shook several out into his hand, tossed them into his mouth, and chewed methodically. He thought something passed before the eyes of the stern man, widening them for a

59

moment, after which the stern man regarded him with a slightly cocked head.

"What's the matter, kid? Don't like a little weather? Bugs don't like it neither, makes 'em hide. So while they're hidin', we're gonna drop some traps on 'em. When they come out in three days, they'll be hungry, and we'll slam 'em."

The smell of coffee reached his nose, and he noticed for the first time the steaming Styrofoam cup perched on the gunnal. He looked back to the stern man for confirmation, but it was useless, for he remained standing out in the rain, cigarette drooping from his lips, simian look smeared across his face.

He turned the engine over as the stern man untied them. The smooth, creamy chug of the diesel reassured him and he decided he couldn't face the coffee alone. He straightened out the boat in the channel and ducked into the cabin for a second, reemerging with an old bottle of coffee flavored brandy. The stern man watched him pour it into his coffee.

"She's backin' in on us," he said, gesturing to the slate gray clouds above. "Gonna thump us pretty good, but not until later. We got at least until night. Cheers."

As they moved out of the harbor channel, the steady clip-clap of the waves slapping the hull changed to a more urgent whack-whack, lifting the boat slightly. The VHF radio crackled with a call to the lobsterman. It was the harbormaster, who assured him a small craft advisory was on its way up. The lobsterman assured him he would be back before they had the flag out the door.

As they cleared the jetty a great clap of wind raced across the water and slammed them, sliding the boat physically sideways and driving the rain like nails. The stern man held tightly to the console and the lobsterman smiled at him. The lobsterman throttled the boat up as they met the waves of the breakwater, which began to lift them and drop them methodically. The broad Novi hull of the boat seemed to enjoy the abuse, splitting and dispelling the waves with ease.

"See?" the lobsterman said, "nothing. Just a little rain."

Squinting through the windshield, which was now little more than a melted blur, the lobsterman repeated the assurance to himself and sipped his coffee. The brandy loosened him and cleared his head. That's a damned thing, he thought, only thing that ever clears my head is the booze. Hope I never stop drinking, or I'll be all screwed up.

The waves that they cleared now began to turn on them and give chase, sometimes breaking over the transom despite the boat's speed. They pitched, rocked, and were pulled quickly away from the coast. The roofed area that extended behind the console offered little protection from the wind that pushed not only the rain, but the sheared tops of the waves into their faces, stinging them. The lobsterman knew that the wind was the lord of the ocean, pushing it at its will, directing the rain and roaring its anger. Its howling had replaced the sound of the engines, and the lobsterman held the wheel tightly.

The stern man was hanging on tightly to a supporting post, the cigarette hanging from his lips no longer lit. His eyes were wide and accusing as he stared at the lobsterman, who took a drink from his coffee cup.

"Well, looka there, he's got a pulse," the lobsterman said, but even if he had yelled it the stern man would not have been able to hear it, for the wind suddenly roared a violent blast, a sheet of rain and blown saltwater smacking the boat from all sides. The lobsterman saw the stern man's lips moving, his mouth open wide, his hand pointing behind the lobsterman's head. But the roar of the storm was deafening, overwhelming, muting everything.

The boat started up on a huge swell, rising almost impossibly. Then, the swell was gone, and the boat dropped furiously down, smashing the ocean, flattening the lobsterman and the stern man onto the deck. The laced coffee was lost.

"Well, that's it!" the lobsterman screamed, barely able to hear himself. The storm had built with frightening speed and intensity, and now they rode the mountainous swells that were everywhere. From his position sitting under the wheel, the lobsterman could see only walls of water and black gray sky. Sometimes they blended together into a single, pur-ple-black manifestation of doom.

Though they were sitting close, facing each other, the lobsterman couldn't see the stern man's face anymore; it was lost in the rain. He turned and pulled himself up in front of the wheel. There was nothing but huge walls of green black water to be reckoned, and the compass spun as if driven by an engine. With a vague idea of land the lobsterman spun the wheel and pushed the throttle forward. He couldn't tell if the engines were still running, or if they had been swamped into the past tense.

When the lobsterman looked back the stern man had disappeared, and the lobsterman thought that odd. The cabin door was open and he could see that the stern man was not in there. Then he realized that a great wall of green water had descended onto the boat between them. For a second, all the sounds of the raging storm were gone. A swishy silence had descended in its place. The water itself was warm, and he reached out and put his hand into it. But the wall collapsed just as in-stantly as it had appeared, hammering him hard.

He closed his eyes, and when he opened them his lobster boat was very far away. Its lines were handsome as it rode out the storm, and he was thankful for having chosen it. It had been a good boat. The swell lifted him like an elevator, and the absence of fear made him giddy. Je-sus, he thought, what a view. I wish I could sell tickets for this ride, I'd make a fortune. It was then that he understood that this was a special ride, and those who took it never got off.

Breathe the water, he thought, it's quicker that way. But his mouth remained welded shut, and his arms methodically treaded water in an automatic attempt to live. It was then, after that slow understanding that being so far from his boat meant he could never get back to it, that panic pounded his heart. His lungs suddenly ached madly, and his lips were pried open as he gasped for air. He tried to swim, but was again crushed by a wave.

How easy it would be to just open my mouth and breathe this water and become food for the lobster I've spent my life chasing.

But his hate for life, his self abuse, his patent disrespect, all of these things lost out against his fear. It was fear that pumped his arms and kicked his legs, fear that kept his eyes shut and lips sealed against the water, fear that propelled him to the surface of the water.

As his head broke the already ragged surface of the water, he gasped, filling his lungs. When his eyes followed, he could see his boat no longer. Finally got you, too. That thought, the thought of his boat gone, the only thing he lived for, almost defeated his fear, and perhaps it would have, given any more time to destroy the control created by fear's command.

But he was lifted from the water, not from the ocean's swell below him, but from a force above him. His back was arched at a crazy angle as he was dragged over the gunnal and back into his boat by the stern man.

The stern man was breathing hard and dripping water as he stared down at the lobsterman. In one hand the stern man held a long gaff, the gaff the lobsterman used to snare the rope under his buoys. In the other, he held the knife he usually kept in its sheath on his belt.

How did you manage to grab me with a gaff and not kill me? the lobsterman wondered. Then he became vaguely aware of rope, lots of rope, was wrapped around him.

He tried to move, pulling at the tangled mess of wet, swollen rope that tied up his legs. But the line ran overboard, ending in line of lobster traps that was being jerked by the storm's caprice. The rope tightened suddenly, dragging him across the slippery deck, slamming him into the transom, pinning him. One leg, his left, stuck up at a crazy angle, an impossible angle, and he watched as it was twisted and yanked by the rope. Fear subsided and the pain took its place.

A scream welled in his throat, grinding his teeth together. Slowly and torturously, his knee was being hyperextended by the violent pull of the rope. He reached down vainly, tugging at it. It felt as if there were an underwater winch trying to drag him back overboard. His jaw finally released, and he opened his mouth and screamed.

"Where's my knife! Where's my goddamned knife!" he screamed.

Suddenly, the stern man was there, on top of him, slashing furiously at the rope. Bracing his own foot against the inner hull, the stern man hauled at the rope, trying to slack it so he could cut it.

As if it could sense the impending loss of its target, the storm redoubled its efforts. A fresh mountain range of angry water battered the boat, sending the stern man skidding against the gunnal. But as fast as he was knocked down, the stern man was back up, slashing furiously at the line.

Jesus Christ, the lobsterman thought, this kid's really going for it. Son of a bitch.

Pain coursed freely through the lobsterman's body, pushing at the edges of his vision, numbing him into a surreal daydream. He was glad he could not see the flesh under his soaked jeans, and that was when he heard the bone in his left leg break.

Never heard that before, he thought, more calmly. Even above the roar of the storm the snap of bone was audible.

As the stern man hacked madly at the rope, the lobsterman searched his face. But all he found was grim determination.

"Why?" screamed the lobsterman. He grabbed the stern man's soaked shirt. "Why are you saving me?"

If the stern man could hear the lobsterman, he made no sign. So intent on cutting free the lobsterman was he that he failed to notice the mess of rope he was standing in. As he cut the last strand of rope and liberated the lobsterman, the rope bunched around his own feet slithered sickly over the gunnel, tightened with a snap around his feet, and ripped him over the side.

The wind diminished then, leaving the lobsterman with a ringing in his ears. With a great effort he dragged himself up onto the transom. Huge black swells still lifted the boat high, and the rain still stung down from the purple sky. But the storm was beat, wrung out. He searched the boiling surface of the water for any sign of his stern man until he could no longer hold himself up.

As he slumped back down to the deck, the lobsterman opened his mouth and let it fill with rainwater. When the drops began to hurt his eyes he closed them and went to sleep.

66

"You're Entitled to the Meat"

When the deer jumped we were driving a low stretch of Route 2. Behind the black outline of the spruce forest the lights of the paper mill washed out the night sky, but the road was dark. A colicky fog oozed thick and thin, dashing us as we drove. It punched out the headlights of the car and stretched out our pupils until they ached.

The road straightened out and cut a path through a wide field. We could see the fog coming and going and it looked like herds of ghosts. It was a place where a deer really shouldn't have been. The country was exposed and a deer had no business trying to cross the road there.

We weren't driving. We were sitting in a car that was moving. My knee braced my body against the passenger side dashboard. Jack was sitting behind the steering wheel with his elbows locked. The light from the fog made him look sick. It was a cool, medical light, dim, and when I looked out the window, at the things moving in the night, at the sliding motion of the fog, and the black gullies that bordered the road, it all made me feel as sick as Jack looked.

Jack rolled down his widow and stuck his face out into the wet wind. Then he brought it back in and did it again. Each time he leaned out the window he pulled the car over the centerline. Each time he leaned back in, the car drifted into the right lane. Finally he gave up and covered his left eye with his left hand.

Neither of us saw the deer. The big Buick shuddered as if it had struck a tree, but it never hesitated. There was nothing to see, a blur in the fog, the thump, then the car returning to its previous speed.

Jack stepped on the brakes anyway and I didn't know we stopped until my nose began to bleed. The windshield was cracked where my face struck it and my neck began to ache.

"What the hell was that?" asked Jack. In the great, black stillness of the night the big Buick idled patiently. The right front tire was almost in the ditch.

"I don't know. I'm bleeding."

We got out and it was cold but the air felt hot and wet, like breath. My tongue felt something syrupy and tasteless and my nose throbbed in time to the racing drum of my heart. We stood there and the fog stopped moving. It fell on us like a pillow. The big Buick's headlights probed it for a few feet, then gave up. There was enough light to see the deer.

There were no antlers, and for a second the deer looked comical. It was lying in the middle of the road about 20 feet in front of the big Buick. Its big rump faced us and its head was twisted back so that it faced us, too.

"What the fuck is that?" asked Jack.

I walked up to the deer and my nose went from hot throbbing to cold throbbing. The blood was already beginning to coagulate.

"It's a doe," I said.

"A deer?"

"A dead dear."

Jack ran a hand through his hair. He turned away and that was when he saw the front of the big Buick.

"Jesus," he said.

The entire grill was caved in. The hood was pushed up and crumpled and the bumper disappeared into the engine. Lime-green antifreeze leaked out onto the road, glowing like the margarita mix we'd mixed with cheap tequila earlier that night. It was a small deer and the big Buick never registered the impact, but the damage was extraordinary.

"That deer did that to that car?" he asked. "What's that?" He pointed to a lump lying next to the dead deer. The deer itself looked remarkably good for having been struck by 3,000 pounds of big Buick. Except for the unnatural twist of its neck the deer might have gotten up and ran away.

I walked over to the lump lying next to the deer. At first it looked like a joke, like someone had left a miniature of the dead deer stuffed in an opaque sack when we weren't looking. Then I realized.

"That's a foal."

"A foal? What the fuck do you mean?"

"It's a fetus, really."

"Fetus? What the fuck are you talking about?"

"The deer must have been pregnant. When you hit that doe, the foal came out."

"Came out? What the fuck do you mean, came out? It was fucking born?"

"It was aborted."

"Jesus." I could feel Jack's neck getting hot from ten feet away. "Is it dead?"

"It was never alive."

"Jesus. Shit."

I could hear his throat close up around the words and then I could hear him retch. When he finished the police came. I don't know how they got there. There were no other cars on the road. The deer was in the middle of the road, and any other cars would have had to have driven over it to get by. There were no other cars after we hit the deer and there wasn't a house for miles. There was the fog and the road and the deer and us. And now the cop.

The cop was old and very heavy and he was smiling. It was one of those "I've got a secret" smiles they put on when they recognize something. The cop hitched up his pants.

"Looks like you got'm," the cop said as he looked over the dead deer. Then he saw the unborn foal. "Preggers, eh?" He clucked his tongue and dug a finger into his right ear, squinting. "Whatcha gonna do?"

Jack and I looked at each other. Jack wiped his mouth and tried to swallow. The cop was smiling.

"What are we gonna do?" I echoed.

"About the meat," the cop said. He looked from me to Jack and he kept up that thin-lipped smile.

"What meat?" asked Jack.

"The deer meat! Jesum!" The big cop gestured toward the deer. "By law, if you run over sumpn', you're entitled to the meat. It's yours." He paused and leaned forward and I thought he might tip over, and then we'd have a bigger mess on our hands. But he just leered, and added, "By law." He walked back over to the deer and I could hear Jack retching again in the darkness.

Post Goddard Fiction: Three New Stories

Author's Preface: The Blame Game

For someone who has spent a considerable amount of time writing short stories—I've been at it for twenty-five years—and for someone whose master's creative thesis was a short story collection that became my first published book (*Name the Boy*), I've written precious little short fiction since earning my MFA in Creative Writing. It is yet another example of the abundance of irony, which, I'm beginning to believe, is one of the building blocks of the universe. In a situation like this, a writer can do only one thing: look for someone or something to blame.

I could start by blaming life, but that's too general. So let's narrow it down category by category.

Category One: I blame publishing. In the spring of 2006, as I was finishing my master's degree at Goddard College, my creative thesis was accepted for publication. That meant that almost as soon as I graduated, I had to begin the long, frustrating process of bringing a work to fruition with a small press. The details were endless and mind-numbing, and I won't go into them here, but until the book came out in April, 2007, most of my time was devoted to getting that book right, then printed.

Category Two: I blame teaching. More consequences of success. Holding an MFA entitled me to teach at the college level, which I did with great relish at Community College of Vermont (CCV). In the fall of 2006 I was hired to teach English Composition. The class was cancelled, but not before I spent gobs of time developing a syllabus and preparing a course. In the meantime, I was hired by CCV to staff the writing lab, which was almost exactly like teaching, except I didn't know what I was doing. I was also teaching at Mt. Mansfield Winter Academy (MMWA), a school for ski racers in Stowe, where I live. I taught there three afternoons a week.

Category Three: I blame work. Did I forget to mention that I still worked for FedEx, part-time, 25-30 hours a week? My days looked like this: 0500: get out of bed, eat some breakfast, go to FedEx. 0600-1100: work for FedEx. 1100-1200: come home and eat. 1230-1500: teach at MMWA. 1500-1800: work around inn (more on that below).

Category Four: I blame innkeeping. Especially on weekends, innkeeping gobbled up vast amounts of time. At the Auberge de Stowe, I performed a variety of tasks, such as bed making, vacuuming, painting, plumbing, basic wiring, woodchuck removal, dog chasing, light carpentry, pump repair, prayer, cussing, and drinking.

Category Five: I blame family and marriage. Yes, that's a job. It takes dedication, thought, and hard work. Your family and your marriage just won't work unless you make them part of your daily consciousness. If you don't, nobody else will.

Of course, I don't blame any of these things for my shocking lack of fictional output; they're all precious and important to me, choices that I've made deliberately. But the lesson here is that life requires choices, and writing--for me--is one of those choices. If I were to focus on my writing the way I really want to, something else would have to be pushed aside.

I have, though, managed to write three new stories, and they're presented here for the first time. I'm taking the reverse approach; that is, the stories are appearing in a book, collected together, before being published in a periodical. They could appear later in some literary magazine, but for now I think this is the best place, the best context, for them. I'm not sure I can comment on them in the larger sense of my writing, except to say that they're a departure from the themed stories that appeared in *Name the Boy*; none of them revolve around the father and son theme. "Up a Sleeve" was the first story I wrote after Goddard, and in many ways it's the biggest departure for me. It revolves around the dissatisfaction a young woman feels with her life, but it's also about the mixed messages society sends us, confusion, and leaps of faith. "The Gore" and "Water and Willow" were written almost simultaneously, and setting is a major character in both stories.

Why didn't I try to publish them somewhere else before placing them here? Motivation. I played the blame game, as described above. And I wanted to take a break from short story writing. I was devoting the few available hours I had each week to the completion of my book on innkeeping, *The Innkeeper's Husband*, and I wanted to write a novel. That squeezed out short stories. It was only the creation of this book that spurred me to complete these three stories. In their completion I understood something about myself as a writer. I may never be a novelist. I don't have that sedentary focus needed to plod my way through such a long treatment of story. But I will always be a short story writer.

"Up a Sleeve"

Mary Ellen wasn't thinking about penises when she saw the man with the missing hand. She was thinking about the time she and Doug went to Cape Cod and rode their bicycles along the canal and stopped at the little lunch shack near the Sagamore Bridge and ate lobster rolls that were overpriced and under-lobstered. It was a hot day and the wind came from the west, strafing the cyclists along the canal, forcing the sweat from their bodies and drying it before it soaked their clothes. She remembered the way Doug looked, so athletic, so tall, the way he canted his torso when he took off his shirt, the way the muscles gripped the sides of his ribs and the way the bicycle seat disappeared into the shiny material stretched across his butt. And she was thinking about how she always chose the wrong man.

Now she looked around the place where she was. The hot breeze she felt came from asphalt, radiating heat between corrugated steel buildings. Instead of gulls bobbing on the water she saw her co-workers herding under a small awning, trying to escape the brutal August sun while they smoked cigarettes back to back during their ten-minute morning break. She pressed herself into the lee of shadow along the side of the building, so that only the tips of her breasts were touched by the sun. Her nipples burned.

One of the cigarette smokers dropped his butt and ground it into the sun-baked hardpan between the buildings. He broke from the group and came towards Mary Ellen, moving sideways like a crab, as if trying to keep an eye behind him, and an eye before him. His black T-shirt hung off a collection of bones that swayed unnaturally against each other, like loose golf clubs in a trashcan. When he reached her, he smiled.

"Mary Ellen, Mary Ellen." He looked back at the smokers, their gray lung spunk hanging in the still heat of the morning. "Mary Ellen, you want a smoke?"

She shook her head and looked away, toward the empty end of the buildings. The alley ended in a scrub of burnt bushes concealing a trash-filled culvert. The motion moved her breasts in and out of the sun, giving them a flash of coolness. She couldn't just run away. She spent enough time avoiding her co-workers so that she was branded a snob. Jasmine, the woman who worked opposite her on the package binder, told her the other day that she ought to come out with her and some of the other girls for a beer after work.

"It might help you get out of here and up to order picking," Jasmine had yelled over the din of the machinery.

"Do you go out a lot after work?" Mary Ellen yelled back.

Jasmine smiled wide and clicked her gum, revealing two rows of teeth that would have been beautiful had they been in the mouth of Clydesdale.

"Yeah, all the time."

"Then how come you're still here?"

That was the end of their chatting.

Mary Ellen got the job at DeWitt's two weeks after Doug stopped re-turning her phone calls. The last she heard from him was when he was in Chicago, on his way to San Francisco to begin work as the editor of a new poetry journal. He said they'd move out there together as soon as he could find a place to live, as soon as he started making some money. She was starting to understand that there was probably no money in poetry at any level, and that Doug probably wasn't going to call anymore.

The man with the black T-shirt coughed and the heat returned to her, bringing the present back to her sweaty skin. She was only wearing shorts and a tank top, but she squirmed in the clothes, and pulled at her waistband.

"Hot, shit," said the man. "I'd like to go for a swim right now. Wouldn't you? Wouldn't that be cool?"

She thought about the trash-filled culvert, the standing pools of slime quivering with mosquito larvae, the rank smell, and she couldn't believe that there were places like this in Vermont, places that mimicked the dying industrial beasts of her childhood, even the urban prison of her college years in Boston. When Doug told her of Vermont, of the places he knew, it had all sounded so idyllic—and it had been, it still was, when she got home to the little run-down shack they rented in Wolcott. But here, close to the only highway this far north, life succumbed to the tragedy of cheap plastic crap.

"There's a little swimming hole over to the Bends," he said. "Nice and quiet, you don't even need a bathing suit or nothing."

She looked at him, at his brown-rimmed teeth, the stubble on his drawn face like a clear cut after a fire. His chest was concave beneath the shirt, and his belt buckle stuck out, pointing toward the culvert as if there were a line pulling him in that direction. A bell rang, and their co-workers dropped their cigarettes simultaneously and twisted them into the ground with their feet. Mary Ellen looked around for the National Geographic cameras, sure that these animals' morning ritual was being filmed for a PBS special.

"I don't think so," she said, moving out into the sun to avoid him on her way back into the building.

The heat made her weepy, and when she got back to her station she turned away from Jasmine so she could bite her lip in privacy. The pain of her teeth sinking into her lip only amplified the pain she felt about

77

Doug. She knew she didn't love him, didn't even want to marry him, but she wished he'd stayed, just a little longer, just long enough to get her out of here. But there was nowhere else to go, no parents to run to, and the rent was due on the dinky shack she was stuck with. She ended up at DeWitt's because they were always hiring, because they were always firing. The work was monotonous, hot, loud, and stupid, packing boxes with machine parts, sending them down a chute. But she'd decided to stick it out for the summer, until she could save enough money to get her car fixed, then maybe she could drive down to her college roommate's in Providence, maybe find another Doug, this one more faithful.

At lunch she avoided the employee break room even though it was air- conditioned. Instead she decided to sit by the shipping dock, where it was shaded and quiet. The dock was at the far end of the building, facing some quiet woods, and a breeze kicked up, a breeze that remind- ed her of that day with Doug on the Cape Cod Canal, where they found a little spot between the rocks at the edge of the water, where Mary Ellen had slipped Doug's tight bike shorts off, and he cried. Those were the thoughts that were wafting softly through her mind, like smoke off a dying campfire, when she saw the man.

He was talking to the distribution manager, one foot in the office, one foot out. As she came down the long wall with the bathrooms on one side and the racks of product on the other, she had a bisected view of his body, but his head was turned, so his profile was cut in half. What she saw stopped her. He looked like Doug, the same long, gaunt hand- someness, the same wave of thick hair atop the angular head, the same way of standing, spread-legged and confident. Even his ear, the one she could see, the left one, looked like Doug's, small and tender, like little girl's.

She had stopped in front of the women's rest room, and since it was lunch, her co-workers were entering and exiting in twos and threes, passing between her and her view of the man who looked like Doug. The effect was like a time-lapse film, his movements exaggerated. She could only see his left arm and hand, clutching a notebook, which he waved for emphasis while he talked to Mike, the distribution manager. The man's image arrested her, bringing Doug back, all of him, bringing back the anger, the pain she felt at losing a lover, the frustration of ending up at this stupid job just so she could feed herself and pay the rent. She teared up with sadness and anger, and began walking toward him, sure that if this man wasn't Doug, he was his brother, and he'd be able to get in touch with him. She bumped into a woman leaving the restroom.

"Hey, missy, watch it—" But she brushed her off.

When she reached the man her mouth opened to speak, but nothing came out. Now she could see him, all of him, and no, it wasn't Doug. Feeling drained from her face, the emotion fell away from her as fast as it had risen, and she dropped her lunch bag. She was close to him, close enough to see how the stubble of his beard grew, close enough to see to see his teeth—nice teeth, white and even, teeth that belonged in the mouth of a tall, good looking man. The expression on his face froze, as if he were in the middle of a laugh. He blinked once and looked at her, then looked at the lunch bag on the ground before Mike came into view. Mike wasn't in the middle of a laugh.

"Yes, ah, Marie, isn't it? Marie? What can I do for you?"

Mary Ellen wasn't looking at Mike. She didn't even hear him. She was looking at the man's right hand—actually, she was looking at the spot where his right hand should have been. He was wearing a short-sleeved polo shirt, and his solid looking arm ended where his hand should have started. But there was no right hand there. There was nothing there, nothing but open space, not a hook, not a prosthetic hand formed into the shape of a mannequin hand, nothing, just an emptiness at the end of his arm for her imagination to fill in.

But there was something. It was something that made her stare and something that made her heart swell with excitement while simultaneously crushing it with dread. It was a truth not quite in her stomach, but not quite in her crotch. It was something close to that place that erupted from within her once a month, something warm and twitchy, crampy and gassy—something magnetic, and it felt like it came into her from the end of the man's arm.

His stump—and that's the word that came to her immediately, even though she didn't want to think of that word, even though she was trying to force herself to use another word, but she couldn't, not yet—his stump was smooth, and rounded, and the skin had pulled back to his arm in such a way so that on one side of the end of the stump there was a vertical seam running for a couple of inches before it disappeared into the wrist. And the end of the stump bulged slightly, giving it a separate identity from the rest of his arm. What it all looked like to Mary Ellen was a penis. A huge, arm-sized penis, emerging from the sleeve of his shirt and ending with a round, engorged head.

"It's Mary Ellen," she said. She was looking at the man's arm that looked like a penis, and she felt her mind split into multiple tracks, like the physical separation of songs on an old vinyl LP record. She could see her thoughts revolving like that, each one a different song, all of them part of the album. There was Mike, her manager, to whom she had just corrected by giving him her name, Mary Ellen, not Marie. There was the man, who looked so much like Doug that the bitter emotion she'd been cloaking with indignation these past weeks rushed back. There was her job, the place where she was standing right now, the present. And there was his arm, a strange, wonderful looking thing that she wanted to run up and grab, feel it, explore it. It was the hit single, with a catchy refrain, a classic, and she blushed at her reaction.

"Mary Ellen," Mike said. He frowned the way a parent frowns at a child for staring at somebody different. "Is there something I can do for you? Mary Ellen?"

Shame overcame her, and she hurried away from them. She kept her head down until she reached the loading dock, out of everyone's sight. Despite the cool shade offered by the trees crowding up beside the building at the dock, the place was shunned by the smokers. Mary Ellen sat with her sandwich in her lap, looking down at the soggy bread and the can of soda by her feet. Several ants moved by the can, each

80

stopping for a moment to inspect the cold, smooth surface before continuing into the spotty ground vegetation. She thought her life was like this, like an ant's journey, stopping here and there to check something out, meandering. But she wasn't part of a colony. She was alone. She'd been meandering and stopping to check things out for a long time. Now she felt like she'd lost her way, she didn't know how to go back, but she didn't know how to go forward, either. She thought she'd have to start smoking and join the others, stupefied in the broiling sun, shivering in the blistering cold.

Tears surprised her, showering her sandwich. She sat there, hanging her head, and the water drooled from her eyes. Her body didn't flinch, there was no feeling in the pit of her stomach, or higher. Just the tears, pouring from her head, a system separate from her other parts, leaking into the humid afternoon.

"Is it okay if I join you?"

His voice startled her, and she thought it came from the within the thick undergrowth a few feet away. The tears stopped immediately, as soon as she lifted her head, as if there were a valve operated by a switch that turned crying on and off with the lifting and hanging of her head. A bone in her neck cracked and her chin came out beyond her teeth. She turned and saw the man with the arm like a penis standing there. His small briefcase was tucked under his left arm, and his left hand held a paper bag. His right arm hung in the heat. Her tears dried up and her heart began pounding, rushing into her throat.

She shrugged and tried to smile. "Sure."

He sat beside her on the loading dock, to her left, and from the corner of her eye she peeked to see how he did it without tipping over. The penis arm stayed at his side, and he used his legs to squat all the way down until his bottom—which seemed to round itself, like a pear— touched the decking. Then he squirted his legs forward and let them dangle. He looked up at her and said, "Best view in the house."

Now that she could hear it, now that she could listen to it, his voice sounded soft and light, like a sunny morning. It rolled into her ears like the tide crushing the water against the rocks, the same sound the water of the Cape Cod Canal made the day she and Doug spread a blanket out in a hidden cove and allowed the sun to enter their bodies. It was urgent and rhythmic, but if you slipped and fell into it, it could kill you.

"I'm like you," he continued. "I'd rather be outside, even when it's hot. Find a little shade, relax. Listen to the sounds of nature, the air moving through the trees. You know, up here, at the edge of the trees, the air's always moving. There's always some kind of breeze to catch. It's not like the southwest. Texas. Nothing moves down there in the summer. Even the heat stops shimmering."

She tried to be nonchalant in her spying, glancing over at him as she took a bite of her sandwich. She wanted to see how he did things. She wanted to see how he ate his lunch, how his hand handled the job, what he did with his right arm. He held the edge of the paper bag with his left hand and plunged his right arm into the opening. The sandwich scooted out onto his lap, and with the fingers of his left hand he quickly opened the plastic wrap and grasped the sandwich. The fingers moved quickly, like a pianist playing an allegro. They were long and articulate, each moving individually, but working together, with the pinky stretching far around the bottom of the sandwich, bracing it. They reminded her of Doug's fingers, how he could stretch his hand across her abdomen, the tip of his thumb reaching the lower curve of her breast, the pinky sliding down through the tangle of her hair, all the way down.

"Another gourmet baloney sandwich," he said, chewing. "I never know what I'll get."

She startled. She hadn't seen a ring on his left hand. "Does someone make your sandwiches for you?" She regretted the words as soon as they were out, but she straightened her back anyway, trying to make herself appear more proper.

"General store," he said. "They have a little deli counter there. I just tell Jen to reach into the case and pull out whatever her hand lands on. And that's my lunch. I'm David."

He put the sandwich down and reached across his body with his left hand. Mary Ellen automatically brought her right hand forward, reaching for his right arm, reaching for the end of the arm, where his hand was missing, where the skin had been smoothed over and healed to look like the head of a penis. His left hand intercepted her, and they grasped each other, awkwardly at first, but he held her until she relaxed, until his long fingers, incredibly soft fingers, gently squeezed the strength from her hand. She felt it come up her arm, not like an electric shock, but rather a warming, a gentleness that spread into her body until it dissipated through the tips of her toes and the nipples on her breasts.

She felt herself smiling, and then she remembered that it was her turn to introduce herself, and her smile vanished. "I'm Mary Ellen."

"Well, Mary Ellen, it's just not true."

"Excuse me?"

"What Mike said. Told me you were a snob when I asked him what your name was. Oops. Sorry about that. I already knew your name when I asked you. Hope you're not mad."

His voice loped like dog turned loose in a field, and the plushness of his voice sounded almost southern, delicate. But she didn't hear the words. She felt them.

"I told Mike that's probably because you're too smart for this place. You don't look like you belong here. Do you?"

"What? I'm sorry, I didn't hear you."

"I was just saying that you don't look like you should be working the line in a manufacturing plant like this. There's an intelligence about you I could see right away. You seem overqualified, just by the economy of your movements. The way you hold yourself, like you've known dignity, and this isn't it. Am I right?"

She looked at him for a moment, wondering who he was, what he was doing here. "I hate this place. I just had to pay the rent. My boyfriend took off, and I don't have anywhere else to go, so I took the first job I could find."

Her stomach fell away from her, torn by the gravity of what she'd just said. Why tell him so much—everything—without knowing who he is? But the words were out so easy, so natural, and she didn't care, didn't care about any of it, and she looked at his arm and she felt warm and happy and there was a little buzzing inside her.

He chewed his sandwich, smiled, nodded. The buzzer signaling the end of lunch sounded inside the plant, and she rose. "Will you go out with me. I mean, would you like to go out tonight, maybe get something to eat? Something besides baloney?" His skin was porcelain and it captured the light opaquely. She had the strong urge to touch his face, to let her fingers disappear into that smooth skin.

He looked up at her, and though the noon sun shone in his face, he didn't blink. He finished chewing and said, "I'd like that, Mary Ellen."

She returned to work but hardly concentrated on what she was doing for the rest of the afternoon. It was like David said, she was overqualified. Her mind rinsed through things, the way he reminded her of Doug, his arm, the way he chewed his sandwich, his arm, his gangly way of talking, his arm, his arm, his arm that looked like a huge penis, the low-frequency buzzing inside her.

How could he not know? She wondered if she missed something there. Surely he's aware of that, of its effect on women—and some men, now that she thought about it. But he seemed so unaware, so regular. Normal. But still. That arm. It was because he ignored it that it became an erotic fixation within her, aligning itself with her humming interior. It was that tingling she felt in her nipples, the way her toes went numb when he shook her hand. She allowed it to happen and she was glad for it because there had been so little to be glad for, and this felt good. She stood at her machine and watched Jasmine and wondered what she'd do with a man whose arm looked like a giant penis. She wondered if she'd know what to do with it, or if she'd just yell "Yee-haw!" and try to jump on it.

"What the hell are you all giddy about?" Jasmine said, but Mary Ellen didn't answer, she just watched the machine play out its string of repetitive motions for the rest of the afternoon. She felt reckless and free of the misery that had held her, like the heat bouncing between the corrugated buildings. She walked by them on her way to her car after the shift ended and hardly felt the afternoon heat. Even though their day was over, her co-workers lingered outside the plant, smoking, as if they were dogs wearing an electronic collar that prevented them from leaving the area of the building, prevented them from doing anything but smoking.

Mary Ellen rushed past them without feeling her legs move, without feeling the hot air in her lungs. She left the space between the buildings and when she turned out onto the gravel parking lot, he was there. Leaning against her car, his left arm cradling his right, almost tenderly, he looked at the plant's long driveway, as if he were waiting for something to come from that direction. Her eyes went to his right arm, the way he held it, the way the end rubbed against his upper left arm, and she couldn't think of anything else. And then she was there, standing next to him, and she didn't remember the ride in his car, how he drove with one arm, or how he knew which car was hers, or the first drink she ordered.

"What's a mojito?" he said.

"I don't know but everyone's drinking them this summer. Everyone except the people I work with, they're still on Marlboros and Budweiser."

He laughed and shifted in his seat. She watched him cross his legs without effort, without moving the rest of his body. She did the same, and she felt her underwear rub pleasantly against her skin, against the right places. Something seemed so odd, so untypical about him, the way he held himself, the way he moved, like a dancer. Or maybe it was the arm. She looked around the little pub. There was a big bar against one wall, very dark, with stainless steel stools. Round wooden tables filled the space against the other wall, and more people came in and filled them, until what had started as a quiet space with only the sound of a golf match on television became a burble of happy people after work. She loved it because the people were so upbeat, laughing, full of life, and none of them smoked. None of them looked like corpses and there were all different types, some business people, some workers, some tourists, and they all seemed free and it made her feel that she chose the right place when he'd asked her where she wanted to go.

It was after her second mojito that she noticed. People filled the pub, the waitress came over to them several times with drinks and appetizers, David got up to use the men's room, and she fixed on the way he swung his hips, as if he were showing off for her. But nobody in the pub seemed to notice his right arm. Mary Ellen fixed on this, to the exclusion of the sounds around her, the faces of the people there. How could they not notice? She sipped her mojito. Can't they see what I see? Can't they see this giant penis, this erotic mass of skin and articulation? Don't they wonder why the end of his arm is shaped like a perfectly helmeted cock? Complete with a rim that she could almost feel sliding—

"Mary Ellen? Are you still here?

David was laughing and looking up at the waitress, who looked back at him, but didn't seem to see the huge cock lying across the table, pointing at Mary Ellen.

"I think we're all set with drinks for now," he told the waitress, and she receded into the thickening crowd. He turned to Mary Ellen. "Is that okay? I mean, you're still drinking that one."

She felt herself smiling as she said, "Yeah, that's fine." Then, she came back, just a little. "You know, I was wondering how you knew that was my car in the parking lot."

"It was easy," he said. "I just looked for the one that wasn't like all the others."

"You mean the ashtray wasn't overflowing with cigarette butts?"

He smiled but he didn't laugh.

"No. I just put myself in your shoes. Didn't you feel it? When I came and sat down next to you—didn't you feel something different? I just used that feeling to home in on your car. Like there was a bunch of you left all over it, just radiating you, and I could feel it. So I went to it."

Her hands circled the glass and the droplets of moisture gathered on the outside became a torrent, soaking her fingers. She felt wet all over.

86

"You had this look of pain, this sad face," he continued. "I just had to find out what that was all about, and I think I did. It's about your boyfriend leaving you, right?"

"How did you know?"

"You told me, remember? But that's not really it, is it? Our boyfriends and girlfriends are forever breaking our hearts, it's what they do. How we react shows the truth about us."

"That's interesting, but I don't think a shitty boyfriend qualifies as a heart-breaker."

David sat back and rested his right arm on his lap. He absently stroked it with his left hand.

"I'm going to guess that it wasn't about the end of a relationship, was it?"

"What's the 'it'?"

"What you're feeling. There's something underneath it, something burning in you, something you want but have never had. That's why you just didn't leave here when your boyfriend left you. It's why you got a job in that crappy place, it's why you're miserable."

Her mojito was gone and she desperately wanted another.

"There's nowhere else to go. I thought Doug and I—I thought, we planned on being together, and there's just no home to go to for me now."

"If it will make you feel any better, you can tell me what happened."

She shrugged. "Nothing. Nothing's what happened. That's what the problem was with Doug. He couldn't do anything. At all. He couldn't love me. At least not the way I needed. And I just couldn't live like that, so he had to leave."

"You made him leave."

She leaned forward and almost put her face into her empty glass.

"He couldn't—I needed something, something he couldn't give me. It wasn't a relationship, was it? How could it be? He couldn't do that, you know?"

Her hands were very tight around the base of the glass and it felt like a smooth shaft in her fingers. She began to move around in her seat, to cross and uncross her legs, trying to get comfortable, but she felt like she was about to combust, to erupt in flames, and even as she had the thought she saw herself tearing her clothes off, ripping them away until she was naked and free to be herself.

"Do you know how hard it is?" she asked in a voice barely audible above the rising din of the pub. "Do you know what it's like to love someone who can't give you the completeness you need, someone who makes you feel like it's you that's the problem, when all you really want is to feel whole, to feel like you're the kind of woman a man thinks about all day long when he's away from you?"

He leaned forward, sliding his right arm across the table, until the tip brushed against her hand, and said "Yes." She had her first orgasm.

In the car ride to his house, she told him about the afternoon on the Cape Cod Canal. She looked out the open window and felt the night air, still hot, but moving, blowing across her face, and she told him all about Doug, how she rode her bike behind him just to look at his ass, his legs pumping the pedals, and how they found a little spot down from the paved path that ran alongside the canal, a little cove, and they blocked the way there with their bikes and she took off her clothes and when she tried to pull Doug's bike shorts off he stopped her. She thought it was a game at first, a way to turn her on more, and he only took his shirt off, which would have been enough for some women, she said, that chest, so smooth, and his tiny nipples, like the tips of pens, and his abdomen muscles braided across his midriff. Her hand slid inside his shorts and she heard him then, he cried, or gasped, or froze, and her fingers knew, her fingers told her, her fingers told her everything she needed to know, saw the future for her, because her fingers found nothing, there was nothing of him, nothing for her fingers to excite, nothing to feed her body, and they stood there in the hot afternoon sun on the Cape Cod Canal, Mary Ellen, daughter of Tom and Jennifer Ryan, naked, with her hand thrust into the Lycra bike shorts of Doug Randal, her fingers searching over and over for something to make her a woman, to make him a man, so that they knew who they were, anything, and finding only emptiness, a vacancy she couldn't understand, and her fingers realizing everything she'd need to know about the future and communicating that back up her arm and into her body, which suddenly broke out in goosebumps.

David lived in a small house not unlike her little shack. It was neat, as she expected, and without lots of distractions, like artwork on the walls or rows of books and CD's. As he tossed his keys on the counter, he started a little narrative, but she interrupted him, pulling him around by the crook of his arm, spinning him into her. She reached up with her right hand and pressed her palm into the back of his neck and pulled his face into hers, his lips against hers, and she was aware of the pose, how it looked like an old Hollywood movie scene, and it felt good. His right hand slid around the small of her back and she shivered, but not with cold, with heat, and behind her closed eyes she pictured his arm, which she now thought of as just a giant penis, a long erection, stretching out from his shoulder, and she began to melt.

She was aware of certain parallels, but none her mind or her body would disallow, nothing to stop her now as she pulled her clothes off with her free hand, while keeping his lips pressed to hers. And she didn't even notice those lips, soft and shaped so differently. Why hadn't she noticed that about David before? How could she miss something like that? But already she forgot it, forgot even the way his waist seemed so svelte, almost concave, as she ran her hand back up his side when she'd artfully managed to strip herself with one hand while kissing him and gripping his neck.

David was talking, David was saying something, he was trying to speak, but she wouldn't let him.

"No, it's better this way, don't you think?"

She pulled him onto her, onto the couch, and if she'd bothered to look up, if she'd bothered to look away from his right arm, away from the end of that arm where the skin was so uniquely folded back over the end of the arm, so that it resembled a huge, erect penis, as if someone had deliberately molded it to look that way, she might have seen his eyes. She might have seen that mixture of surprise and terror there, contained in their widening, like the eyes of a child who's about to dive into the pool for the first time.

But she saw nothing except herself. She saw her hands, working together on the right arm, sliding up and down it. She saw the inside of her body, liquid and bloody, an infinite collection of cells all pointing in the same direction, all pointing out from the intersection of her thighs, which she parted now, and drew the end of David's right arm into her. And as he spoke to her she heard nothing, none of his confession, his apology for not telling her sooner, his desire for her without wanting to hurt her. She didn't see him pull off his pants with his left hand to reveal nothing but underwear that matched her own, because she had everything she wanted in his right arm, and she moved the arm into her, her body convulsed once, and she relaxed, her bones coming unjointed, her mind untethered, and a thick, silent darkness wrapped around her, until she fell away into a place where she wasn't alone anymore.

"The Gore"

Jedward crouched in the hedge behind the basketball hoop and watched the front door of the rectory. It was an ornate front door, with four panes of glass divided by a crucifix of wood. On the crucifix was a real, wood-carved Jesus, complete with drooping head and anguished look, looking like he was about to meet his maker. In order to open the door to the rectory, you had to grab Jesus' right hand, and when you did, the nail that pinned his hand to the cross jabbed into the palm of your hand, drawing blood more often than not.

"It's a fine way to remember the Lord's suffering," said Father Mc-Cleary, whenever someone—usually the mother of a toddler with a bleeding hand—complained about the aggressive door to the rectory. It wouldn't have been a big deal had the catechism classes been held somewhere else, where the door handle didn't make you bleed. But Father McCleary insisted on having the classes in the rectory, because he had a colostomy bag that needed to be emptied every five minutes due to the amount of vodka he consumed throughout the day. And Father McCleary insisted on leading the prayers at the start of every class. He told his parishioners that he had so little else to do in this tiny parish in

Vermont's Northeast Kingdom that he needed to justify his job every way he could.

Jedward's plan was simple: Suzy Fourchette, a nurse from St. Johnsbury, had gone in to make a confession; he'd wait for her to come out, then he'd run in the church and poke the padre in the colostomy bag with a broomstick, rendering him befouled. This would give Jedward the critical seconds he needed to change the wayward priest's views: Jedward had startling news to share. For Father McCleary was not the Irish Catholic he claimed to be; he wasn't even the Roman Catholic his clerical collar claimed him to be.

Father Bathbar "Bill" McCleary was born Bathbar Jehousafits, the son of a traveling Northeast Nominationalist preacher named Trafalgar Jehousafits, himself a wayward Presbyterian. Bathbar—or "Bill" as he preferred to call himself since his dismal defection to the great unwashed religion, as Jedward called the Catholics—came to his Irishness and the priesthood in an unusual way. While traveling through New England with group of carnies attached to a regional fair, Bathbar, Jedward, and their father, Trafalgar Jehousafits, stopped in a little fishing village called Green Harbor. Trafalgar thought that the stop was precipitous, for when he learned that Green Harbor was swarming with papists, he saw an opportunity to convert the freaks to a legitimate following.

Instead, Bathbar, suffering all the usual rages of a 16-year old Nominationalist with no sexual outlets, ran away from the fair with a sassy redhead named Suzy McCleary. Just when Bathbar was getting the hang of Suzy, she became pregnant. Suzy's father, a local fisherman named Max "Mental" McCleary, who operated a fleet of three draggers, hinted that Bathbar's hands might end up in bait bags if he didn't make things right, so Bathbar drove Suzy to Vermont for an abortion. This was not what Mental McCleary had in mind. As Bathbar waited for Suzy at the doctor's office, he spied her father's pickup truck pulling into the parking lot, and the hulking man piling out of the truck with a gaff in one hand and a 40-ounce bottle of Narragansett in the other.

Bathbar went out the back door, but he didn't go home. He went west, rightly guessing that a fisherman would never turn his back on the sea. For twenty years Bathbar drifted through the country, finding work as an auctioneer in Wichita, a roustabout in Wyoming, and a deck hand on a crab boat in Dutch Harbor, Alaska. But he only made real money when he took up his father's legacy of preaching. Soon he was following the county fair circuit around the lower 48, preaching the word of God, or anything else that would draw a paying crowd, making enough money to buy his own Cadillac, and staying with one outfit only until his drinking got him kicked out.

By now Bathbar had begun calling himself Bill McCleary, in honor of his first love's surname. One summer he followed the fair circuit up to Vermont, a place he hadn't seen since he fled the doctor's office in Brattleboro all those years ago. The place held powerful memories for him, and he considered leaving his traveling ways and staying there, when he fell ill.

At first diagnosed with Crohn's disease, Bathbar—Bill—was subsequently diagnosed with colorectal cancer, and underwent a TME—total mesorectal excision. While recovering in a hospital in St. Johnsbury, Vermont, he met a redheaded nurse named Suzy Fourchette, who took a shine to him when she first read his chart.

"McCleary was my maiden name," she told him. "Where are you from?"

"All over," he told her. He was simultaneously frightened and delighted that the former Suzy McCleary didn't recognize him as the frightened boy who left her with her feet in stirrups more than twenty years ago.

"Hmm," she said, still studying his chart, "it says here that you're a minister. What church?"

Bill, long proficient at talking fast on his feet, remembered a boarded up Catholic church named Our Lady of Perpetual Agony in a little town called Avery's Gore. He'd stopped there a month ago while catching up to the fair when his Cadillac overheated. He noticed the church because it was the only other building on Main Street, directly across from the gas station/general store/snack shack/town hall/school house/Masonic Lodge/adult bookstore.

"Our Lady of Perpetual Agony," he blurted out to Suzy. Old feelings erupted inside him as he gazed at her.

"Oh, you're a Catholic priest. How come it doesn't say that on your chart?"

"I was delusional when I got here."

Bill—or Father Bill, as he was now calling himself—was outfitted with a colostomy bag and pronounced cancer-free. As he recovered, he spun a tale for Suzy about his church in Avery's Gore. He said he was trying to raise money to fix it up, to make it a symbol of hope that everyone in the region could look to. Bill secretly hoped to lure Suzy there, where he could reveal himself to her, and perhaps pick up where they left off. On the day he was discharged, Suzy wheeled him out to his Cadillac.

"Please come and see me in Avery's Gore," he implored her. "It's so lonely out there."

"But what about your congregation?"

"There are six other days in the week."

Father Bill drove away, stopping first at a state liquor store to pick up a bottle of Absolut Citron, then to Avery's Gore, a triangle shaped township in northeast Vermont forgotten by everyone except the one person who lived there, Mary Sullivan. Father Bill discovered this interesting fact when he drove back into Avery's Gore and stopped at the gas station/general store/snack shack/town hall/school house/Masonic Lodge/adult bookstore to get a bite to eat. The placemats were advertisements for the local businesses, and every business began with the name "Sullivan," like Sullivan's Service Station and Sullivan's General Store and Sullivan's Snack Shack and Sullivan-at-Law and Sullivan School and Sullivan's Adult Bookstore.

When the waitress/mechanic/town clerk/butcher/elementary schoolteacher Mary Sullivan asked, "Whatcha doin in these parts, Padre?" Father Bill answered, "I'm your new parish priest. Burlington sent me down to reopen Our Lady of Perpetual Agony to serve this community."

Mary set the coffee pot down and frowned at him. "That doesn't seem likely. I think I'd've heard about that." Mary had a voice that sounded like a tuba stuffed with socks, and when she crossed her arms before her truck-tire sized breasts she looked as big as a mattress. Father Bill wiped the corner of his mouth with his napkin and smiled up at her.

"Well why don't you come over to the church tonight and I'll tell you all about it."

Father Bill had his hands full with Mary Sullivan. Herself a lapsed Catholic, she began showing up for mass—and showing up in his bedroom—forcing Father Bill to improvise on the spot.

"That doesn't sound like the mass I remember," Mary told him.

"Maybe if I got some sleep I'd come a little closer."

"Are you sure you're a priest?"

"Are you sure you're a Catholic?"

Soon Father Bill was entwined in all of Mary's businesses. Avery's Gore was so small—barely a square mile—that all Mary's business came from folks traveling to and from St. Johnsbury to work. And that's where the parishioners came from. At first, Father Bill objected to having real Catholics come to mass, as opposed to Mary. But Mary saw it as a way to lure people into town on Sundays, her slowest day of the week.

"I serve more breakfasts, sell more gas, wrap more meat and rent more porn on Sundays than any other day of the week," she declared, after promoting the catechism classes, which she herself taught, and which drew more people in on Sundays. And it was into that world of roadside religion and pancakes and colostomy bags that Jedward Jehousafits came with a broomstick one Wednesday morning.

Jedward had been looking for his brother for over twenty years—since Bathbar left and their father died trying to win a bet from a Kentuckian by getting a congregation of dogs to bark the Lord's Prayer. When the dogs wouldn't cooperate, Trafalgar Jehousafits became enraged and cuffed one of the dogs, and it bit him. The dog turned out to be rabid, and Trafalgar died foaming at the mouth in a dirty little hospital in Meigs County, Ohio.

But Trafalgar left a will, and in it he left his two sons vast amounts of money with the single stipulation that they build a church in their father's honor. "Through my own weaknesses I have dragged these boys around the Americas pursuing ill-gotten gains," he wrote. "It's is my wish that they share in my wealth, but before they do so I require them to create, in my name, an everlasting church, a monument to righteousness."

Jedward knew that his father was adept at swindling hicks out of their last five bucks, but he was not prepared for the amount of money he and his brother stood to inherit: two million each. When Jedward—who was three years older than Bathbar, 19 at the time of their father's death, asked the attorney how this was possible, the attorney said "Junk bonds." It was the end of the 80s and Trafalgar had invested his money as shrewdly as he'd swindled people out of it, playing the markets for all they were worth, amplifying his investment many times over. Upon the old preacher's death the money was moved into a conservative trust.

And that's where it stayed while Jedward combed the country, searching for his brother in order to satisfy the terms of their father's will and collect their windfall. But Jedward wasn't motivated by any brotherly altruism. He, too, had finally rejected his father's life, and spent the last twenty years working on a lobster boat Down East on the Maine coast. When Trafalgar's lawyer found him, Jedward's arms were buried in a bait box filled with codfish carcasses. When Trafalgar's lawyer outlined the stipulations of the will, Jedward raised his bloody arms to the sky and said, "Hallelujah!"

Finding his brother had been more difficult than Jedward ever ex- pected. He started where he and Bathbar had ended as brothers—the little fishing village of Green Harbor. That's where he encountered Max "Mental" McCleary, a walrus-sized man with tiny black pebbles for eyes and catcher's mitts for hands. When Jedward told Max he was looking for his brother, Max went mental. It was only after promising to bring him back to Green Harbor that Max dropped Jedward to the deck of his boat. Max turned and looked out to sea and said, "I am going to kill that boy for what he did to my daughter."

"Did he hurt her?" Jedward asked cautiously, rubbing his neck and getting up from the slick deck of the lobster boat.

"He wrecked her life."

"Where is she now?" Jedward was already thinking that Max's daughter might lead him to his brother. Max suddenly brightened and turned away from the ocean.

"Oh, she's a successful nurse at a hospital in St. Johnsbury, Vermont."

Jedward frowned.

"I thought you said he wrecked her life."

Max darkened and his fists clenched. "He got her pregnant and then took her to Vermont for an abortion. She'd be married with children by now if it wasn't for him. Now she's just successful. It's terrible, and I'll kill him for it."

Jedward carefully left the boat. He'd spent the past twenty years around lobster fishermen, and he knew how unstable they were, given to blaming everything and everyone but themselves for their own misfortunes and the vagaries of hunting crustaceans on the ocean floor. He left Mental Max stewing and staring out into the ocean. He thought that Suzy the nurse might be as good a place to start as any. By the time he pulled away from Green Harbor he was excited, and he didn't see the rusty pickup truck following him up the highway.

When he arrived at the Northeast Kingdom Regional Medical Center in St. Johnsbury, Vermont, Jedward had a plan. It was so strange to him and his experiences that it sounded brilliant: he'd tell the truth. He'd find this Suzy and tell her he was Bathbar's brother and that he was trying to find him and that they were going to inherit two million dollars if they built a church. And then he'd wait for "it." "It" was what his father, Trafalgar, had taught he and Bathbar. "It" was human nature, the incessant need to not only survive, but outdo, defeat, exceed, the other guy. "It" drove

97

sober men to drink, chaste men to sex, and peaceful men to war. "It" also filled Trafalgar's pockets throughout the years, and now Jedward intended to cash in on the compounded interest of "it."

When she looked up from her post at the nurse manager's station on the third floor of the hospital, Suzy's natural reaction was to move her hand to the security button next to the phone. Pushing that button would produce several uniformed officers within two minutes. But there was something familiar looking about the disheveled man coming toward her. He was smiling, almost bashful, as he approached, and moved her hand away and smiled back. She thought he looked lost.

"Hello, Suzy," he said, and she immediately taken back. Not only did this man look familiar, but he sounded familiar. And now he smelled familiar, the smell she grew up with: fish. As the daughter of a lobster fisherman, she was imbued with the knowledge of that smell, and it brought her back. It also reminded her of how she got here: the boy who got her pregnant, her father's rage, finding solace in school, the failed marriages, the unfulfilled longing for something lost.

"Do I know you?" she asked.

"Well, no, not exactly. But I think you know my brother."

And Jedward launched into his tale, a long explanation of the story of him and Bathbar and their father's final wishes and the money. And when he was finished, Suzy thought of Father Bill and his desire to fix up the church in Avery's Gore. For now she didn't say anything to Jedward about Father Bill—there was something weird going on, because she'd had the same feeling about Father Bill that she'd had about Jedward, though with Father Bill she just thought it was because he had her maiden name. There was just enough strangeness going on to make her want to drive out and see Father Bill.

Suzy shrugged. "I'm sorry, Jedward, but I never saw Bathbar after... well, after he left me. It was a long time ago."

Jedward thanked her and went out to his car in the parking lot. He watched the employee entrance for two and a half hours, until Suzy emerged. And then he followed her as she drove west on Route 2, to

Avery's Gore. He stayed just far enough behind her so that she wouldn't notice him, but he was so intent on following her that he failed to notice the rusty pickup truck smelling of fish that was following him.

Father Bill—Bathbar—was unprepared when Suzy showed up. He thought he'd have to go back and find her, after he'd swindled Mary Sullivan out of everything in Avery's Gore. But in Mary Sullivan he'd met his match. She was shrewd and cautious, trying to manipulate him as much as he tried to manipulate her. They had reached an unspoken standoff, and the tension rolled around the little dot of their town like spring fog. The only place Father Bill could escape the iron rule of Mary Sullivan was inside the church. Despite the fact that there were no official parishioners during the week for Our Lady of Perpetual Hope, Father Bill had posted a schedule for the sacrament of confession. In the small office at the back of the church, he'd found some ancient paperwork left by the last administrators of the church, with a schedule for confessions. The last pastor—Father James Sullivan, if Bill were deciphering the faded handwriting correctly—offered residents of Avery's Gore opportunities to confess their sins twice a day and three times on Saturdays. This puzzled Bill: how much trouble could you get into in this narrow gap in the woods, and how many people were around to get into that trouble? That's where Bill's ignorance of Catholics failed him; he didn't understand that all a Catholic needed to sin was a body and the breath to fill it.

What Bill really needed was time alone in the confessional with his bottle of Absolut vodka—or, as he called it, his bottle of "Absolution." There he could sip quietly and escape Mary's oppressive eyes. So he was startled when he heard the doors to the church open, followed by a sharp exclamation as blood was drawn from another unsuspecting penitent. He was even more surprised when someone entered the confessional and said, "Forgive me Father, for I have sinned."

Jedward, waiting in the bushes by the basketball hoop, wanted desperately to see what was going on inside. He snuck around to the back and listened, but could hear nothing; he couldn't even hear the rusty old pickup truck rolling to a stop in front of the church. He tried the door to

the office and it opened quietly. Inside he found a desk piled with papers. He tiptoed over to the only other door and entered the sacristy,
though he didn't recognize it as such; to him it was just a room with a
sink and a crucifix on the wall. But now he could hear muffled voices
coming from the inside of the church. He poked his head out and found
that he was looking out at the dozen or so pews that formed the church.
He was on the altar. To his left were the confessionals, and he could see
a woman's feet under the curtain of one side, but he still couldn't hear
what was being said. He removed his shoes and padded over to the
other side of the confessional, and slipped in.

By now, Mary's curiosity was piqued. Three cars in Avery's Gore on
a Wednesday was a new record, and she had to find out what that clown
of a phony priest was up to. She'd decided to tolerate him as long as he
was making her money, and the whole religion thing proved to be a boon
for her businesses, except the Masonic Lodge, which never really
seemed to come into its own. As she sat in the gas station/general store/
snack shack/town hall/school house/Masonic Lodge/adult bookstore, she
saw one car pull up and stop near the playground. A woman got out,
wearing what looked like nurse's scrubs. She walked directly to the
church and looked at the schedule for confessions posted beside the
door. Then she grabbed the handle, yelped, and pulled her hand back
quickly. Mary chuckled to herself. That's what you get for going near a
church, she thought. The woman disappeared inside and Mary lost her
humor. What would some out-of-towner be doing in that shithole church
in the middle of the week? She didn't believe for one minute that she
was going in for the phony confessions Bill had posted next to the front
door; she knew he went in there to be alone and play with himself or
drink or whatever. Mary waited and watched for a few minutes, and
when the woman didn't come out right away, she decided to go see what
was going on. She was just about to lock up the gas station/general
store/snack shack/town hall/school house/Masonic Lodge/adult bookstore when something stopped her.

Another car pulled up, and a wild looking, bearded man got out and looked around, then snuck up to the church, watching it from the basket-ball court before disappearing around the back. Now Mary knew something was going on, and it was all going on around Bill—or because of Bill. She cursed herself for letting him into Avery's Gore, and was again about to exit the gas station/general store/snack shack/town hall/school house/Masonic Lodge/adult bookstore when a third vehicle pulled up in front of the church. A broad-shouldered man got out of a rusty pickup truck with Massachusetts plates and looked around, his head stretching up as if he were sniffing the air. Her heart skipped a beat; he was incredibly handsome, rough looking. He reached back into his pickup truck and pulled out a gun, a pump-action shotgun, she thought. She started to feel squishy inside. The man walked up to the doors of the church and pulled them open without hesitation or exclamation. This is going to be good, Mary thought, and she locked up the gas station/general store/snack shack/town hall/school house/Masonic Lodge/adult bookstore and hurried across the street before she missed something important.

Back in the confessional, Father Bill knocked back a swallow of vodka and tried to see who was sitting on the other side of the curtain. The voice sounded familiar, but it wasn't Mary's, and what other woman had he spoken to lately? Was it one of the mothers who dropped off her child for catechism? He thought he should say something, but since this was his first confession, he was at a loss for words.

"Father?" came the voice again. And then the curtain slid back, revealing Suzy Fourchette, the nurse, to him. He gasped.

"Suzy?"

"Billy, why did you leave me like that?"

"Pardon?"

"Billy, it's me, Suzy, Suzy McCleary, and I know you're not a priest, so you can stop with all this—" She gestured to the inside of the confessional, then looked at his Roman collar. "I've known who your were since you were in the hospital. You must have told someone your real name when they admitted you, because it was on your chart. St. Johnsbury isn't brimming with Jehousafitses. It wasn't an accident that you ended up under my care, Billy."

"You knew? You knew all along? But why didn't you say anything?"

"What could I say, Bill? I was shocked at first. I mean, imagine seeing you in the state you were in—the state you are in—and then hearing you give my name as yours. You must have still felt something for me."

Bill bowed his head. "You're right. I've just lived an awful life, and when I saw you at the hospital, it brought back all those feelings from when we were kids, the good and the bad feelings. I've thought about you every day, how I left you there like that. I'm sorry—can you forgive me?"

"Oh, Billy." She reached through the curtain and took his hand. "Of course I can. But you've got to get out of this place. Don't you know what happens in Avery's Gore?"

He didn't have a chance to answer. The curtain on the other side of the confessional flew open, revealing Jedward.

"I'll tell you what's going to happen in Avery's Gore," said Jedward. Bill reacted with confusion and surprise, but only because someone else was on that side of the confessional; he was shocked to see a bearded face so close to his own. Suzy reacted with recognition. It was the man who came to see her earlier that day at the hospital; it was Bathbar's brother. Things came together for her, and from the look on Jedward's face, things were coming together for him: the church they were sitting in, their father's will, the money. In the moment before Bill—Bathbar— finally recognized his brother, Suzy and Jedward exchanged looks across the confessional, and Suzy was embarrassed by the thoughts racing through her head, that Our Lady of Perpetual Agony would be the perfect church to fix up, and that all that money would then go to Jedward and Bill. She felt terribly guilty, but then Bill interrupted her.

"Jedward? Is that you?"

"Yes, it's me. Who else would it be?"

Bill leaned back against the wall. "Holy shit. What are you doing here?"

"Ask her." Jedward nodded toward Suzy

Suzy put her face in her hands and cried. "Oh, Bill."

"What the hell's going on here?"

Jedward told him about their father and the money and the stipulations of the will and the church. He paused and looked around and said, "This church would do nicely."

"Is that what you thought?" Bill asked Suzy.

"Of course not, Bill. I thought about you. How could I have thought about anything else after you left me all those years ago?"

Bill looked at his brother. "You know I don't exactly own this place."

"Well who does? We'll buy it from them."

A sour expression covered Bill's face. "That might not be as easy as it sounds."

The door to the church flew open, and Mental McCleary came in, cursing the blood flowing from his right hand. In his left he held a shotgun.

"Goddammit!" he bellowed. "What the hell kind of church is this?"

Jedward, Bill, and Suzy emerged from the confessional to see Mental McCleary shaking the pain from his right hand.

"Dad!" Suzy said. "What are you doing here?"

"I came to kill the bastard that left you at the doctor's office alone after he knocked you up!"

Suzy shook her head. "Dad, that was twenty-five years ago. I think I've moved on from that. Put the gun down."

Bill was astonished. "You really earn your nickname every day, don't you?"

Mental McCleary turned red and shouldered the gun. "Now I'm going to blow your fucking head off!" But he didn't. The barrel of a revolver snugged up behind his ear and stopped him. It was followed by the voice of Mary Sullivan.

"Nobody's going to blow anybody's fucking head off," she said. "Except me, maybe." She reached around and took the shotgun from Mental McCleary and placed it in a pew. "Go stand over with them," she said.

Mental McCleary shuffled his bulk over to the others while Mary checked out his swagger. "Now, somebody needs to tell me what's going on in my town." She looked at Bill. "Let's start with you. What the hell are you doing?"

"I was hearing confessions," he said.

"You were the one doing the confessing," said Jedward.

"Be quiet," Mary said. "All right, let's start over. Introduce yourselves to me, and tell me what you're doing here."

By the time they'd finished all of them were seated in the pews. Mary had put the revolver away, but she was still facing the other three.

"How much money will you inherit?" she asked. "And don't lie, because I'm also a lawyer, and if you want to buy Avery's Gore from me I'll do the research on you and your father's will."

"Two million," Jedward mumbled. "Each."

She thought about it for a minute, then looked at Mental McCleary. "How's the lobster fishing business?"

"It sucks. I'd rather own my own fish market and sell overpriced swordfish to the tourists."

Mary softened. "How'd you like a business partner?"

"How much you got?"

She looked at Jedward. "A million."

Jedward shrugged his shoulders. "For a million, I want the deed to the whole town. The land, the church, the gas station/general store/snack shack/town hall/school house/Masonic Lodge/adult bookstore. Everything."

"Works for me. Mental? I mean, Max?" Max "Mental" McCleary would have cried, except the dollar signs soaked up his tears.

"One more thing," said Jedward, before they adjourned the meeting. "Who's Avery, and what's a gore?"

"Avery was my first husband. He and I bought this whole area, which is a triangle of land bordered by Knowlfield, Brookstone, and Silas. And that's what a gore is: when they surveyed the land for the individual town grants, there were stipulations about how much land could be granted for each town. The new towns couldn't exceed that area, so there were leftover parcels of land, triangle shaped, called gores. Avery and I bought this one and built this little place."

They all got up and walked outside, into the sunshine. Just then a car sped by. Mary looked at her watch. "Rush hour's starting. Don't forget the speed limit through town is 25. And you're the new sheriff, so don't hesitate to pull them over. I make a nice income from that. Once they start slowing down, they start stopping, and that's where you make your real money. Right, Bill?"

Bill didn't know what to say; he looked from Suzy to Jedward to Mary. He tried not to look at Mental McCleary. Mary and Mental went into Mary's house to help her start packing, leaving the three of them alone. Bill suddenly remembered something.

"Suzy, back in the church, you asked me if I knew what happened in Avery's Gore. What does happen here?"

She shook her head. "It must have been a legend, just a story. The people I work with all say this place is haunted, that strange things happen here. I guess they're half right." She turned to look at the church, and Jedward and Bill turned with her. "Anybody know anything about building a church?"

"Water and Willow"

Margaret looked out the small window at the vast swale of grass sloping away from the trailer. Where the land bottomed out a small creek flowed westward, into the dying sun. A single willow tree grew there, shading the small wooden bridge. A rope still hung from one of the branches, and Margaret remembered the small chair swing that used to dangle from its end. Her father had built it for her and her twin sister, Madeline, for their tenth birthday. It had been a hot summer, and the creek was down to a trickle. But the willow tree kept what was left of the water cool, and the girls spent the hours of their summer days swinging in that shade, fighting with each other, talking about the boys they'd marry some day.

Margaret's bloodless lips pressed together at the memory. Her hands rolled an apple over and over under the water drizzling from the faucet. When she finished, she reached for a dishtowel that wasn't there, and she caught sight of her hand in the afternoon light. It glowed red with rawness, and the joints swelled until they looked like gumballs trying to burst free from her skin. Her fingers clawed the fruit, and the palms of her hands were misshapen, overdeveloped from years of milking cows. She dropped the apple.

As she bent to retrieve it, a low moan came from the far end of the trailer. She hesitated at the sound, and then she felt something familiar: pain. It shot up her back, through her legs, down her arms. She winced and closed her fingers around the apple, and heard the moan again. This time it carried her name, softly: "Maahhhgrittt."

As she straightened up the pain went away, and she was reminded of her penance. Only when she was standing, or working, was she free from pain. Lying down, sitting, any form of relaxation brought with it the pain. She put the apple down and shuffled down the narrow hall to the back bedroom.

"Maahhhgrittt."

She stopped in the small doorway. "I hear you. What do you want?"

Clutter hid the floor and the first four feet of the wall, where a single bed wedged itself. A thick bureau held a chattering television, which was buried under a mountain of magazines. The floor between the bed and the opposite wall was stacked with newspapers, piles of clothes, and fishing and hunting gear: rods, tackle boxes, guns and gun cases, and boxes of ammo. Margaret entered the room only to bring Walter a tray of food, or to retrieve it. The light came through a high window, and the beam caught the dust particles twisting through the air. The room smelled of rotting vegetation, a sweet, earthy smell that she didn't mind. It was the only thing she could stand about the room.

"Can you help me up? I need to get to the bathroom."

She looked at him and rolled her tongue around her gums. There were spaces in there, gaps where there used to be walls of smooth, hard teeth. There were gaps on Walter, too. There was emptiness where a leg had once existed below his right knee. There was uselessness where a left arm had once been, crippled from a stroke. The arm hung flaccid and aimless, withering from disuse.

"The doctor said you're to help yourself, lest you start putting on weight and lose that other leg to the diabetes, too."

"But Margaret, I can't do it. I can't. I need your help."

"You were fine this morning. And you didn't have any trouble getting yourself drunk last night. You'll figure it out. I'm going to pick up mother, and I'll be back in an hour. Make sure you clean yourself up."

"Oh, shit, Margaret, why are you bringing her over? She hates this place, and I hate having her. Why do you got to always do things like this?"

His whining disgusted her, and she could never remember clearly why or how they had first fallen in love. She picked up her keys and walked out to her car, a crisp June wind nipped at her cheeks. Does summer ever come to this part of Vermont? she wondered. It hadn't for the first fifty-five years of her life. There was no reason to believe this year would be any different.

She drove alongside the north branch of the Passumpsic River, a broad stream that flowed down to St. Johnsbury and the Connecticut River. She remembered hot days from thirty years ago, days spent in the deep swimming holes cut along the banks of the river. She remembered Walter then, taking off his shirt to reveal his farmer's tan, just about the most exciting thing she'd ever seen. And she remembered other things, too, things that came before the present. Her memory said, "You see? It does get hot here in the summer, you just don't remember."

"More than likely it never got hot here. We were just too young and stupid to feel the cold." The sound of her voice in the empty car surprised her, and she startled herself, as if she'd been asleep at the wheel. She'd been talking out loud to herself more and more lately, and it bothered her. Her mother had always talked out loud to herself, and as a girl it drove Margaret to embarrassment. She'd be sitting in her room, reading, or talking on the phone, and she'd hear her mother, yammering away, talking to the dust on the refrigerator, or to the bathroom door. It was like the woman had no inner monologue, everything was externalized. Margaret had spent a lifetime fighting the habit, but lately she'd noticed it slipping into her life. She vowed not to let it happen, they way she'd let Walter happen.

109

After ten minutes in the car, the pain returned to her back, her legs, and her shoulders. It was a terrible, burning pain that didn't throb with her pulse, but flowed steadily and relentlessly, like the Passumpsic River beside the road she traveled. The pain came to her more and more these days, and her nights were spent in motion, rising and walking, moving around to stop the pain. She didn't dare go to a doctor; she'd seen enough of the inside of hospitals over the past year of Walter's decline. And she didn't trust any diagnosis a doctor might make. She'd watched while Walter was diagnosed with enough problems to kill a tractor. Then she watched while he fell apart one piece at a time. No, she thought, that won't be me.

The road rose away from the river then, and the huge brick building that housed her mother came into view. Riverview Manor was an assisted-care facility housed in a former textile mill along the river, at the edge of Caledonia City. It sounded nice—manor implied something stately and dignified—but it was really just another institutional place, like the elementary school she went to: tiled floors and walls that were constantly being washed and disinfected to remove the puke deposited there daily. Her mother, Dorothy, hated the place, and Margaret took some small satisfaction in that. It wasn't a cruel or unloving impulse that formed that contentment; rather it was a sense of balance. Her mother fancied herself a woman of wealth and standing, when she was really no more than the school bus driver she'd been most of her life.

Margaret parked the car and walked ahead of the breeze, which didn't feel as cold down here. Her mother was already waiting for her by the front desk, and Margaret was thankful: she wouldn't have to walk down the long hallways with her footsteps echoing back at her; she wouldn't have to smell the industrial cleaners used to kill the smell of dying; and she wouldn't have to see her mother in her room, that tiny closet, the cold single bed. The breeze followed her in as the automatic doors swished open and her mother exclaimed.

"Oh, God, close that door, it's frigid outside!" the old woman said, her voice high and grating and tremulous.

110

"Mother, I can't close the door, it's automatic. It closes by itself."

"Well, I see that you haven't changed. Just as sassy as ever. Oh, how did I ever get a daughter like you? I'm so ashamed."

"Come on, Mother, let's go."

Margaret offered her arm to her mother to help her get up from her chair, but Dorothy waved her off, trying to lean forward on her cane and pull herself up. She couldn't get her emaciated frame far enough forward to balance on the cane, and she slumped back with a cry. Margaret looked over at the front desk nurse, who was watching the scene with a purse-lipped objectivity that said she'd seen this act played out a thousand times, and she knew how it would end. It would end, Margaret thought, they way every one of these individual dramas would end, the way it ended for all of them, her, her mother, the nurse, everyone. Margaret watched the nurse and wondered if she knew what was going through her mind right now. She wondered if the nurse had seen this so often—maybe even experienced it herself—that she knew what was going through Margaret's mind, that she could see the movie playing there, the movie where Dorothy falls face first into the cold tile floor and Margaret's soul is released into heaven.

But the desk nurse looked back down at her paperwork, oblivious to Margaret's little drama. She felt insignificant and useless. She held out her hand to her mother and Dorothy took it this time. The shock of her mother's frailty always surprised Margaret. She almost pulled too hard, and thought that if she did yank too hard on her mother's hand, the whole arm would come away from the body. Either that or she'd throw Dorothy through the plate glass window of the automatic door. Her mother clung to her elbow as they walked out into the late spring sunlight, making whooping noises about how cold it was, and Margaret thought suddenly how much warmer it felt than when she got here. When they reached the car, Dorothy looked at it and sniffed.

"I see you're still driving this old rust-bucket."

"It's the same car I had last month when I came to visit you, Mother. I'll probably have it next month when I come, too."

"I'm so embarrassed to be seen in such a dilapidated vehicle. They're probably all watching me now, laughing." She gestured back at Riverside Manor. No they're not, Margaret thought. They're probably all bitching about the pudding they're going to be served for dessert after lunch today.

"I shouldn't be surprised," Dorothy continued. "I don't know what happened to you. This car. That man. And her." The old woman gestured across the river, to a low brick building. There were two ambulances parked outside the building. "You know I can see that place from my window. Terrible. Reminds me of you every time I look over there."

"Mother, it's a rehabilitation facility. Dawn's recovering from an accident."

"A motorcycle accident," said Dorothy, wagging her finger at Margaret. "She fell off a motorcycle. She was drunk." Her eyes brightened. "Ah, you didn't think I knew, did you? I know all about it. Word gets around, which is a good thing, because you don't tell me anything. Oh yes, I know she was drunk. With another one of those men she's with. Probably drugs, too. Oh, yes. That's a fine daughter you raised."

"I raised her the same way you raised me, Mother."

Dorothy covered her mouth with a hand and widened her eyes with shock. "Oh! How could you say such a thing? Why do you always say such hurtful things to your mother? Oh!" And she began to cry, her bony fingers covering her pinched face, her sobs lost on the breeze. Margaret looked around the parking lot but saw no one. It would be easy, she thought. She could just sweep her foot under her mother's legs and the old woman would go straight down, smash her skull on the pavement, and die. And that would be the end of it. Margaret imagined herself telling the police or whoever what happened: "She just collapsed. I tried to catch her, but she went straight down."

Instead she looked across the river to the low brick building that housed her daughter. Another project, she thought. She'd have to come visit Dawn sometime this week, watch them wheel her out, and listen to her sobs as the girl lamented her situation. It's too bad Mother can't go over and endure her, Margaret thought in a moment of inspiration. Maybe they'd cancel each other out.

She helped her mother into the car and got in and drove back up the road that rose and fell with the river's meanders. She hoped that Walter had at least closed the door to his room, but when she helped her mother up the stairs and into the trailer, she immediately saw he hadn't; he'd hobbled out on his crutch and trailed magazines and newspapers behind him. He was in the small enclave that passed for a kitchen, standing in front of the sink. He was smiling, and he waved when Margaret and her mother entered.

"I made sandwiches," he said, brightly.

"Oh, God," said Dorothy when she saw him.

Margaret looked up at the clock. She'd been gone barely an hour, but somehow Walter had managed to get drunk. Or maybe he was drunk before she left. He was leaning against the counter, one empty pant leg pinned up to his back pocket, one useless arm dangling aimlessly below his shoulder. She was again seized with the thought of how easy it would be sweep her foot under Walter, to send him crashing to the floor, cracking his skull on the counter's edge on the way down. It would be so easy to explain, and nobody would care if a diabetic drunk died in a double-wide up here.

"Come on in, Mother. Here, have a seat and I'll see what Walter's made for lunch."

"I made sandwiches," he said again. He hopped and held on to the edge of the counter and looked around as if he'd forgotten where he placed something. Margaret came over and she could smell the ripe, rotting fruit smell of the alcohol on him. He kept his bottles hidden, and he probably had two or three buried in the mess of his room. Walter looked from Margaret to the counter top, where a bag of bread lay open, the white slices spilling out. A jar of mayonnaise was next to it, unopened.

"I couldn't get the mayo jar opened," he said. He was still smiling but his tone was dark. "You know, I've only got one good arm, so it's kind of hard to open jars."

"Walter, go sit down at the table. I'll make the sandwiches."

Walter hopped over and sat down across from Dorothy. She pretended to fix her hair and ignore him, but he kept smiling and looking at her.

"Oh, God, look at you," Dorothy said, her voice exasperated. "Still missing half your arms and legs, I see."

Margaret dropped the knife with mayonnaise on it, but held on to the edge of the counter, refusing to turn around and involve herself. Walter would have to deal with this on his own.

"And that hair," Dorothy continued. "I don't know how you do it. You got all this land when my husband died, and what did you do with it? Frittered it away on God knows what. And now you're left with this." She gestured to the cramped inside of the double-wide.

The smile stayed on Walter's face. He leaned back and smoothed his hair with his hand. "Well, Dorothy, maybe we wouldn't be in this predicament if you hadn't gotten yourself into so much, um, financial trouble."

Dorothy sucked her breath in sharply and narrowed her eyes, the wrinkled skin bunching like an untidy pile of cold cuts. "Don't you dare!"

"Oh, but I do dare. You see, we need to keep the playing field even here. Yes, you and your gentlemen friends managed to suck all the money out of your own bank account, so Margaret and I had to sell off some of the lots of land to bail you out. Not to mention the cost of that luxury condo you live in now. Who do you think pays for that?"

"Don't you bring my friend Edward into this. That was a misunderstanding, that's all. He said he'd repay that money."

"Oh, I'm sure. As soon as he's done fleecing the next rich old bag."

"And you shouldn't be talking about anything. Look at those children you raised. One's dead from drugs and the other's a vegetable in that loony bin across the river from me. You've got no right to talk."

"That's enough from both of you." Margaret set down a plate with a sandwich and potato chips in front of each of them. "Eat your lunches and be quiet."

Walter and Dorothy looked at their plates but didn't move. Margaret hadn't made a sandwich for herself, and she didn't sit down with them. Instead she turned away from them, washing her hands. She looked out again at the willow tree. Now, in the fuller light of midday, the tree looked warmer, and the pale green of its foliage seemed radiant. She thought that maybe Madeline was in that tree, looking back up the hill at her, and she wished her sister hadn't died, that she was here to help her with their mother.

She thought about going outside the trailer, about leaving Walter and her mother alone inside to consume each other. She could imagine walking down the slope of the lawn, the trailer at her back, as she moved toward the willow tree and the rope swing. It was tempting to think of the liberation of that simple act, but she knew better. She knew that leaving the trailer meant leaving the conflict, and that the willow tree would look different up close. Only through the window above the sink did it hold the magical quality that she needed to hold. She didn't linger on how that could be possible; she only accepted it, the way she accepted her mother and her husband. They were things that simply were.

She finished drying her hands and turned around to the table, which was suddenly quiet. What she saw was like the memory of a disaster, something lived over and over again in the mind, like the memory of her sister falling off that tractor on a hot summer day, like the memory of identifying her son's body in a Newport funeral home. Her mother and Walter were quietly eating their sandwiches. Neither of them appeared to acknowledge the other, both intent on their sandwiches and chips, and they seemed to Margaret like babies that just needed to be fed. All their noise and anger had been about food, about nourishment, about hunger. If it were always this easy she'd keep a supply of sandwiches in her purse.

Walter and Dorothy didn't speak again; Dorothy's cackles diminished as Margaret helped her down the stairs and into the car. Once on the road Dorothy became quiet, and Margaret checked on her several times. The old woman seemed to be following the river beside the road intently, as if reading some message there. When they reached the bend in the road that led away for a few miles, she turned to Margaret.

"What kind of sandwich was that?"

It sounded ridiculous to Margaret. How could her mother not know what kind of sandwich she'd just eaten? But Dorothy was leaning toward Margaret, her face wide and bright.

"It was sliced turkey with lettuce and tomato."

"Oh." Dorothy settled back into her seat and crossed her arms tightly across her withered chest, closing her eyes. Her face relaxed and Margaret thought she fell asleep for the rest of the ride. When they arrived at Riverview, Margaret got out and went around to open up her mother's door.

"Come on, Mother, we're here." She expected theusual outburst about returning to the assisted care facility, but Dorothy didn't move.

"Mother? Come on, time to get out. We're here."

She reached for her mother but her fingers found only a cold, rigid body strapped into the car seat. She recoiled and covered her mouth. She turned and looked around the parking lot, but they were the only ones there. And then she heard the river rushing by, relentless, continuing, and she cried for the memory of her mother.

Scenes from a Novel:
A Master Class in Fiction

The idea is terrifying: take a novel in progress and hand it (in this case, a ten-page section of it) to one of my fellow writers for a critique. Exposure is total. Risk is everywhere. Opportunity for humiliation abounds. So why do it? To paraphrase a candidate Clinton T-shirt, it's the learning, stupid. And I'm not talking about your learning, though that may become a nice ancillary to this exercise. I'm thinking of myself, and my novel aspirations. Let me explain.

Every writer wants to be a novelist. That's because writing a novel is considered the "toppermost of the poppermost," as The Beatles used to say of their desire to have a hit record. As there are everywhere else with living things, there are hierarchies within the writing world. And while the sexy factor for all other kinds of writing—short stories, plays, memoir, nonfiction, journalism—is debatable, what's not debatable is that the novel is king of composition.

It wasn't always like this. Storytelling, when it shifted from the oral to the written tradition, was necessarily more compact. Works like *Beowulf* and *The Canterbury Tales* showed a lack of central story cohesion, something necessary to a long work like a novel. Some consider *Don Quixote* by Miguel de Cervantes the first example of a novel; others defer to *Robinson Crusoe* by Daniel Defoe, or *Pamela* by Samuel Richardson. More likely is that these things evolved slowly, incrementally from each other, so that by the beginning of the 19th century even the fledgling United States could boast true and important novelists like Washington Irving (*A History of New York, The Life and Voyages of Christopher Columbus*), and James Fenimore Cooper (*The Pioneers, The Last of the Mohicans, The Prairie*).

Just when the novel became the *ne plus ultra* of writing genres is impossible to say, since most of the great novels ever written have never been read by most people, and if some novels weren't taught in high school, none of the great works would have been read. What made the novel sexy was its accessibility in form to the masses, and that included the detective novel and romance novels. Many people read novels today, and most read for pleasure, for the desire to be taken away. And it's that imperative that drives the novel to the top of the heap.

So it was natural for me, as a developing writer back in the early 90s, to think that I might be a novelist, too. After all, I was living in France, which is where all writers go to start their careers. It made sense. I began writing novels at a terrifying clip. In the three years I lived in France I wrote four novels: *Illegal Evidence, The End of Bay Ave, A Regular Guy,* and *A Modern Man.* A couple of years later, while living in Montreal, I wrote two more: *To Die Upon A Kiss* and *Ragged Claws.* But writing a novel does not a novelist make. Though I had no trouble writing novels, I never really warmed up to the form. Two of those novels—*To Die Upon a Kiss* and *A Modern Man*—were published at online sites in the late 90s, when we were all supposed to make millions from the Internet. It never happened for fiction writers.

And even though I survived the writing drought of the beginning of this century, when I all but abandoned hopes of having a career as a writer, I am continually drawn to the form of the novel. Even though I understand that I am a natural born short story writer, the literary offspring of Ernest Hemingway and Flannery O'Connor, I still fall into the novel trap. Just this winter, after I finished *The Innkeeper's Husband*, a nonfiction book about innkeeping, I immediately launched into another novel, with the dubious title of *Penguins on the Mountain*. It was my first attempt at a novel since I abandoned the writing of a book called *Angels in Vegas*, which I chucked into a drawer after being accepted to Goddard College.

Writing a novel has become the same thing for me: I get a third, or halfway through, and I lose interest. My characters start to piss me off, the story seems unsustainable, and distractions creep into my life. Usually those distractions take the form of new stories, short stories, which need to be written. And with the writing of this book, I've discovered a need to diversify. I enjoy writing in all kinds of genres, in both fiction and nonfiction. About the only thing you won't get out of me is a poem. As Harry Callahan said in *Magnum Force*, a man's got to know his limitations.

After Goddard, one of my screenwriting friends began extolling the virtues of a book called *Save the Cat,* by Blake Snyder. He swore by its logical approach to structure. He's now a successful writing working in Hollywood, and his mantra hasn't changed: "Structure, structure, structure." I read the book, and suddenly the problem with my unfinished novels became clear: They lacked structure. They were sodden with character study, but no story. And without story, nobody would care.

Another thing happened about this same time. For the first time I watched *The Power of Myth*, an extraordinary documentary with Bill Moyers and Joseph Campbell, the author of *The Hero with a Thousand Faces*. The documentary is a conversation between Moyers and Campbell about Campbell's mythic hero structure. This structure is what's behind successful works of all kinds, including movies, plays, and books. The hero's adventure drives storytelling from a basic human place, a seminal location embedded in humans, requiring only the accoutrements of the writer to fashion an original tale. This was what was missing from my novels: structure.

This relationship with the novel intrigued me, and I thought that I must not be the only person—the only writer—out there who grappled with the form. When conceiving this book, I wondered how I could include various kinds of writing. Though I wanted to include examples of a novel, I knew I couldn't put an entire novel in; nobody would read it. Then two things occurred to me.

On a trip to Florida, I brought a book to read. Though I knew I'd never read a book on vacation because we had way too much planned, I took it on the off chance we'd find ourselves delayed at an airport. True to my prediction, I hardly touched the book until one Sunday afternoon when we were sitting by the pool. I picked up the book and opened it and looked through it a little, then began to read the introduction. I don't think I made it through the first page of that introduction before I realized that it was exactly the kind of book I wanted to put together. The book was called *Slumgullion Stew: An Edward Abbey Reader*, and besides incensing me by having such a great title that I couldn't use (I've always wanted to write a book called *An Edward Abbey Reader*), the book's form inspired me to create the book you're reading now.

In *Slumgullion Stew*, Abbey includes some excerpts from a couple of his novels. He laments this, complaining that a novel can't really be excerpted for any good use, that too much is lost by removing a part of the book from its context.[3] But he included the excerpts anyway, and the effect on the rest of the book was positive. I thought I'd do the same thing, but I had an idea to go a step further.

When I was in graduate school, I attended the Master Class in Fiction. The way the faculty handled that was to ask for samples of student writing, which would then be anonymously critiqued during the class. Usually the professor would focus on one aspect within the sample to highlight a teaching point. I thought that would be a great way to look at a couple of samples from novels I've written. So I've given the samples to a couple of writer/teachers to critique. Knowing the intent is important here: I'm not doing this to better myself or the novels; I'm using it as a teaching moment, an opportunity to look at what a working, moving, breathing writer goes through, internally and externally.

The two novels I've chosen to excerpt have never been published. The first excerpt comes from *Ragged Claws*, the second from *Angels in Vegas*. In terms of timing, or chronology, *Ragged Claws* was written around 1998, *Angels in Vegas* in 2004. I hold no pretensions about either of the books; I've moved on. Author, editor, and teacher Nancy McCurry critiques the first excerpt. Author and teacher Max Shenk (*What's With Her?*) critiques the second excerpt. The biographies of the critics appear at the end of their critiques. It goes without saying that I'm deeply grateful to both of them, and though I'm unable to compensate them directly for their participation in this book, I've promised them a piece of the action, so make sure that you buy several copies of the book so they can make more money.

An Excerpt from *Ragged Claws*

Critiqued by Nancy McCurry

(Note to readers: Nancy's edits appear in bold, italicized text, within brackets, after the highlighted portion of the text to which she's referring.)

Prologue: The Sea

When the rain came it strafed the green ocean swells with deep pockmarks. The wind blew the rain in slanting sheets that came in and out of focus, as if someone were shaking a great gray curtain. A jetty jabbed out into the tortured surface of the sea, a stubborn black finger accusing the weather. At the very end of the jetty, the place the ocean reserved for its most cinematic explosions of salt and foam, a small figure crouched against the push of the wind.

Beyond the mouth of the harbor the sky and the ocean shed their differences, morphing into a blueblack, horizonless bile. Appearing and disappearing like a legion of reluctant ghosts, foamblown whitecaps struggled to break the storm's canvas. A strong gust of wind nearly toppled the boy into the ocean and he sat down on the wet rocks to steady himself. *[Bring the reader closer to the "small figure" before stating he's a boy. We still see just a tiny form way out.]*

The sea was overtaking the jetty and pounding it with deafening ferocity. The boy knew *[this moment establishes the scene's Point of View character]*the waves would be predictable, and he counted them off, one, two, three, then a bad one, which he braced himself for, then one, two, three... He also knew that the jetty would be gone in another hour, swamped. His eyes stung with salt spray and bullet-hard rain but they never wavered from the spot on the horizon he knew it would come from.*[the reader needs to know what "it" suggests. Too vague. Missing an opportunity]*

The wind blew up beyond hurricane force and the sound it made as it ripped across the tops of the spattering waves before slamming into the jetty rang hollow and empty and loud enough to hurt. It was the sound of a locomotive dying. He pulled the hood of his slicker tight around his face and blinked and in his back he felt a tightening like electricity.

It was out there. He couldn't see it; he felt it. It lurked out there, brooding in the storm, and any minute now it would appear, slow and wavering, but growing larger, until the chug of the engines could assert itself above the storm.*[This moment suggests there's something with an engine coming, but I don't know if the writer is still referring to the metaphor of the locomotive, or if there's a literal aspect I should be understanding, but am missing. Frustrating. Question: If the reader is told what the boy is waiting for, might it offer more conflict/tension than this ambiguous image?]*

He was leaning forward when the wave caught him. It was a queer wave, coming from behind him, from the lee of the storm, and it toppled him face first onto the slick rocks. His face *[change one instance]*slid forward and then it stopped and he felt the cold smooth rock pressing back against his cheek. Far off he heard the bell on the H-buoy ring with drunken irregularity: *Clang...clang-clang...c-clang-clang.*

When he got up there was nothing to see. The wind came hard and turned the raindrops into razors that ripped across the surface of the water. There was no horizon because there was no sky and no sea and he was only ten feet from the end of the jetty but he couldn't see it. He could only feel the rain probing his slicker, looking for a way in.

A voice reached him. He turned and carefully retreated along the jetty, back toward the safety of the wide, flat beach. He stopped only once, to assure his footing, but he never looked back.

His mother never stopped calling him.

"Sweeney! Sweeney!"

I: The Lobster

Sixty feet below the tempest that shattered the surface, the environment couldn't be more different. **[Can't conjure that image. Might add: ...that shattered the surface of the bay...]** *On this night, Cape Cod Bay was a wild dichotomy.* **[Might flip sentences] [*The writer might state clearly that we're at the bottom of the sea here. Orientation in scene setup is paramount.]**

On the rocky bottom, visibility was less than zero. **[Reader is still ungrounded]** *The current, reflecting the distant agitations of the raging surface, twitched as if teased, swishing capriciously up one moment, pushing across the sandy crevices the next. Ambient water temperature hovered around 38 degrees Fahrenheit.*

In a small space under a slick black rock that was one shade darker than the pitch-black gloom of the ocean floor, the female lay still on her side. **[This stabilizes my perspective. Make sure your reader can always "see" what you're talking about. It's their right.]** *Deep within her the last of her gastroliths have formed, and her old hard shell,* drained of the calcium needed to keep it integral, cracked between her tail and body.**[Say what this is. If the reader has to guess, we'll guess wrong, then feel stupid. Not a good way to start a relationship]**

For the next half-hour the female Homarus americanus *performed a miraculous feat: she squeezed her soft inner body out through a break in her old hard shell. When finally free of her old exoskeleton, the female lobster lay totally helpless in the shadow of the big rock.* **[Now we can see what we've been wondering about. Why the mystery?]**

A few feet away, not unknown to the female, a big, barnacle-ridden male was keeping tabs on her progress. His long antennae were reaching out, tasting the water, feeling her stress. Now, as she lay defenseless, he advanced on her.

Using his huge crusher claw with the precision of a surgeon and the tenderness of a lover, he rolled the female onto her back. First his antennae, then the microscopic cilia on the underside of his tail lead him to her, and something short of mating takes place. When it is over, he has transferred spermatophores to a receptacle between the bases of her last two legs. And the invisibility of the cold, black water was their only witness. **[Super nice. Writer might revise the scene from top to bottom allowing the reader to be the voyeur and sense the tension and conflict sooner.]**

Part One: Boston, April

1: Before coffee

And now the Saab won't start.

It is part of a lamentable morning of aggravating dominoes, which began toppling when a power outage left him with a flashing and useless digital alarm clock.

It continued with the hot water tank--electrically heated, of course, except for this morning when the power went out. Now he wants to strangle the genius who came up with the idea that everyone in this luxury high rise Brookline condo should have their own hot water supply,. For $2,500 a month, he wanted hot fucking water.

And now this piece of shit Swedish airplane with wheels won't start.

He considers first the steering wheel. His huge, wide hands clench it at 10 o'clock and 2 o'clock, his knuckles the color of vanilla ice cream. It gives a little. I can just rip it out, he thinks. Like pulling the guts out of a fish I can just rip the whole column right out. Then I can snap the shiny black doors off their hinges, rip the leather seats out, collapse the dashboard, tear the hood off and piss on the goddamn engine. Thirty-five thousand fucking dollars. Jesus.

What would Dad think?

With a growl Sweeney dispatches the inner voice. *I don't care what my father would think about this car.* He never had thirty-five cents--never mind thirty-five grand--to rub together. *[Italicize the inner thoughts, or quote it and let Sweeney say it out loud]*

As if a long buried switch had been flipped somewhere, thoughts of his father--nothing more than brief flashes, really--had been trickling into his consciousness. He defeated the paternal memory this time by fantasizing about dismembering the Saab with a framing hammer.

But instead of demolishing his car with red fury, Sweeney takes a deep breath and urges gravity to drain the blood from his throbbing head. I need to have a better day than this. I need this day *badly.[Writer should find a way to off-set the inner dialogue. Right now the string looks like, and feels like, a breach in PoV. Any further instances will be grayed.]*

His sweating palms loosen on the steering wheel and he pulls his tie away from his raw neck. Then he reaches over to the real wood panel on the Saab's dashboard and knocks three times deliberately.

Already he feels better. In control. Thank God for wood to knock. I need my control today. Of all days. Christ.

The Saab starts on the next try.

He squeals the car's tires through the dark garage *[the garage comes as a surprise. Note this in the setup]*, bursting out into the bright blue spring morning, waving to the building's parking attendant as he bottoms out going up the exit ramp. Pulling out onto Beacon Street, he pushes a button on the stereo. In the trunk, a CD changer selects a disc at random, its anti-shock laser beam easily picking up the digitized musical message, sending it up to the Blaupunkt, which pumps the music through the ten speaker system.

Some fully caffeinated Steely Dan, Bodhisattva.

The pounding beat energizes him, dissipating the rage and replacing it with an excess of blood that manifests itself as an erection beneath his Brooks Brothers slacks.

Well all right, Sweeney thinks. Now we're getting somewhere. He guns the engine, feeling the turbo kick in and propel him down busy Washington Street. Someone in a Chrysler swerves to avoid broadsiding him. The driver leans on the horn and mutely curses Sweeney. From behind his one-way privacy glass, Sweeney laughs and gives the Chrysler the finger.

Out of his glove compartment comes a pair of Ray-Bans. He checks his look in the rear view mirror, runs a hand through his thick, wavy hair, and thinks, *Not even JFK, Jr., had a do like this!*

He blows through two red lights, leaving a crescendo of angry horns in his wake. The exciting pulse of the music urges him on. Gone are the anger and frustration. This will be a good day, I can feel it now. Steely Dan's backbeat pushes through his blood, warming his skin.

Nearing Kenmore Square, the traffic becomes too thick for his bobbing and weaving. He's locked in. Shit. The song ends. Shit*fuck.* He checks his watch. The complexity of the Breitling chronograph still confuses him. The flash on his right ring finger doesn't.*[?? What does this mean?]* He hits a button on his cell phone.

"Hi, Vicky," he says before his secretary can offer a greeting. "What are you wearing?"

"Excuse me?"

"I said, 'What are you wearing?' You see, I'm driving to work in the buff, and I'm just sitting here, working the gearshift and thinking about you. I'm thinking about what you look like under all that hair, under those turtle necks and frilly collars."

"You'd love that, wouldn't you?"

"Hey, c'mon, all my other secretaries let me sleep with them."

"I'm not them, am I? Would you like to hear what your day is looking like?"

She's totally noncommittal. Inscrutable. Dammit.

"That and so much more."

She briefs him on the various meetings and phone calls he must return. One thing, however, stands out: the Lachman account. The biggie, he remembers. A cool sweat cracks his skin.

This is when a man approaches his Saab and begins washing his windshield. The man has drooping, milky eyes and a dirty bandanna around his head. His fingers are gnarled turds.

"Thanks Vicky," he says to the phone. "See you in a few."

"Take care of that gear shift for me, Sweeney," then hangs up. She got me, he thinks. The man washing his windshield distracts him. He flicks the wipers on and powers down his window.

"No thanks, buddy," he says to the washer.

"Too late, man, I'm finished. That'll be a buck." The washer smiles a black smile and holds out a filthy hand.

Sweeney recoils and hits the washer fluid switch, sending a stream of blue liquid up into the man's face.

"Did you say a buck?" Sweeney says harshly. "I thought you said fuck, as in 'Fuck you,' which is exactly what you can go and do, you prick."

The window washer staggers back a step, pawing his eyes. A pick-up truck with two men in it are stuck in traffic next to Sweeney. They are watching the scene unfold as traffic refuses to budge. The one in the passenger's seat is wearing a Boston Bruins ball cap. He leans out his window and says to Sweeney, "Hey, you're the prick, buddy."

Sweeney drops the Saab into neutral, yanks the parking brake up and jumps out of the car. The other man jumps out of the pickup truck, a big smile on his stubbled face. In his right hand he has a 22-ounce framing hammer.

The driver of the pickup, a triple chinned convoy of fat, yells "Go get 'em, Davey!"

In the back of the pickup truck there is an overturned wheelbarrow. Red bricks are splayed around it, and everything is covered with a fine, gray dust. *Potato monkies!* thinks Sweeney. *Bricklayers!*

And there is something else in the back of that pickup truck, something that jumps out at Sweeney with the power to arrest: empty cans of Schlitz beer.

*Schlitz beer! I didn't think they made that piss any more!***[Good use of italics here]**

As a deep part of his gray matter reels from the slap of the image of the beer cans **[Wordy. Trim]**, the conscious part tries to keep the bubble from bursting.

Instantly his mind flashes his opponent's biography: most likely a blue collar native of Revere, our bricklayer enjoys polishing his Camero, getting drunk by four p.m. every day, slapping his gumchewing girlfriend in the mouth and pissing his pants whenever the Red Sox get close in August. Sweeney imagines that the bricklayer thinks he is easy pickins: a guy in a suit driving a Saab.

Well, today is your unlucky day, chump.[Suggest cutting. Back story stops the energy.]

That is when events vapor lock. The deep part of his mind erupts messily into his reality. A torrent of deja-vu cascades over Sweeney, swamping him with cold heat. With his right hand on the frame of the car and his left tearing the tie from his neck, Sweeney freezes. Even as the thick necked bricklayer advances on him and raises the hammer, he remains still.

He sees the man, and the hammer.

Yet he sees nothing.

He sees someone else with a framing hammer. He sees another pile of Schlitz cans. He sees a boat, and he sees his father...*[perfect]*

*

That was the day the wind skipped down the length of the Cut River, cutting countless scallops across its dark green surface. The wind was a bully, strutting in from Duxbury Bay, hissing wildly through the dry marsh grass. It reached up and stuck a finger in Sweeney's chest and said, "I dare you." Then it ran away with its tail between its legs, laughing. *[great]*

It was late April but it felt like early March, chilly enough to make your nose run, not cold enough for a hat. The Cut River emptied into a harbor swollen with the tide. The boats rode impossibly high on the water, above the land. It was sunny, with a sky the color of polished steel, giving the light a polarized quality. It was a flat, bright light, making everything look like a cheap postcard.*[nice]*

It was one of those clear, snapping days that made you wish for summer without hating winter. *[This near-slide into second person is a jump from the last segment. Not sure it's warranted.]* The *Ragged Claws* was hauled out behind Fran's Clams.*[You'd have to say what the Ragged Claws is here. I'm guessing it's a boat, but the reader can't be sure.]* Behind Fran's Clams there was a dirt ramp for launching boats into the Cut River at high tide, and there was a large, dirt parking lot that cost five dollars to park in during the summer. Right now it was empty. Empty save for the *Ragged Claws*, propped up on a dubious frame of wooden vees. *[The writer might cut that first reference to the RC and just stick with this introduction.]*

Standing up on the deck of his father's dry docked fishing boat, Sweeney felt the cool wind run through his straight mop, urging his head to turn. His eyes moved across the empty parking lot until they came to rest on the building that was Fran's Clams. *[We need a basis in time here. How old is Sweeney now? In the scene setup be sure to*

131

state, clearly, Who's on stage, What's going on, and When/Where we are.]

Fran was a 300 pound septuagenarian who ran the fried food and lobster joint called Fran's Clams. She was rarely seen outside, spending most of her time sitting behind the take out counter, scowling, drinking gin and chain smoking Kent 100's. Her face was hung with red pocked dewlaps and her eyes were pools of curdled milk behind impossibly thick glasses.

Sweeney brushed the hair from his eyes and wondered if Fran knew that someone had spraypainted the word "BEARDED" between the words "Fran's" and "Clams" on the rusting tin sign that hung off the building. As the wind gusted, the oxidized chains creaked and Fran's lewd sign made a thin, lonely sound that was somewhere between the call of a whale and the screech of braking tires. *[nice, nice, nice]*

He stood there, looking at the sign swinging in the bright, flat light.

Until his father said, "Hey."

His head jerked around. Under the cool gaze of his father's polished rock eyes Sweeney felt the way he always felt in this man's presence: infantile and obvious.

The sun was high above them but his father's shadow extended out in all directions, engulfing Sweeney *[?]* in its chilly umbra. As he stood with his hands on his hips down there with the engine, his father ran a hand under his nose and scratched the stubble of a three day old beard. A thick wool watchcap was pushed down over his sun wrinkled forehead in a gesture that exuded aggressive indifference. Sweeney's father and the engine were of about equal proportions, and where one ended the other began.

He **[this pronoun, initiating the sentence, confuses the reader. Are we looking at Sweeney or the father?]** had recently watched a PBS special on gorillas, and it struck him that his father greatly resembled one of the big silver backs he had seen: massive upper body, scowling black brow, long, thick arms punctuated with gnarled fists the size of baseball gloves, bowed legs. The only thing his father had that the giant male gorillas of central Africa didn't have was a Tiparillo cigar jutting from clenched teeth and a case of Schlitz beer *[_____ **something is missing here. Maybe a case of Schlitz at his feet.**]*. It seemed to Sweeney that the beer and cigars were infinitely regenerating, never totally disappearing, the same way a lobster will grow a new claw after the original is ripped off.

The beer came in cans, which sat in a shallow cardboard box. The box held twenty-four cans, a case. As his father worked he would rip a can free from the plastic retaining ring, down half of it, then place it on the deck beside him. A minute or two later he would rise again from the black hollow of the engine hold, drain the rest of the beer and casually toss the can into the corner beneath the hauling wheel. Half the cans from the case had been emptied.

"Hey" was all his father said before turning back to the dirty diesel engine. *[I cut this because the following sentence seems to contradict it.]* Sweeney expected to hear "hey" three or four more times. And each "hey" would betray the gentle accent of Ireland. He wondered if that was why his father spoke sparingly. Was he ashamed of his pure Irishness?

Standing close to his father, he could feel a strong pull, something like gravity. The closer he got to the man, the more the rest of the world was blotted out. He's a ripple in space and time, thought Sweeney, and everything that gets too close is sucked in and dumped into another dimension. He closed his eyes; the impression behind them was indelible: eyes the color of smoke from a wet fire, planet sized back. He sighed and opened his eyes again.

For a little while Sweeney bent closer to his father. Occasionally an empty beer can would be tossed in the direction of the hauling wheel. The ritual was repeated in silence. His father's economy of words was unrivaled, and Sweeney wondered if words had been rationed along with everything else during the war.

Eventually he tired of watching his father twist nuts and grunt at belts. In the cabin he found the worn remnants of an old hockey stick.

His father kept Sweeney's old sticks on board and used them to scrape the mung from the decks after a day of fishing.

The hockey stick fit into Sweeney's hand the same way the glass slipper fit Cinderella. The stick was magic and its spell flowed up through his hands and arms until it coursed through his veins and lifted his feet from the deck of the boat.

At least that was the way Sweeney felt every time he picked up a hockey stick.

He lifted one of the empty beer cans with the blade of the stick and set it upright on the deck. Then he crushed the can with his foot, forming an aluminum hockey puck.

Soon his silent father melted away and Sweeney, deftly carrying the crushed can up and down the deck on the blade of his crude hockey stick, was embroiled in hockey thoughts. This weekend he had two games scheduled: one tonight and another tomorrow morning. Both were against the Duxbury Pee Wee Red Wings, whom Sweeney and the rest of his Green Harbor teammates referred to as the Doucheberry Pee Pee Ring Dings. *[nice]*

As he glided up and down the deck of the boat, he closed his eyes and felt the puck--the crushed can--sticking to the blade of his stick. Opponents slid away from him easily and his wrists flicked almost imperceptibly, sending the puck into the net--the crushed can through the open door to the forward cabin.

"Hey."

Sweeney looked up. His father was leering at him from the engine hold.

"Another beer."

Sweeney popped his father another beer, another can of Schlitz. The empty can rolled down the deck to his feet. He thought the brown label looked like dog shit. Stupid, insipid dog shit. He crushed the can and shot it out of the boat and watched as the wind took it and bounced it into the water.

He'd never forget how much he hated the sight of Schlitz beer, how much he loathed the sight of the long, slender cans with the simple brown labels.

*

Digitized, compacted and stored neatly in a dusty, unused corner of his brain, the manifestation of his past is returned to its mental storage bin without Sweeney really knowing that it is trundled out in the split second before the confrontation begins.

There is a man holding a hammer and there are cans of Schlitz and just for a second Sweeney wonders how a cold Schlitz would taste right now.

He blinks, and...

...the bricklayer raises the hammer and brings it down viciously at Sweeney's head. The grotesque claw head of the hammer never finds its mark. Snapping out of his dream, Sweeney slips to his left and buries his right fist into the bricklayer's gut. Then he drops him with a magic left to the chin. The bricklayer's Bruins hat flies off, revealing a tangle of thin, greasy hair trying to conceal a bald spot. His bloody face bounces off Sweeney's shoes.

Sweeney takes a deep breath. He looks up at the driver of the pickup, who is gaping at the scene. Then he looks back down at the beaten laborer. "Now I've got to get my shoes shined," he says, and climbs back into the Saab. Angry, his left fist red and swollen and hurting, he cuts off two lines of traffic on his right and turns up Brookline Ave, catching Lansdowne Street.

New music comes thrashing out of the speakers: Van Halen, Hot For Teacher.

And now, for the first time in a long time, Sweeney wants booze. He craves it. He desires it. His heart lusts after it pruriently.

Inside his mouth his tongue swells under a torrent of saliva. Scotch, bourbon, beer, vodka, wine, his mouth becomes a playground of booze. He doesn't just crave a drink; that he can and does handle from time to time. Right now, he wants a total drunk, he wants to be utterly shitfaced, pie-eyed, gassed, completely fucked up. He smashes the steering wheel

135

two times and grits his teeth. *Think of something else*, he commands: Vicky's breasts.

The Saab screeches under the Green Monster of Fenway Park, bending into Hemenway Street. His breath comes in hot gasps. From a side street he picks up Mass Ave, then turns onto Columbus Ave. *[There's something labored here.]* Sweat sprouts beneath his eyes, stinging his slick skin, tingling his lip. He begins to pick out all the liquor stores and bar rooms along his route. He adds the rest of Vicky's licentious body to his sexy countervision, throws in his wife and murders the booze craving.

By the time he realizes he's still breathing with an adrenaline induced velocity, he's all the way to Kneeland Street, catching Atlantic Ave and turning onto State Street, pushing up past the Old State House, before at last finding Court Square and the almost secret entrance to the company parking garage. Don't stop, don't stop, don't stop, his mind charges. He noses the Saab into its spot between Al Simpatico's Mercedes and Mike Anderson's Lexus.

The cinder block wall before him plays out the sexual fantasy that he used to cancel the alcohol flash. Then, it too fades away. As he regains control over his breathing, he realizes that it has been a long time since he's craved total annihilation through total inebriation. He thought that was a feeling that was gone for good.

What a morning! A blackout! A cold shower! A fight! And no coffee yet!

To remedy that, he steps sharply to the elevator, which opens onto an alley full of upscale shops. The three floor ride up promotes controlled breathing. He steps out of the elevator smartly. People look at him, his stern face, his power outfit, his physical presence. People *move*. Cafe au Lait is at the end. Even before he's inside he sees her.

Rather, he sees her feet. He always starts with the feet, and she's got'em. Ankles. A flaring calf. Demure knees. Pornographic thighs. He knows the rest. His renewed erection presses against his belt buckle.

He walks up behind her. Slips a hand around her waist. Cups a

136

heavy breast. Drags his tongue across her ear. Presses himself through the millimeters of fabric that separate them.

"Mmmm," she says, "if you're not Sweeney, we're both in trouble." She reaches back and runs a hand through his distinctive wave of hair.
[She's a waitress?]

"Vicky asked about my gearshift this morning, babe," he whispers around his tongue.

"Tell the little slut to find something else to shift or I'll have her for lunch."

"Now that's something I'd like to see."

Behind the counter, a white-toothed, olive-skinned man says, "Next!"

She slips from his grasp. "Your regular?" she asks him. "Double decaf latte and a number 22," she says to the man behind the counter.

Up on the board, Sweeney sees his daily bread, and the tale that describes it:

No. 22: Double Jamaican Blue Coffee...22 ounces of the intense Jamaican blue bean, a bean so potent that to pick it without plastic gloves is to invite teeth clenching disaster, a bean so volatile that Congress tried to classify it as a Class B substance, a bean so unstable it must be double sealed and shipped packed in Styrofoam drums. We roast our Jamaican blue beans twice, extra slow, over a fire fueled by the vines from which the beans are picked. Then we double brew the coarse grind, infusing it with steam from a fine ground boil. To drink Jamaican Blue you must show a love of coffee, you must show courage, and you must show proof that you are over 21 years of age.

His pulse quickens and his erection fades. Ahead of him, Suzy **[get her name in sooner]** pays for the coffee, hands him his oversized designer cup and they sit at one of the small tables lining the outer walls of Cafe au Lait.

"There was no hot water this morning," he says, grimacing as he sips at his steaming coffee.

"I showered at the gym." *[Who says that? Sweeney or Suzy?]* Her pale blue eyes look frozen with boredom as she scans the coffee shop. Painted fingernails adjust the cuff on her blouse. *[who is she to him?]* Her lips are together in a motionless, flat way that suggests nothing. She is utterly illegible. "What happened to your hand?" she asks without looking at him.

His eyes flash down to the red swelling that betrays his knuckles.

"Slammed it in the car door."

Now she looks at him. Now he has her Arctic Ocean eyes on his. The remnants of his erection retreat completely, leaving him sexless and impotent.

"You've got the Lachman account today, don't you, babe?" *[Suzy says this? Direct the reader]*

"Thanks for reminding me." *[Suzy is his assistant?]*

She looks back down at his hand. "Try not to hit him. I've got my eye on a little black Carrera."

He sits back and laughs. "Says she who makes more than her husband." *[Let the reader in on this sooner. Feels like a trick]*

Suzy smiles but it is an allowed smile only. Although her lips part and her cheeks blush, her eyes are unchanged. She reaches up and touches a drop of sweat on his temple.

[Give him a beat (motion) here so the reader is looking at Sweeney, not Suzy] "I'm not having the greatest morning," he says. "About ten minutes ago I was dying for a drink--no, not a drink, a barrel of booze, something I could dive into and gulp my way out of."

"You look great now, babe."

"I put you and Vicky together on top of me and *presto!* Craving gone."

"You replaced one addiction with another." She looks at her watch. "I've got to run. Eight o'clock bullshit session." She stands and kisses him, letting her fingers drift down to his crotch. *[Keep this text wrapped in one paragraph]*

"Is Connor still giving you shit?" he asks.

"Not since I told him I was married to Sweeney."

Finally her eyes seem to warm. He sees her pupils dilate slightly. He pulls her to him *[stage this scene so the two are standing up]* and kisses her hard on the mouth.

"I might be late tonight, babe," he whispers.

"I'll keep it warm for you."

After watching her leave, he takes his coffee and marches down the alley that leads to his building. His erection is roaring, better than ever, and he seriously considers stopping off at the men's room to service it.

About the Critic:

Nancy McCurry teaches creative writing at Rio Salado College in Phoenix, Arizona. She is also the owner of All About Books, a book editing service. Over the years, Nancy has edited hundreds of novels for copy and content, sheperding scores of authors to publication. Nancy holds an MFA in creative writing from Goddard College.

An Excerpt from *Angels in Vegas*

Critiqued by Max Shenk

(Note to readers: Max's narrative critique appears at the end of the excerpt.)

Part One: Vegas

Chapter 1

Where I'm from, life was never satisfactory. Where I'm from, time and tide take life as easily as the sands wear away from the beaches. Where I'm from, sometimes, people die. Or worse, they live. They out-live their time and their usefulness and yet they remain. They remain because somewhere, sometime, long ago, someone asked them to be a man. And they replied.

I come from Marsh Vegas. Viva Marsh Vegas. Leaving Marsh Vegas. Fear and Loathing in Marsh Vegas. The City of Lights. Vegas by the Sea. Vegas-upon-Atlantic. Green Harbor in Vegas. A place full of men and fishermen. Not really Marsh Vegas, but Marshfield. Marsh Vegas is the moniker given to the Town of Villages by the locals, a cynical, twisted way of highlighting just how different Marshfield, a sleepy little fishing village southeast of Boston, and Las Vegas, Glamville, really are. The moniker is a tribute to the lack of action in town, and the parochial attitudes contained within. I know, because I helped forge many of those attitudes. I'm a twelve-year-old boy, and one day it was my turn to bust out of Green Harbor, one of the villages of Marshfield. I didn't do it like everybody else.

On the day my mother asked me to be a man, the weather was tropical. Rain fell in silver sheets while I watched her from the kitchen window. She struggled to pull a grimy metal trash barrel up the exposed cellar stairs. Above her the torrents overflowed the gutter and spilled down freely. Her clothes quickly drenched, and the curls of her hair obliterated into lifeless mattes. I watched her impatiently. When she reached the top step, I sighed and went out to help her.

By the time I got around to the back yard she had given up. The barrel tipped over and rain pounded trash into the mud. I saw cool water on her face. Her shoulders rounded into submission and she stood motionless save for the soft shaking that accompanied her sobbing. Without words I righted the trash barrel and began putting the spilled trash back into it.

"Oh, *Mathieu*," she said. She was barely audible above the roar of the thunderstorm. There was no lightning, but the thunder shook our lives and fought with the slap of the rain for cacophonic supremacy.

"Oh, *Mathieu*," she repeated. I tried not to look at her but I was finished picking up the trash. Despite the warmth of the morning my soaked skin chilled. In a rare display of directness she took me by my shoulders and held her face close to mine. I could no longer rely on the din of the storm to supersede her.

"I'm going to need you, *Mathieu*. I'm going to need your help now. You're going to have to be the man around the house now."

Her crying punctuated her words. Each sob spilled out and mixed with the rain and the humidity and fell upon me in a deluge.

"I'm so sorry, Matt. *Mathieu*. I'm so sorry, but I'm going to need you to be the man around here now."

I looked up at her. I was still a boy, and I said the only thing I could say. "I know, ma. I know."

I dragged the barrel past her, down the long driveway, where the rain lashed it efficiently. For a long time I stood at the end of the driveway, not wanting to go back. The rain beat through my clothes, through my skin, and thunder filled my heart. I was twelve.

*

I remember quite clearly the night my father left us. It preceded that stormy morning when my mother ordained me with the burden of alpha male. Unlike the other times he had left, this time there was no mounting apprehension, no confrontation, recrimination or tears. This time the fight between my parents spread out on the first floor of the house beneath our second floor bedroom, different because of the cadence of sounds that deviated from the normal rhythms of their arguing. This was not the standard fight.

The standard fight usually began long before my father arrived home drunk. It featured my mother's weakness for alcohol and cigarettes, and my father's incredible selfishness. For my mother, afternoons would descend into misery one Virginia Slim 100 after another. As shadows lengthened and it became evident that Dad wasn't going to make it home, or even try, vodka provided her with a vessel to sail on while she smoked. And when Dad did show up on those nights, Tommy and I headed upstairs.

He would announce his presence with a growl. We hid under the blankets. We could picture his straight, white teeth in a vicious smile as he berated Mom. We could hear him kicking chairs around and snarling, and we could hear Mom snipping back, and then Tommy and I would cry. "Please don't say anything to him, Mom. Please just leave Dad alone. Just don't say anything to him and he'll calm down and forget about it and we can come down." And we cried together and hugged each other under the blankets but Mom never stopped talking, ranting. The normal condition of her voice was high and edgy, but after an afternoon of booze and butts and anxiety it was grating and unnerving. She kept yipping and shrilling until finally Dad roared and thundered out of the house. He never hurt her, never touched us, but Tommy and I would cry ourselves to sleep anyway, terrified by a generic fear, a ruthless and relentless malaise that worked faster than a glacier, but slower than a backhand across the face.

But the night that Dad left us was no was no standard fight. That night, my internal fight-o-meter was rocking off the scale and there was nothing I could do to stop it.

What set this fight apart from the others? Was it the straw breaking the camel's back? Or was it the collective agony that had hardened our family's arteries like plaque until our most vital organ simply rebelled in a macro-infarction? Tommy and I didn't know, and we didn't immediately sense the difference: we only knew it was bad. Only hindsight could provide us with answers, but the answers led us in circles.

Watch while I close my eyes: even now I can see him pulling up the driveway that night. He sits in his truck with the dome light on for almost fifteen minutes, smoking, tipping a beer can up, crushing it, smoking, opening another, then rummaging around the truck. And I can see Mom watching him, waiting, muttering in her own tongue, hyperventilating a half pack of Virginia Slims. She sits on the edge of the bay window in the family room. In the middle of the bay window is a large, double-globed lamp. Reflected in the lamp are the headlights of my father's truck, bent and elongated by the curve of the glass, stretching out towards my mother, never quite reaching her.

My eyes voluntarily open. For me, it is much better to dream with them wide open. People will tell you they don't want to see it coming, but I don't believe that.

I had a decision to make. Downstairs, in the kitchen, on top of the almond colored refrigerator, was a flashlight. Tommy and I needed that flashlight. The longer Dad stayed out in his truck, the darker it became inside, and we needed an emergency light source. We needed supplies, too: Saltines, from the cupboard next to the sink. With the flashlight, and the Saltines, and a book, we could ride out the night. But I didn't want to run into Dad.

I wasn't worried about my mother seeing me. As these storm fronts approached she became catatonic. To Tommy and me she was a barometer. When the French language invaded her, we knew the pressure was falling and the tension was mounting. Slowly she would disengage herself, as she had done this night. And just before my father showed up, silence, a sudden end to the Latinate chattering.

After removing my sneakers I edged down the stairs. In the dining room I checked on my father: his form in the cab of the truck. Without pausing for a glance into the family room I glided to the refrigerator, my heart thumping painfully. I collected my goods and was about to head back upstairs when I saw her. Still seated by the double-globed lamp in the family room, watching him, waiting. I didn't know what I was looking at for a moment. Then I realized: she wasn't smoking. I put my head down and ran up the stairs, damning the sound of my wake.

"Mom's not smoking," I told Tommy. Already he was digging greedily into the Saltines. We were under a huge Boston Bruins quilt stretched between our two twin beds. It was a narrow space and the overhead light glowed incongruously through the fabric the way a distant star might light a planet from another galaxy. We were lightheaded and warm from rebreathing our own exhalations.

"Really?" he said, through a mouthful of crackers. "What's Dad doing?"

"Just sitting there," I said. I tested the flashlight.

We heard the front door open. We looked at each other and stopped breathing. I reached out from under the quilt fort and switched off the overhead light. In the dark we were safe. We waited.

But we heard nothing. We waited some more. Not even a footfall was discernible. I stuck my head out from beneath the quilt. In the vast darkness of our room there was nothing to encumber the sound of the house. But there was nothing to be heard. I retreated. Tommy's face lit up when I held the flashlight on it. The uneven light gave him a regard beyond his years, but his eyes, big as saucers, splayed with little boy fear. I was about to say something when we heard it.

It wasn't a bark. It wasn't a cry or a yelp. Nor was it a shout. I can go on and say what it wasn't, because it wasn't anything. Anything wasn't it. In the few seconds that it happened, I struggled with what it wasn't the way astrophysicists struggled with black holes before they new what they were. There was a sound from below, and then we could hear my father coming.

The fear in our house touched everything around it, a presence as heavy as the humid night air, as real as the walls around us, and it preceded my father up the stairs, but just barely. He crashed through the door and stood for no more than a second, unevenly backlit by a naked bulb. His barrel shaped chest heaved unevenly and a small muscle on the right side of his jaw flexed in time with his breathing. Sweat soaked his mangy T-shirt. His hair was matted with it and his face glistened. Tommy and I backed into a corner. He scanned the room but passed over us. In one swift, economical motion he grabbed the portable black and white television and pounded back down the stairs.

The night closed around his retreat, diminishing him as he left. First we heard the slam of the front screen door, then the television crashing into the bed of his pickup truck with enough force to shatter the screen. The driver's side door, which never caught closed, was slammed six, seven times, until Dad swore at it with such color and ferocity that it must have complied, for the next sound we heard was his wheels squealing out of the driveway. The fading acceleration of his truck into the hot night was the last we had of him.

Tommy and I were surprised. We considered ourselves connoisseurs of parental conflict, a profession born of the necessity of self-preservation, for it was in our best interests to be able to analyze and react to any situation that might arise. We made a living from our distanced eavesdropping, communicating silently with each other through a range of facial expressions: intense apprehension as the opening salvoes were launched; surprise at the tone or depth of disdain that was leveled by either Mom or Dad; grim rectal constriction as the fight reached its routine crescendo.

"What was that?" Tommy asked. His bright, round, blue eyes held nothing but curiosity. Torment never knew his face. His was world was a giggling place, even in the acrid atmosphere of our parents' marriage. Because their fights usually ended up with apology and tears, Tommy was never prepared when my father stormed off. And after witnessing the way Dad stormed up the stairs and ripped the television from the wall, Tommy looked stunned. I thought it was about the worst he'd ever looked.

I didn't know what to say to Tommy. That was a first for me, for I always knew what to say to Tommy. I was his older brother; his protector and prosecutor; the corrective lenses through which he viewed the world. But I was as shaken as he at the sight of my father, wild-eyed and detached, tearing the television from our room and disappearing into the night.

So we stayed there in our rambling room that took up the whole second floor of the brand new custom cape my father had begun building five years earlier but had never finished. We sat in the harsh glare of the single bare bulb, which hung from the ceiling, occasionally looking at each other, until finally we fell asleep. We fell asleep in the sticky night air waiting for the thunder and lightening and rain to come, waiting for a cold front to come through and break the awful heat wave.

*

The day that my father left began in an unusual fashion. That morning he did not try to make his own coffee. That morning he had preceded the alarm out of bed. That morning the rusted out Ford pickup had turned over and caught the first time, leaving me in my bed, alone in the graying light of a predawn summer morning, alone upstairs with the sounds of my brother's deep breathing. It was the morning my father's boat sunk.

In Green Harbor, a small community attached to the larger bedroom town of Marshfield, boats didn't just sink. Tsunami didn't just appear at the H-buoy and swamp the fleet. Boards in the hulls of sturdy Novi lobster boats didn't dry up overnight and spring leaks. Barnacles didn't chew their way through steel-hulled draggers, sending them to the bottom. Yet boats did sink in Green Harbor.

A boy doesn't know why a boat sinks any more than he knows why an old man dies. The effect is startlingly clear; the causes remain mysterious. I knew only the things I could steal from my parents, the sorrow and the joy of their lives together. I knew about the end of the month, when the money came in, and the beginning of the month, when the money had to go out. Month changes were stressful transitions. Anger and cynicism are learned fast, matched with certain vocabulary words, pieced together into a quilt of reality that formed the ebbs and flows of our existence.

"Your father's boat sunk," my mother told me the morning before the night my father left. I'd heard it before, but always with someone else's name in the subject line of the sentence. It was always, "Duke Mc-Cluskey's boat sunk," or "Jimmy Duggan's boat sunk," and the revelation was always made late at night between my mother and father, over cigarettes and rye whiskey. And though it was never explained to me in detail as a boy, my knowledge of the circumstances surrounding a sunken boat was implicit: sabotage.

Sabotage was a word of the sea. It ebbed over your lips and slapped the jetty that protected the harbor. It drifted in on a nor'east seabreeze and cooled a hot day. Sabotage was as much a part of the lexicon of the fishing community as were the terms of profanity that punctuated their conversations. Sabotage was currency and it was wheeled as freely as sex and physical violence, paid out and called in. I didn't know what a sunken boat meant; I knew only what it stood for.

When you're twelve, you can't interpret the subtleties. You have only your gut, not yet fully evolved or stocked with situation retrieval material. Everything is open, everything forms, so that when my mother said, "Your father's boat sunk," my analysis was simple: trouble. Pain. Drinking. Late nights in the kitchen with cartons of cigarettes and quart bottles of Early Times and strained whispering.

Morning developed slowly, with languid imprecision. Heat built deliberately. I felt it beneath my feet, felt the heat coiling itself up, composing itself for the main event. The ground conspired with the sun that day to radiate up into me, to scald us. Out in the backyard Tommy hit a basketball with a golf club. Each time it hit the basketball the club bounced back and flew from his hands. Even that early in the morning I under-stood the heat's intentions. Above Tommy the sky shone white and cloudless, yet the sun was not visible. It blanched the scorched grass and shimmered the atmosphere. Even sideways it was hot.

That was all my mother said to me that morning. She was lost be-hind the smoke of her cigarette. Her face was vacant; not a foreign look for my mother, and her voice was thin and distant. Much of what I re-member about my mother is predicated by the presence of cigarettes: lipstick on a white filter; curling ash; a small leather cigarette purse. It was a barrier between us, keeping me at a distance and keeping her medicated.

"Your father's boat sunk," she told me, and then she was gone. Only a twist of cigarette smoke remained to sign the space where she had been.

I know that my mother thought I was only twelve years old. In fact, I was. But not to my own mind. Inside, I was light years ahead, anticipat-ing her actions. Only a little of it had anything to do with my size. I was tall and broad shouldered for a boy of twelve. People routinely mistook me for a young adult. Most of the time this was amusing, making me feel special in a good sort of way. But many times it was isolating and dis-tressing, setting me apart from my peers, creating unwanted expecta-tions. I never used my size to my advantage; the thought never crossed my mind. I was just tall and lean and I had the huge hands of a man, and that was who I was.

As she walked across our quiet street to the Millers, I imagined that my father was the subject of the upcoming conversation with Mrs. Miller. From my perch beside the bay window in the family room I watched them talk through that hot afternoon. Only their heads and shoulders were visible above the Miller's porch railing. Both posed in identical fashion, right hand held high with a cigarette between the index and middle fin-gers, in order to minimize the distance between smoke and lungs. My mother did the talking. She waved her hands about while Mrs. Miller nodded constantly, pausing occasionally to puff her cigarette or raise her drink glass to her mouth.

Out on the kitchen table sat an old Royal typewriter. The years had rendered it clunky and vaguely grotesque. I wanted to go to it. Sitting in the glare of the bay window was uncomfortable and sticky. I wanted to sit before it and let my fingertips fall gently into the cups of the keys, to feel it push back at me when I tried to turn thought into script. Paralysis gripped me, for I wanted the act, not the spirit. So I contented myself with the dream, the possibility. I felt warm, not hot.

That day I had my newspaper, my typewriter and my television, and I wanted it to be all right. I felt badly inside, but that was far away. There, in the present, with the sports page open and the house quiet, I was all right. Inside, the house was relatively cool. Through the back door I could hear Tommy out in the back yard. His self-narration sounded like deranged ranting from a distance. I checked on him from time to time, wondering how he could stand the heat, wondering if he remembered that Dad's boat had sunk, that Dad was gone.

*

It was after five that afternoon when my mother finally came home. Tommy and I watched television while she fixed herself another drink and lit another cigarette. The ice clinked in the glass, the lighter grated as she flicked it, then there was the soft pop that accompanied her first deep lungful of smoke. Those sounds were dear and familiar to me and they bred contempt with zeal normally reserved for familial relationships. It was my belief that if my mother and I ever became separated in a noisy cocktail lounge I would be able to find through her the smoky din by listening for the sounds of her ritual cigarette lighting.

"What are you boys watching?" she asked. She was standing in the doorway of the family room. Before I could reply, she answered herself.

"Those idiots. I thought I told you not to watch those idiots. Tommy, you're too close to the television."

Tommy sat cross-legged on the floor about three feet in front in front of the television, his mouth slightly agape. His eyeballs extruded from his skull and his pupils dilated as he watched Moe slap the shit out of Curly while Larry looked on with horrific bemusement.

My mother's voice floated out flatly, with a bloated dissonance that rendered her as grainy as the Three Stooges on the television screen. She sounded as if she were as enraptured by the show as Tommy and I were. My eyes stayed riveted to the screen so I strained to catch a glimpse of her from the corner of my vision. Although I knew what I would find I felt compelled to try and look, to verify what I already knew.

By the time I turned my head she was gone. The screen door slid open and closed on its track, followed by a deck chair being dragged across the planking of the back deck.

After a few minutes I went to the kitchen and looked out onto the back deck. She sat with her cigarette held high in one hand, a drink held high in the other. I followed her gaze across our yard, across the street to the Miller's deck. By changing my angle I could see Mrs. Miller and her husband, a large, red-faced local cop with a barrel chest and a shock of prematurely white hair. He paced his deck and rubbed his huge belly with one hand. In the other he held a can of beer. I went back inside and told Tommy it was time for dinner.

"What are we having?" he demanded of the television.

"Cereal."

"Cereal?" Now his trance was broken and he turned to me. "Why are we having cereal for dinner?"

I shrugged. "Mom's tired. We're having cereal."

"I don't feel like having cereal."

I frowned. What a bullshit artist this kid was. He'd say anything just to be contrary, to get attention. "Good for you."

We ate our cereal in front of the television, the evening news. Darkness brought an inexplicable intensifying of the day's heat and humidity. The atmosphere was absolutely soaking, painting us with sweat. Tommy and I went upstairs. We didn't want to be there when Dad got home, but we were.

*

151

Sometime before dawn, long after my father had come and gone, the thunder came. Preceded by pink waves of silent heat lightening that danced across the ceiling of our bedroom, it rumbled in the distance as it always did, slowly drawing near, more cinematic, the lightening whitening, the noise unbearable, the violence terrifying.

With the arrival of the first fat raindrops, the peepers and crickets ceased their racket. The drops sporadically slapped the thick vegetation, helping to mitigate the crash and bang of the storm. As the rain intensified the thunder was slashed with ever brighter lightening, until I could see the underbelly of the clouds illuminated in the dead of night.

I closed my eyes and let the storm come. It raged around us, invoking the same terror in me that all thunderstorms invoked, a sheer, unencumbered terror, a plain fear that needed no thought, only shelter, only prayer. And I wondered if even that would help. Nothing ever stopped the thunder. Nothing.

Chapter 2

I could never imagine how my mother landed in Green Harbor. She was small and slight and dark-haired and though she had mastered enough English to make her accent all but indiscernible, she was miscast in this land of Irish Americans, this place affectionately referred to by the locals as the Irish Riviera.

Her past was mentioned only obliquely, en passant, to sidestep the questions of my brother and me as we grew up. Her family, she said, were also fishermen, from Marseilles, and she came here with her mother when she was twelve after her father vanished at sea one winter.

Like many small creatures my mother was hyperactive, hypersensitive to danger, skittish and flighty. This she balanced with her drinking and smoking. For all the time she spent shadowing Tommy while he learned to ride a bicycle, or standing beneath our tree fort while we pounded nails, she spent an equal amount of time posed with a cigarette between her fingers and a tall glass filled with vodka and something— soda, some kind of juice, or vermouth.

An equal amount of time was also spent over at Mrs. Miller's. As well as being our neighbor and my mother's primary foil, Mrs. Miller was also a high school English teacher. By this arrangement her summers were free, and she spent them out on her back deck, removing as much clothing as she could and tanning her lithe body and drinking with my mother. "Matt, honey," she was fond of saying, "some day I'm going to have you in my English class. Then I will open doors for you and show you things you didn't know existed." She liked to smile and run her fingers through the hair on the side of my head when she said this.

Mrs. Miller was also one of the great "ya" listeners of all time. While my mother flitted out her apprehensions in a sentenceless, punctuation-free monologue, Mrs. Miller sipped her own drink, smoked thoughtfully and replied, repeatedly, "Ya, ya. Oh, ya, sure." Like my mother, Mrs. Miller was a transplant. She liked to say that the country she came from was even farther away than my mother's native France—at least temporally.

"In Georgia, darling, we have a certain way of doin' things." That was Mrs. Miller's favorite saying. After an afternoon of vodka tonics and cigarettes, she would drawl that one out and muss my hair and tell me that once I got to her English class she was going to really teach me. Sometimes her fingers would linger in my hair, running down the back of my neck gently in a way that made me tingle in areas far removed from either Georgia or France. She would smile at me while she did this and it was then that I learned that smiles didn't always mean happy or funny. This smile wasn't mean—it was something else. Something that had to do with the tingling. If my mother ever noticed this she didn't say.

Mom's Americanization was lost on me. A twelve-year-old boy doesn't have the reference points for comparison. Your mother is your mother and your father is your father and nothing more. I knew she was French and that her name was Claire and that her family name was Rochette but that was no big deal. My father's grandfather had come from Cork and I had many friends who were first or second generation Americans, specifically Irish Americans. Our foreigness was precisely what made us American.

That she found and married my father only added to her mystery. In her limited references to her childhood she described her own father--the maternal Marseilles grandfather I never met--in exactly the same terms she used to curse my father's shortcomings: a foolish fisherman, a damned liar, a selfish bastard. In my twelve-year-old mind, I wondered how she could speak about her dead father with such reproach and enmity, since when she lost him and was brought to the United States by her mother she was only twelve. I knew why my father engendered those reactions in her. For the most part, they were deserved.

In 1975, in Green Harbor, a small fishing village south of Boston, my mother, a surreptitiously hard drinking, chain smoking, hyperactive bundle of nervous energy, and my father, a Boston Irishman, subject to all the strengths and weaknesses accorded that title, an alcoholic from the womb, a man who moved to Green Harbor, a.k.a. the Irish Riviera, at the age of twenty to escape, in his own words, all those "fuckin Irishmen" that had been his family and friends growing up in Dorchester, were no different from any other family I knew. Except, that is, in one respect. My parents were the first ones to divorce.

It didn't happen the day after my father left us and it didn't happen that summer. Legally speaking it never happened at all because my mother never got beyond the actual filing of the papers with a lawyer, which she did on the Friday after my father left us. But in Green Harbor it was as good as done, and the distinction between separated and divorced was not observed. In the eyes of the community Mom and Dad were done.

In the beginning I thought the idea of having divorced parents was cool. It would be something I could tell people, something that would make them feel sorry for me, and by extension, like me. Finally someone would pay attention to me, and I would practice saying it to my image in the bathroom mirror.

"My Mom and Dad are divorced."

I would make the longest face I could, as if the buzzards were circling my carcass. Then I would imagine their reaction, their sympathy, their attention. I would imagine the divorce as some sort of badge of courage I could wear, something that distinguished me above the others, some tragedy that I had survived and come through with flying colors.

But that's not how it worked out.

*

Much later that day the rain finally stopped. We were left with a steaming jungle. The atmosphere remained so liquid that breathing was difficult. I had not thought much about what my mother asked me that morning. What was a man? Already I felt that I possessed the resignation needed for the job, the quiet acceptance of life's lousy little turns without fuss that all real men had. I knew that the clarity I felt within would be enough—and more—to satisfy the job requirements.

Tommy and I met after lunch—more cereal—out in the tree fort. It was still raining, but softly, the drops drumming indifferently on the plywood roof of the place that Dad had nailed together.

With Mr. Miller--an off-duty cop--leading, a search for my father among the barrooms and flophouses of Green Harbor was initiated. This might not sound like much of a challenge in a village like Green Harbor, but don't be fooled. In Green Harbor you couldn't drive more than half a mile without passing a bar. There was the Webster Room, which became the Helmsman, which became DJ's, which became Brian's Place. And there was the Dockside, which became the Compass Rose. And the Roadhouse and Checkers and Bonnie Parker's, which became Rafferty's. And the Shoals, which became the Captain's Two, which became Jennifer's, which became Biaggio's. And the Rexicana and Plett's Pub and the Breakers and the Venus and the Fairview—which only recently burned to the ground. And there was the Ranch House, which is still the

Ranch House and is exactly what it sounds like: a real rummy's ono-matopoeia.

And let's not forget the civilized drinking clubs of the middle class, the Disabled American Vets, the American Legion, the Knights of Colum-bus, the Benevolent and Fraternal Order of Elks, the VFW, and those communal stalwarts, the Masons. There were more obscure places to drink, too, places like the 9-hole Webster Hill Golf Course, and the GHYC —the Green Harbor Yacht Club—which boasted no yachts, but plenty of Schlitz and peanuts. Those were the places that men could go to on a Sunday morning and get a bottle of Budweiser for fifty cents.

You just couldn't go thirsty in Green Harbor. And I still haven't men-tioned those places where you could get Schaeffer To Take Out: Pad-dock Package, Brant Rock Liquors, the Green Harbor General Store, Ocean Bluff Packet, Leo's Liquors, Marshfield Liquors, Hubbard's Cup-board, Blanchard's.

None of these places ever really went out of business. Oh, they changed owners and themes, and maybe they were dark from time to time, but they kept living, like an earthworm whose pieces keep wriggling no matter how often you slice it up, or a lobster that keeps regenerating its claws no matter how many times you rip them off. It was almost as if the ground beneath these places was hallowed, anointed with booze and tears and pain and divorce and blood and abuse, and no matter what was erected atop that stained soil, the liquor would flow.

If you were sober and thirsty in Green Harbor, that was your own fault.

My father remained undiscovered after his boat had sunk. The mys-terious sinking, which in my mind had sparked the night of my parent's separation, eliminated the logical place to find Dad. The boat was where he slept on the nights when the fights with my mother were bad, and on the nights when he was just too drunk to get off the boat and into his pickup truck. Without the boat for a beacon, he was unfindable.

Because of the concentration of barrooms around the town pier, the beaches and the waterfront in general, there were nights when Dad never returned home. Tommy and I knew because we had been out with him, out pulling lobster pots all day. A lobsterman's day never ended, his life was non-linear, circling over and over again throughout the same rhythms.

Steaming out of the harbor at six in the morning, I would watch my father as alert and alive as I had ever seen him. The boat was fueled, replacement traps were piled on the transom, and his notebook was consulted. The notebook contained LORAN coordinates which fixed the position of his sets—lines of ten lobster posts marked at each end by a buoy painted in the distinctive colors which identified the set line as belonging to the lobster boat *Claire*.

On board, as we steamed out of the harbor, he was the model of efficiency, setting up the bait box, checking the bilge and filling the live tank, steaming quickly to the first set. It wasn't until ten o'clock or so, until he'd finished off his first sixpack, that things began to go downhill. There were times when some of his sets would remain out for months at a time, and when he finally stumbled across them, or when someone had told him to pull his damn pots or have the lines cut, the pots would be barnacled and brimming with dead lobsters, starfish and crabs.

After selling his lobsters for cash at the pier, Dad would make his way down to the Ocean Café. Most nights he wouldn't make it out, but if he did, the Helmsman or the Breakers would catch him. Losing his truck, he would often stagger back to the *Claire* and sleep in the tiny, stinking forward cabin. That's where he could be found spending his life in a circle of being drunk, recovering from being drunk, or getting drunk.

But now, with the *Claire* presumably mired in the soft marshy mud at the bottom of the harbor, no one knew where to look for Dad, least of all Mr. Miller the cop, a drinking companion from the neighborhood but someone who never mixed with my father's fisherman drinking partners. Those were two different classes of alcoholics.

*

In the first few days following my father's departure, a thick, numbing fog enveloped Green Harbor. What had begun as a line of summer

157

thunderstorms blew up into a sou'wester which stalled offshore, backed into the Gulf of Maine and whipped itself up into a proper three day blow, a rare summertime nor'easter. By the time Saturday arrived the rain was coming in sideways, slashing and cutting in the fashion of a November storm. There was talk of a hurricane off the coast of Florida racing up the coast to join the burgeoning summer storm, but the two systems ultimately repelled each other.

All around Green Harbor sweatshirts came out of drawers and the Cadillacs with Florida plates parked themselves alongside the rusting pickups of the locals outside the barrooms. Mr. Miller gave up the search for my father after one day. A police cruiser rolled up to the Miller's house and a cop carried Mr. Miller up the front steps like a bag of cultured mussels, depositing him on the front step for Mrs. Miller to deal with.

Of course, my mother went straight over to the Miller's after the police brought their fallen brother home. The foul weather denied me my usual view of Mom and Mrs. Miller smoking and drinking and fretting the afternoon away, but I could picture them in the Miller's kitchen, Mrs. Miller saying over and over again, in her Southern drawl, "I just don't know, Claire, I just don't know."

Desperation was not on my mind. That word was too big even for a smarty pants like me. But that afternoon in the cold wind and the fog that obliterated summer, with my father gone and his boat sunk, with my Americanized mother across the street trading cigarettes with a fretting neighbor whose husband was lying in an alcoholic coma, things didn't look all that great.

That weekend my mother sent Tommy and me to our grandparents.

*

Grampy drove down to pick us up and on the drive back up to Quincy we played the license plate game. For every license plate we spotted on the highway that had two of the same numbers in a row, we got a nickel. Three numbers in a row and we got a dime. Four in a row meant a quarter. Out of state license plates were worth a dime, except in summertime, when their value plummeted to a nickel due to the influx of tourists. A plate from Alaska or Hawaii was worth a Kennedy half dollar on the spot, something that had only happened once, but Grampy was true to his word, pulling over in the breakdown lane and producing a freshly minted half dollar.

Grampy loved that game, not using it for a distraction to keep a couple of boys quiet during a car ride, but genuinely getting into it, paying himself when he spotted a plate with three 5's, slapping the steering wheel when Tommy and I fought over who saw what first.

Whenever we were in that car, a '69 Galaxy 500, there was a baseball game on the radio. It didn't seem to matter what time of the day or night, if there was a ballgame inhabiting the airwaves, my grandfather would pull it in. Once, on the way to mass in the morning, he flicked on the radio and on came some announcer describing an at-bat from Chicago.

"But Grampy," I said, "there are no ballgames in the morning, not even on the west coast."

Grampy winked and smiled and drew his jowly face up into a smile. "Armed Forces Radio, kiddo. They're replaying a game from last night." This explanation delighted him and he slapped the steering wheel and issued his laugh, which was somewhere between a cackle and a yelp.

That aura of continual baseball extended out of his car and into my grandparent's house. Radios infiltrated every corner of the house, all of them tuned to the station that broadcast Red Sox games. There was a radio on the table between the two chairs my grandmother and grandfather spent their days occupying. It was a beauty, a Philco Multiband that could pull in the BBC, AFN and anything else that skipped across the atmosphere. There was also a radio on the nightstand between their beds, a radio in the kitchen next to the stove and one on the dining room table. Outside there was one atop the rusting aluminum patio table. At any given time one or more of these radios would be turned up to maximum volume, blaring a ballgame. My grandparents were partially deaf, and in the olden days, the way you overcame deafness was with volume.

"You're deaf because you have all the goddamned radios turned up so loud," my father would bellow when we visited them en famille.

That day, when we arrived at my grandparents' house in Quincy, my grandmother was on the porch roof. A pile of asphalt shingles was beside her and her mouth was filled with roofing nails, which she promptly spat out.

"Dad!" she called to Grampy. "Dad! Did you bring my water?"

He waved her off impatiently. "Of course I did. For chrissakes, do you think I'd come back without it?"

Grampy removed two plastic jugs filled with seawater that he must have filled before he picked us up. He shuffled into the house, leaving the car running and his door open. I reached forward from the back seat and turned off the ignition and Tommy and I climbed out.

"Come on in boys while I soak my feet."

By the time we got inside, Grammy was sitting in her chair, her feet immersed in a basin filled with seawater. She reached out and flicked on her radio and Curt Gowdy's voice thundered into the room, snapping with static and nearly drowned out by the ambient babble of the ballpark. The volume was set at an excruciating level, so loud it distorted the already fuzzy transmission. The effect was stunning. No ballpark was ever as real as Grammy's radio turned all the way up. Grampy came in and before plopping into his chair, he gave my grandmother a glass of iced tea that had no ice and didn't smell like tea. He sunk into his chair and began reading the newspaper.

Tommy was already deep into the National Geographics. My grandparents had been getting National Geographic since the magazine's inception, and they had never parted with a single issue. Not that they had bothered to catalogue or store them in any useful way. They just had hundreds and hundreds of them, most of them in piles behind the sofa. Tommy tore through them until he found his favorite, the August, 1969 issue entitled "Up the Congo." Inside there were several photographs of the local women doing the washing down by the river while wearing nothing more than a swatch of burlap around their hips.

Grampy must have been tired because when I looked up again the newspaper was covering his face and deep snores issued from beneath. Grammy was doing a crossword puzzle from the stack of game magazines that stood beside her radio on the table. When she saw me look up she smiled and put down her pencil.

"Matthew, come here, dear." She patted the arm of her sitting chair, motioning for me to sit down. She had been doing this since for as long as I could remember, and even though I was a man sized twelve year old, she insisted I come as close as I could.

"Do you know," she said, "that when you're father was a boy he used to sit right where you were sitting and read. Read, read, read, that's all he wanted to do. That and fish. Do you like to fish, Matthew?"

"I like to read, Grammy."

Up close I could really see my grandmother's age. Her face sagged and her eyes showed rims of red around the bottom lids. They must have been blue, those eyes, but now they were cloudy, as if high cirrus clouds, precursor to a storm, had moved in. She thought about what I said and took a long drink. Now I could smell the distilled grain on her breath. You didn't come from Green Harbor and not know what that smell was.

"Well, I suppose you could be a writer of some kind," she said. "Or, you could enter the priesthood. Imagine that."

Up came the glass and down went another long drink. It was then that I realized just how big the glass was. Not just a regular tumbler, this was a glass that a German would find suitable for beer drinking: tall and wide at the top, it must have held close to a quart of liquid. In this case, rye whiskey.

"You know, someday you could become the Pope." Then she would hesitate a moment, and say, "Well, only Italians can be popes, but you could become the Cardinal. Imagine: a cardinal for a grandson. And if not a cardinal, a bishop. What an honor to be a bishop."

And then she would pause and take another drink and look at me with those milky eyes and I loved her but I just wanted her to say it and get it over with because I was beginning to feel uncomfortable. I knew she was drinking but I didn't know that she was smashed. I just thought that was the way everybody was.

"And if not a bishop, my dear," she would finally say, "at least a priest. There's no shame in a family having a priest. Imagine that." With that said she downed the rest of the glass of whiskey. In those moments I was always unsure. Unsure about how to feel—happy because my grandmother loved me in that milky, distant way that grandparents have, or confused because she seemed so unnatural, but I was not well enough equipped to detect and identify her flaw. Around my grandparents I mostly felt ambivalence. I knew I loved them, but they, like most of the adults in my life, seemed separated from me by a frustrating distance that I could never overcome.

I drifted away from her as she turned to Grampy.

"Dad!" she bellowed. "Dad!"

Grampy awoke with a violent start, sending the newspaper flying.

"What? What? What is it?"

"Dad!" she yelled. "Dad, you've got to get dinner started. And refill my glass!"

*

That night I wondered where my father was. Though his boat sunk and he disappeared after that terrible argument, foul play was not something that entered my mind. Such was my father's existence that I simply assumed he was kicking around Green Harbor somewhere, hiding out in a hovel above a bar somewhere.

Downstairs the radio blasted out a ballgame. From the bedroom came my grandfather's equally loud snores. Only in the cramped front bedroom that Tommy and I shared when we stayed there could I find refuge from the din. I opened a window and in came the sounds of the traffic out on Route 9, a perpetual ribbon of cars running in and out of Boston. But those sounds were distant and manageable, and they floated in on a cool breeze that filled the room with energy and hope.

Tommy was asleep on the bed beside me beneath a pile of National Geographics. There was so much around me, so much humanity, so much life, yet I felt none of it. I felt vastly alone, I felt like the image at the far end of a telescope, extended beyond the grasp of palpable reality, gone, gone. Tommy was there in the bed beside me, but he was gone. Downstairs Grammy was weaving her way through Curt Gowdy's rendition of a Red Sox game, but she was really gone. And the smartest of us all, Grampy was snoozing away. He knew when to get out.

It was just me and the house. Just me and fifty years of married life, the lives of my grandparents, of my father and his brothers. The wallpaper began to speak to me, and I began to listen.

That was good wallpaper. It had to be, to stand that much abuse. It had been there since my father was a boy. I know because he never failed to tell me when we were there together. "Look at that wallpaper. Last forever. Not like the shit they make today." My fingers brushed across it, and I could feel its depth. It was textured, vertically ribbed, reinforced with some kind of cloth, I imagined. I could see Grampy hanging it—

I checked that thought. It wasn't Grampy who did all the work around that house, it was Grammy. My earliest memory of her was seeing her up on the roof on a hot July afternoon, a mouthful of roofing nails, three or four bundles of shingles scattered about her, while she nailed a new roof on. She was raised by a carpenter who expected his girls to be able to do everything he could. As a little boy she had regaled me with stories of how her father had taught her everything, from hammering nails to fixing car engines. When she told me these stories of her girlhood she would always laugh at the wrong parts of the story. She would tell me that her father had her carrying some boards and a load of them dropped on her foot and she would laugh, saying, "Oh, did that hurt!" It didn't seem to me that kind of pain would be amusing.

I lay there and I looked at that wallpaper. It was like no wallpaper I had ever seen, nor have I ever seen any like it since. It depicted a duck hunter coming through a stand of reeds in a salt marsh. As in all wallpaper, the scene replayed itself over and over again in a pattern, ad infinitum, until the whole wall was covered in early twentieth century duck hunter.

My eyes were drawn to the duck hunter. The light from a streetlight outside the bedroom window lit the wall beside my bed. I moved closer to the edge of my bed and studied the figure on the wall. He was featureless the way a clown is featureless, with only thick representations of his eyes and lips, which gave him an exaggerated look. The more I looked at him, the more grotesque he became, his lips thickening, his eyes blackening, the entire image decomposing before me, until he became so menacing that I had to turn away.

That's when I heard the whisper.

It wasn't a call, and it wasn't a voice. It wasn't the wind, and it wasn't anyone moving about upstairs. I was doing well at identifying what it wasn't, which left me only with what it was. With all the noise from the ball game on the radio downstairs and my grandfather's snoring and the cars whizzing by on Route 9, I shouldn't have been able to hear a whisper. But I did. It came from the closet.

In my grandparent's home there is a front bedroom, a back bedroom, and a tiny middle bedroom opposite the bathroom. To get to the middle bedroom you have to walk down a long, claustrophobic hallway that looks as if it was an afterthought to the original construction of the house. The hallway is dark, without lights. The only way it can be navigated is to turn the bathroom light on. But that only illuminates half the journey. The door to the middle bedroom must be left open, for the lights from the cars on Route 9 are what guide you the rest of the way to the bedroom. Once there, an old fashioned push light switch turns on a harsh overhead light. A small lamp on a nightstand next to the bed can then be turned on, giving the room a gentler light, and the painful overhead light can then be outened.

Besides the gymnastics required to get to the middle bedroom at night, the only other outstanding feature it possesses is its access to a huge closet that runs the length of the eves on that side of the house. It is the only storage space upstairs. When I heard the whisper again, it was coming from that closet.

I know I should have felt fear. That crazy wallpaper had upset me again. But the whisper sounded familiar. Tommy? No. I had just left him sleeping in the other room. Not even the tricks of an old house could have carried his voice through walls, around corners, down halls. The whisper persisted as I drew near the closet door, and as I opened it, it stopped.

Soft light from the bedroom spilled into the closet opening, illuminating a small square of floorboard. The closet itself is little more than storage space among the eves of the house, and the closet door is nothing but a half door opening into it. The heat from the day, woody and stifling and aching to escape, rushed out to me in something close to a gust of wind. My body went rigid and I began to tingle. I was stuck to the floor, grounding some current, unable to breathe.

And then it was gone and the breath came back to me. I nearly choked on the air, which was full of tannic dry rot from the roof rafters and tarpaper and ancient boards that made up the inner roof of the house. It was sooty and dusty and it grated the back of my throat, eliciting a spasm of coughing that I managed to cover up by burying my face in the crook of my arm. When the coughing subsided, I swallowed and crawled in.

Somewhere to the right of the closet door on the inside of the closet was a light. I felt around vainly for the string before giving up. Finally, I had to move the lamp from the nightstand as close to the closet door as possible. This allowed just enough light in so that I could see the closet light was broken, the ceramic base cracked off, the bulb missing, the chain gone.

Inside I could see the outlines of many boxes, of stacks of old newspapers. I could see the dark tips of the roofing nails that stuck through the sheathing from the outside. I reached for the closest box and it tipped over. A gun fell out.

For a moment I blinked at the gun. Then my eyes moved past it to several framed photos. They were military units, soldiers posing casually in the field, most with cigarettes dangling from the corners of their mouths, all wearing camouflage in various states of undress. I quickly found my father among them. And something else.

At the time, I didn't know what a diploma was, or how it was presented. But there, along with the photos, was an unmarked diploma folder. Inside it held a piece of paper stating that my father had been cited for valor in the face of the enemy. And then I heard the whisper again, from deep within the eves under the roof. I stifled a scream and fell backwards out of the closet. I closed the door and turned out the lights and got back to my bed next to Tommy.

The steady pace of his breathing soothed me, and although I lay awake for a long time, thinking about that gun lying on the floor of the closet, thinking about my father in a war he never told me about, sleep finally overcame me. Sweet, dreamless sleep.

A Critique of *Angels in Vegas* by Max Shenk

If I were critiquing this work in a peer group, or as an instructor, the first thing I would want to know is this: where is the story going? What is going to happen? What I've read is twenty-some pages of very compelling, rich, absorbing, beautifully-written detail and backstory, but where is it taking us? To what is it building? Of course, I have the advantage of knowing you and knowing what you think is wrong with it, and, from what I've gathered (and now read), it's the same thing that vexed the three 3-ring-bindered "novel" that I carried around and tinkered with for six years: great characters, compelling backstory, every element you need in a good book, but dodging the big question that you and another writer friend challenged me with. What happens?

What has already happened, of course, is that Dad has left. The boat has sunk. (Or "Dad sunk the boat." Important distinction, and the

166

narrator's awareness of this distinction might be a key to what this book could be.) Is this the major event in the book? If so, we've already taken away a big reason for a reader to keep reading: they already have the answer to the question "what happens"? So, instead of the reader being propelled by curiosity about finding out what happens NEXT, instead we're getting a story of WHY it happened and HOW it happened. The story of why and how here is beautifully written, intriguing, and believable, but as a reader, it doesn't propel me in quite the same way as a feeling of knowing something is going to happen, wondering what is going to happen, when it's going to happen, how it's going to unfold... and having the writing and the expose and the character development and dialogue and action all working together to build momentum and create anticipation and curiosity. Is the story going to evolve toward another event, or is it going to devolve from this event?

If "Dad sinking the boat" is the big event in the book, should it be revealed at the beginning? Or held until the end?

This event may seem so inevitable a conclusion to the writer that he thinks "Well, I might as well just give it away at the beginning." But how interesting is a story when we know what has already happened?

There is, of course, the Lieutenant Columbo theory of storytelling: that you tell at the beginning what happens, and the reader knows all along what the solution to the mystery is. But keep in mind that in these stories, the "story" wasn't the murder; the story was the capture of the culprit. Big difference.

If Dad's sinking the boat becomes the book's destination instead of its starting point, even (especially) if that destination isn't clear to the reader, then a reader will want to keep reading to find out what happens next. It creates a different kind of momentum. It seems to me that structuring the book so that the big event occurs at the beginning not only takes the mystery and fun out of the book (yes, even in a serious work like this, there is FUN in it for a reader), but it makes it harder for the writer, because you've got to find things to hold a reader's interest aside from "the natural chronological arc of a story."

Chronology vs. backstory. That is the question I would ask. Which is easier to write? Which is more compelling to read? Which propels you forward, and which by its very nature pulls you backwards?

I think a key to this is VOICE. I like Matthew's voice, but I wasn't sure that it was the voice of a 12-year-old boy. Was it supposed to be? It sounds, as the chapters progress, as if this is a much older Matthew looking back from a safe distance at what happened. My confusion comes from a line on the first page of chapter one, end of the second paragraph: "I'm a twelve-year-old boy." Present tense. If the book was structured chronologically, the 12-year-old boy's voice would come more naturally. He would, by nature, be naive to certain realities in the world and relationships around him. But those realities would be revealed to him as the story progressed, just as they would be revealed to the reader.

One of the best pieces of advice about writing came from a friend of mine who's not a writer, but is a voracious reader. (Judy Gimpel. Might as well give her a plug.) Judy read some of my "novel" and said "I thought the chapters were too long. When I read, especially if I read before bedtime, I want short chapters. When I get to the end of a chapter, I want to feel like I've reached a pause. If the chapter goes on and on and on and I'm tired, sometimes I just can't make it to the end, even if I want to." It was one of the first things that made me step outside of the way I saw the work as a WRITER and inhabit the way that a READER would view the work. How does a reader read? Where do they read? When do they read? Under what circumstances? Not everyone (and in fact, nobody with any sense) reads like a grad student. They carry the books with them, sneaking a page or a chapter here and there, or take it to bed and read a little bit before nodding off. What Judy was telling me, in so many words was that, as a writer, I need to structure my book to work with that instead of against it.

Think of Jan Berry and Brian Wilson. Brian Wilson had a car radio speaker in the studio where he recorded the Beach Boys' hits, so that he could play mixes of the tracks through the same sort of speaker that most of his listeners did. Jan did Brian one better: one of his friends was Roger Christian, a DJ at KRLA in Los Angeles, and Jan would take acetates of Jan and Dean records down to the station and have Roger play them over the air, so that Jan could hear what they'd sound like on the air. If he liked what he heard, he knew he was done; if not, he'd go back to work.

Both of these artists took their music out of the vacuum of the studio and did everything they could to bring an awareness of the listener's experience into the creative process. That's what we need to do as writers sometimes: think like a reader.

Anyway, when I read this, I found myself wanting chapter breaks almost everywhere you had an asterisk break.

Of course, if this was a work for a class, I'd be harping about DO NOT NOT NOT TRUST SPELLCHECK. ("Not not not" is a triple negative, so I'm covered.) Their are a few places wear you use the wrong real word. I'd cite examples, but, alas, I stuck my red pen in storage. YOU go find them. Proofread, proofread, proofread. The story itself is told with care; so should the drafts be presented with technical care.

I think that's it. Except that, yeesh, why is this thing in a drawer? Take it out and gut it, pull it apart, put it back together, and make it the work that you want it to be. What's here is great, and deserves to be even better.

About the critic:
Max Shenk is an author and teacher. His first book is a collection of stories called What's With Her? He teaches writing and composition at the Community College of Vermont, and he has master's degrees in education and creative writing.

Part Two:
Critical Writing

Literary Criticism

What I Like About Annotations
and
Why I Still Practice the Art
and
Why I Teach My Students How to Annotate

I confess that I knew almost nothing about annotations before I started writing them. I knew vaguely how to annotate a text I was reading, but I wasn't up on the form. But once I figured it out, I loved it. An annotation is a brief paper—about 500 words—focusing on one aspect of a reading, something that stood out for you as a reader and writer, something that appealed to you. In the annotation you zoom in on that one aspect and question why it appealed to you, and you find out what it means to your writing.

I love the guerrilla aspect of the annotation: get in, make your point, get out. Annotations focus your writing skills; they're like batting practice. You see so many pitches that you begin to discover your strengths and weaknesses, and you begin to work on them. You also learn something about yourself as a writer, because you're often wondering why your lingered on the use of imagery in that last book you read. Why did the author do that? And why did it jump out at me like that? Is there something going on in my own writing that reflects that? By allowing those questions, then answering them, the process of discovery is initiated.

I teach the annotation process to all my students, regardless of the class I'm teaching. It's one of the most effective tools for bringing readers to an awareness of the text. The most exciting part comes when all the students read the same piece, annotate it, then share their writing with the rest of the class. Students are amazed that other people had vastly different interpretations of the same reading. It shocks them, and broadens them, pushing them into more reflective and productive territory, no matter what the writing assignment.

Many of the annotations that follow did that for me; all of them changed me as a writer and a thinker. The view you're getting from the annotation is inside-out. I hope you've read some of the books here so that you can compare and contrast my annotations with your own interpretations.

"The Power of Synchronicity"

When the emotional arc and the narrative arc of a story synchronize, something special happens. The reader forgets about the plot and begins to truly understand the characters, their motivations, their inner selves. This is the place of great fiction writing, and it's found in *Blood Lines*, by David Quammen. The most dramatic example occurs in "Walking Out," the first story in the collection.

When thinking about narrative and emotional arcs, the sequence and consequence of events and actions hold the key to believability. The narrative arc of this story follows a definite, logical path. David, an adolescent boy, is picked up at a train station by his father. The two are going on a week long hunting trip. They drive to a cabin, then embark on a moose hunt in the Montana mountains. Reading the story, one can almost hear the voice inside the author's head asking, "And then what happens?" They hike to a remote camp the next day, and the day after that, they hike high up the side of the mountain to hunt. There they encounter a sow grizzly bear with cubs. David accidentally shoots his father, gravely injuring him, and in the middle of a snowstorm hikes down the mountain with the dying man on his back. But when they reach safety, it's too late: his dad's dead.

Reading through that narrative summary, there's a lot of places for emotion. And it's the emotional arc that holds all the best parts of this story. Right away there's tension between David and his father. David's parents are divorced, and when David's father asks if his ex-wife passed any messages for him, David says, "She said…she said I should give you her love."[4] It's a lie; David's father figures it out instantly, when in the next line he says, "Oh…Thank you, David." The formal abruptness ends the discourse, and gives us insight into the characters' emotional place in the story. David doesn't want to be there: "I don't want much to sleep in a hut," he said, and his voice broke with the simple honesty of it;[5] his father doesn't really, either: "He pretended to believe that the boy would be glad."[6]

But they reach an understanding, and after the father tells David of his own terrible experience moose hunting, they have this exchange:

> "Why did you tell me that story?" the boy said. "Now I don't want to shoot a moose either."
> "I know," said his father. "And when you do, I hope you'll be sad too."[7]

173

David realizes that he must go through with this, so he steels himself to the task: "Now I'm just hunting moose with my father...Few boys in Evergreen Park have ever been moose hunting with their fathers."[8] Then tragedy strikes: David accidentally shoots his father. Given their strained relationship, the importance of this event cannot be overstated; it's the emotional climax of the story. It's also the narrative climax:

> He was afraid his father was going to die. He wanted to beg him to reconsider. The boy had never before seen his father hopeless. He was afraid. But he was no longer afraid of his father.[9]

This can only happen when David turns an emotional corner in the narrative: he's got no choice. The story demands that he act to save both their lives, so he makes that emotional leap that changes him forever:

> The boy knew he was supposed to feel great shame, but he felt little. His father could no longer hurt him as he once could, because the boy was coming to understand him. He did not want the boy to feel contemptible, but he needed him to, because of the loneliness and the bitterness and the boy's mother; and he could not help himself.[10]

After that point the emotional arc follows the narrative arc to a resolution. Being able to see the two arcs in step with each other enlightens the importance of their relationship in a well-written story.

"The Moment of Change"

Creating a sense of longing in his characters gives James Joyce the opportunity to approach his stories from a complex, less obvious place. It also allows him to highlight their superficiality as a by-product. He reveals this quality of desire in different ways. Sometimes it's expressed as fatalism; sometimes as hope. But the result is a desperation, an emptiness that moves through the writing and leaves the reader with a sense of vastness that's not apparent on the surface.

In "The Sisters," Joyce uses hope—embodied by the narrator, a teenage boy—to illustrate the longing for the life of Father Flynn. Joyce leads off the text with a direct reference to hope, setting the tone for the story to come: "There was no hope for him this time: it was the third stroke."[11] Though there's no medical certainty that three strokes always result in death, Joyce uses the third stroke like a third strike in baseball. But even after that, the narrator needs more proof, more than the two candles in Father Flynn's window, more than the word of Mr. Cotter. Only when he reads a printed report of the death does he believe it: "The reading of the card persuaded me that he was dead."[12]

In death, the priest's sisters reveal his longing. His health had been deteriorating, but when he broke a chalice, "They say that was the beginning of it,"[13] the "it" referring to his mortal end. After that, Father Flynn becomes nostalgic, yearning to return to the place of his birth. He knows he's dying, yet he longs for the past he can't have. It's fatalism, and like hope, it's one of the ways Joyce expresses longing in this short story collection.

In "The Dead" it's the weakness in the otherwise strong Gabriel that Joyce uses to show a character's hunger for some unfulfilled aspect of their personality. Gabriel is drawn as a strong, staid man who does and says the right things. But when he sees his wife lost in a moment of reverie while listening to music, Gabriel struggles to order the moment, to put a name on his wife's feelings. In his arrogance, he imagines himself an accomplished painter, and names the painting.[14]

But later, after he and his wife have returned to their hotel, he finds her still overcome by passion. The song reminded her of a boy named Michael Furey who loved her before she met Gabriel. This is something that he can't control, and it enrages him. He wants to have what Michael Furey has over his wife, but he realizes it's impossible, that there's no separation between the living and the dead. Gabriel's longing for that passion causes him great sadness, knowing he can never be to his wife what Michael Furey is to her.

These examples of longing cause the characters to reveal a change within themselves. In "The Sisters" the narrator realizes that Father Flynn longed for a part of his life that he could never get back, and when he broke the chalice he broke the ties to that part of his past. In "The Dead" Gabriel Conroy's longing for control of his life leaves him desperate for access to a part of his wife's feelings that remain forever closed to him. The longing within a character can be used as a vehicle for change, as Joyce has done in this collection, and by that change will the story have deeper, more complex meaning.

"Precision"

At crucial points in the short story collection *Heart Songs*, Annie Proulx chooses distinctive words that set a hardscrabble mood for the characters and places. The words call attention to themselves through their originality, and this attention focuses the reader's expectations for the tone that follows in each story, and in the collection as a whole. But Proulx doesn't simply sprinkle these words haphazardly. She uses them deliberately, at important junctures, to set, emphasize, and echo the content.

She begins this technique in the first sentence of the first story, describing Hawkheel's face in the driest of terms,[15] using words that arrest the reader and invoke a sense of aridity (in a pointed and plain sense), a laconic character, and of wildness, like a character from a James Fenimore Cooper novel. Hawkheel proves to be laconic and dry, to the point of self-destruction and insanity.

At the beginning of "A Run of Bad Luck," Mae, while preparing to fry porkchops in a cast iron pan, adds the grease using more sonic description.[16] That simple word choice gives us an image that sets the tone for the story. This isn't *haute cuisine*. This is backcountry living. Proulx then uses echo to drop in like-sounding words and phrases in the middle of the story.[17]

Proulx's technique sets the tone for the story right from the opening line, and her hard-bitten word choice isn't limited only to nouns. Names of characters and places also experience the treatment, such as the opening of "Stone City."[18] These names and vocabulary set an unmistakably rural tone to the writing.

Whether the words are contained in a simile, a metaphor, or used in details to form an image, they do the work of tone setting. This distinctive vocabulary reflects the chiseled hardness of the characters, the hardness of their lives, the ruthless mercy of the land.

"Emotional Consequence"

Describing the relationship between fathers and sons leads writers into convoluted places where craft and content don't always meet. But when those elements succeed in coming together, the result is so emotionally satisfying, so rich and beautiful and touching, the enduring image stays with the reader forever. Ernest Hemingway does this in *Islands in the Stream*.

In the first story, "Bimini," Hemingway's technique of deliberate pacing characterizes not only the development of the story, but the mounting emotion as Thomas Hudson, the book's protagonist, anticipates the arrival of his sons for a summer visit. The story begins with a distracting fight scene that lasts nearly 50 pages. The scene introduces us to Roger Davis, Hudson's best friend. After the fight, Hudson and Davis spend the night talking, and the result of their dialogue is an understanding of just how important the boys are to Hudson, how empty his life is without them. This justifies the time the author spends in that opening scene. The relationship between the two men is a complicated one, and it needed time to be shown, so that the scene that came after it would have the emotional impact the author wanted.

When the boys arrive, Hudson treats them as adults, engaging them in long, meaningful conversation. Once again Hemingway lingers through the scene, drawing it out over 20 pages. Two things happen during this conversation. First, the boys feel heady and important; it's exactly the kind of food growing boys really need. Feeding a boy's confidence gives him the stuff he needs to handle his own emotions as he grows, and Hemingway shows Hudson doing this well. Second, it assuages the guilt Hudson feels about his broken family. Showing this relationship in such a true light allows Hemingway to move to the next stage of emotion, and this is where he shines.

Hemingway subtly shows us Hudson's flaws, while simultaneously foreshadowing something terrible. While watching from his boat while his sons snorkle around the lagoon, Hudson makes sure his gun is handy, in case of sharks: "It was really too good a gun to keep on a boat but Thomas Hudson was so fond of it and it reminded him of so many things, so many people."[19] This *is* a poor reason to keep a gun on board; it shows Hudson's romantic nature, his biggest flaw and the reason he's twice-divorced and living without his boys. This all becomes clear when a shark attacks his middle son, David.

When the shark shows, Hudson shoots at it as it approaches David. Over and over Hudson misses, and now we get to see true emotion:

> He felt sick to his stomach, as though something had hold of him inside and was gripping him there, and he shot again; as carefully and steady as he could; knowing full well what the shot meant; and the spurt of water was ahead of the fin. The fin kept right on with the same awful motion.[20]

Hudson's boatman, Eddy, does what Hudson fails to do when he shoots the shark dead. And the consequences of that appear a few pages later, when, after everyone goes to bed that night, Hudson sits

awake and considers his life. He's desperately lonely, painting and drinking his life away in some kind of exile on Bimini. And he reveals how he
copes:

> His life was built solidly on work and on the living by the Gulf
> Stream and on the island and it would stand up all right. The
> aids and the habits and the customs were all to handle the lone-
> liness and by now he knew he had opened a whole new country
> for the loneliness to move into once the boys were gone.[21]

Hudson's despair about being apart from his sons ruins his life, and
his existence becomes a series of time between their visits: "They would
go away at the end of their stay and he would have the loneliness again.
But it would only be a stage on the way until they came back."[22]

Hemingway shows throughout this book how craft and emotional
consequence meet, and he shows the result. The set ups he uses are
long, and what holds the reader is the beautiful, spare prose, prose that
reads like poetry. The emotional payoff is breathtaking, justifying the
buildup, and demonstrating the intense insight the author has to his subject, and to his metier.

"Authorial Insights"

By his own admission, John Irving isn't a short story writer; he's a
novelist. By the time *Trying to Save Piggy Sneed* was published, his
novel output exceeded his short story output.[23] The short stories he includes in *Piggy Sneed* come from the early portion of his career
(1969-1980). What makes this "collection" noteworthy is the author's
thoughts included after each story.

As a collection, these stories offer nothing in the way of theme, and,
with the exception of "The Pension Grillparzer," they reflect nothing of

what we recognize as Irving's writing hallmarks: bears, wrestling, Vienna, prostitutes, orphans, abortion. But they do offer a glimpse into a time in Irving's writing when he was transitioning from minor writer to JOHN IRVING. That's what makes the author's notes so relevant.

Three of the stories—"Interior Space," "The Pension Grillparzer," and "Weary Kingdom,"—are long: 30-40 pages. For the purposes of publication, these are no-man's land lengths. But Irving explains that many of these stories languished in his bottom drawer for years before they were published.

He loathed the unprofessionalism of "Weary Kingdom."[24] He did, however, offer master's level instruction about what he learned from the story, discussing the importance of minor characters in the third person, arguing their importance to the plot.[25]

Insights like that make a long, boring story like "Weary Kingdom" come to life. I went back and read it again, keeping the author's self-criticism in mind. A dozen new doors opened up for me; the story remained the same, but the elements (such as the character of Celeste) took on new form for me.

Irving isn't a kind self-reviewer, at least where his short stories are concerned. Each of the author's notes contains at least one aspect of criticism that shows his critical mind at work. This indicates that Irving the Writer never rests—he's always rewriting. That's the real lesson of this collection of short stories from a novelist. Halfway through writing *The World According to Garp*, Irving knew his future was in novels, not shorter forms.[26] His reflections make that distinction irrelevant to the student.

"A Time to Show, A Time to Tell"

Show, don't tell. It's standard advice that students of writing hear constantly. It's easy to dispense such advice, and expect it to be absolute. But is it always true? Are there times when writing can tell, as well as show? Yes, as long as the showing deepens the telling, and as long as the author has command of her story.

Carson McCullers has such command in *The Ballad of the Sad Café*. And throughout the collection of stories she uses the intrusive narrator's voice to tell, or instruct, the reader, then to show. By this method she creates great drama, a magnifying of the story's effect.

In a complicated setup to describe the marriage of the character of Miss Amelia in "The Ballad of the Sad Café," McCullers' narrator gives a two-page primer on the difference between the lover and the beloved, the former portrayed as carnivorous, the latter as tragic. The description is entirely divorced from the characters of the story.[27]

The story then launches into Miss Amelia's marriage. The telling of her marriage to Marvin Macy can be taken as the "showing." The story is told through description of the events. Taken in small parts, it appears that the narrator is simply reporting on the things that happen. Stepping back and looking at the entire tale of Miss Amelia's marriage allows the reader to see a bigger story. It's how the author shows what's happening. Looking at the writing of this story is like looking at a fresco. Up close, individual tiles stand out; these are the places of telling. When all the "telling tiles" come together, a greater picture appears.

In other places in the collection, McCullers alternates showing and telling to hit the reader from both places. "The Sojourner" opens with lyrical imagery, conjuring an almost dreamlike state.[28] That's the showing. It's immediately followed by the telling, a series of declarative sentences.[29] The imagery of the first paragraph portends something. By following that up immediately with a telling paragraph, that notion is amplified.

Sometimes It's Important to "tell" in a story. But sometimes, using that "telling" as part of the "showing" creates a deeper, more dramatic result.

"Elements of Mastery"

To see what makes a short story successful, one has only to read a few of Chekhov's stories. His style is simple, without adornments or tricks or "Ah-ha" moments that reveal the author's cleverness. Chekhov's writing invokes the wisdom of one of his contemporaries, Oscar Wilde, who said, "The purpose of the artist is to reveal art while concealing the artist." Chekhov not only accomplishes this, but he makes the stories turn in a way that causes the reader to forget the fiction. And that's the mastery of short story writing. Evidence of this technique is found in the story "A Calamity."

"A Calamity" is the story of two people who are in love with each other, but married to someone else. One (Ilyan) knows it, and has surrendered to the misery of this knowledge; the other (Sofya) denies it, proclaiming the opposite with every breath leaving her lungs. Chekhov wastes little time setting up this story; in the third paragraph, Sofya begins her denials, imploring Ilya "please stop pursuing me!"[30] Throughout the story she denies what's between them, proclaiming at various points that Ilyan's feelings are wrong, that she's happily married, and in love with her husband.

Ilyan knows different. He's surrendered to the knowledge of his love for her: "I admit frankly and honestly that I consider my behavior criminal and immoral."[31] Ilyan can do nothing but suffer without her love returned. This tension forms the spine of the story; all the other flesh hangs off it. The story is resolved only when Sofya accepts the change from within herself. After she tries to rouse her husband's emotions, but fails, she gives up, and thinks of Ilyan: "She sat down by the open window and gave herself up to desire…All her thoughts and feelings were directed with one accord toward a single object."[32]

This change happens without Ilyan present. Removing Ilyan from the scene of her change removes the melodrama from the story, strengthening its reality. Chekhov knows that in affairs of the heart, change doesn't come from without, but from within, from that lonely, painful place that we all must face alone. He removes any evidence of himself from the story, allowing the struggles of his characters to take over and guide the story. He knows it's their story, not his.

"Sex, Love, and Madness"

How do questions of sexuality manifest themselves in literature? More importantly, how can this topic be rendered in a way that avoids the lurid, the prurient, while allowing access to the art of the characters involved? In *The Garden of Eden*, Ernest Hemingway employs some of his well-known literary methods to accomplish this. But in the posthumously published work, he also deviates from what's been taught as his classic style. This deviation succinctly reflects the torrid mess of sexuality depicted in the novel.

Ostensibly a *ménage-a-trois*, the relationships upon which the story is based are more deeply disturbed. David and Catherine Bourne are newly married, and on vacation in the south of France in the 1920's. What at first appears to be the passion of young lovers quickly morphs into a mismatched relationship where one partner, Catherine, wants to change her sexuality, and the other, David, goes along because he loves her so much. One day Catherine has her hair cut like a boy's, and that night she forces her and David to switch sexual roles, as she becomes the man. With an economy of words Hemingway masterfully describes how Catherine sodomizes David.[33]

This moment pivots not only the change in Catherine, but the change in David. He does these things because he loves her. And later, when she brings another women into their relationship, he again reluctantly acquiesces. But this time it's more than just Catherine cutting her hair and "getting on top." This time there's another person involved, and as Catherine's hold on sanity plummets, David allows himself entrance into the vulnerability of the other woman, Marita.

Hemingway handles these moments not just by writing around them; rather, he writes about the results. Writing about the results of the acts allows him not only to sidestep the lurid possibilities that would undercut the literary level of the writing, but also to focus on what's important to the story: the characters, not the acts.

In the story, Catherine's struggle with her own sexuality becomes the outward expression of her deteriorating mental state. Her instability drives David and Marita into a closer relationship that in turn drives Catherine more mad. According to the publisher, Hemingway wrote this book between 1946 and his death in 1961.[34] Social mores of the times demanded an obtuse approach to densely erotic subject matter such as this. Yet the blunt approach to the topic is on display everywhere, even when secondary characters like their innkeeper object to their arrangement. In the end, Hemingway achieves what he wants in the book by using a tried and true Hemingway technique: he leaves them all in a bar, drinking.

The Critical and the Creative: An Overview of the Relationship
Between Critical Writing and Its Effect on the Creative

There are many things we all do in life that nobody taught us how to do. They are the things that make us who we are, the activities that define us, and we came to those actions and pursuits in a natural way, a way that when we look back on them, we have a hard time describing what we see. We just know that those things that make us who we are exist, as the dust of the universe has always existed. The things we do inform us and our actions as individuals, and while most people may never look back in reflection and ask why, the power of those interests never diminishes.

All writers are informed. The world manifests itself for them, and they become a prism through which it is focused. While this does not suggest that their art is merely a deflection of someone else's inspiration, it does acknowledge a debt to the influence of others. This is where critical writing enters the scene. By examining the works of others, and by not only asking the mechanical questions—why does this author succeed with this technique, or why not?—but by asking the deeper questions, such as "Why did I select this work to examine?" The writer gains immense and invaluable insight into themselves as an artist, and as a person. The awareness of this relationship between the critical and the creative is imperative if a writer is to develop to a stage approaching mastery.

When I arrived at Goddard College, I was surprised at the emphasis placed on critical writing. The demands are considerable: forty-five annotations (2 pages each), two short critical papers (5 pages each), and a long critical paper (20 pages). That's 120 pages of critical writing in about a year and a half (the last semester at Goddard is spent almost entirely in the revision of the creative thesis). That means that you're constantly reading while you're constantly writing. I think my bibliography had over a hundred books in it by the time I graduated, which averages out to a book a week over a two-year span.

I was not a person who shied away from critical analysis. It was something I'd done on my own my whole life. It was an activity that defined me. But the surprise for me was discovering the connection between what I was reading and my own writing. In my first semester, I wrote both of my short critical papers. I remember sitting down with my advisor and discussing the focus of my writing at Goddard, and telling him that I wanted to explore the relationship between fathers and sons in my writing. He suggested I read *Fathers and Sons* by Russian author Ivan Turgenev. At first this sounded too obvious to me. But the book changed me. It showed me how an author could use big themes—metathemes—to encapsulate the structure of the story. In the case of Turgenev, I focused on the role of nature in the story.

By the time I wrote the second paper, I had a more clearly defined idea of what I'd be writing for my creative thesis. I knew I'd be writing a thematically connected collection of short stories, and I began aiming my readings at such collections. That led me to Andre Dubus, one of the most influential writers in my bibliography. In his collection *The Times Are Never So Bad*, Dubus explores the role of fathers in their relationships to their children. What stood out for me was the role of faith in these stories. That's the theme I concentrated on as I wrote about the collection. After I wrote the paper I saw a strong pattern emerging. In writing about Turgenev's *Fathers and Sons* I examined the role of nature in the story, coming to the conclusion that "Nature is this book's religion, its God." In *The Times Are Never So Bad*, Dubus uses dogma—in this case Catholicism—to collide with his characters' actions, highlighting the weaknesses of both.

With my long critical paper "From Pip to Garp: A Look at the Literary Relationship Between John Irving and Charles Dickens," I was able to really dig into an author I adored—Irving—and discover something about myself I never expected. In the paper I showed how Irving was influenced by Dickens, but I also revealed how I'd been influenced by Irving, how his writing shaped me and directed me.

Gaining that knowledge from those authors and their works would have happened whether I wrote the three pieces you're about to read or not. The difference is that by lingering and reflecting, by asking myself "What is it about this work that appeals to me?" I arrive at an awareness of myself previously unknown. It's an amazing process for a writer, and as a teacher I've even used it in undergraduate composition classes to help students learn where the power of their writing comes from. So here are the two short critical papers and the long critical paper. See what you can find for yourself in them.

The First Short Critical Paper:

"The Character of Nature in Fathers and Sons"

Nature has always been a powerful element of good writing. It can be archetypal (the Garden of Eden), allegorical (*Moby Dick*), or even metaphorical ("To Build a Fire"). All too often, nature becomes overused to the point of banality ("It was a dark and stormy night"). In the hands of a masterful writing, however, nature can become a character itself, bestowing upon the *dramatists personae* traits representing larger questions of the world around them. Such is the case in the novel *Fathers and Sons* by Ivan Turgenev.

There's early evidence that Turgenev deliberately colored his characters as characters of nature from a letter he wrote to A.A. Fet, dated 6 April 1862. In it, he poses rhetorical questions about the book's characters. He answers himself when he writes, "I'll tell you one thing, I drew all those characters as I would draw mushrooms, leaves, and trees."[35]

When the book was written in 1861, Russia was on the precipice of change, a change that would ultimately lead to revolution. Russia, an agrarian giant, was being left behind as the rest of the world mechanized itself during the industrial revolution. With its feudal system of landowners and peasants, Russia was anachronous to the rest of the world. In 1860s Russia a new movement of thought was afoot, and that movement is embodied by Bazarov, the hero of the book.

Bazarov is a nihilist, an empiricist who believes in nothing he cannot quantify. Beyond that, Bazarov spurns the past, represented in the book by his father Vassily, Arkady's father Nickolai, and Arkady's uncle Pavel. The fathers of Arkady and Basarov have decaying estates staffed with peasants. But the peasants just aren't what they used to be. When Arkady and Bazarov journey to stay with Arkady's father, the old man confesses to them that he has had "a lot of bother with the peasants this year. What is one to do?"[36]

The theme of the new peasant representing the natural past doesn't go away, either. Later, when Bazarov and Arkady travel to Bazarov's parent's home, they come upon two peasants standing by the side of the road "abusing each other." Bazarov remarks dryly about their loose tongues and observes that his "father's peasants are not too much oppressed."[37]

This is the essential nature of the book. The past, the fathers, the peasants, the land, those are all things that are changing. They must change, for in the new world, the Bazarovs will rule. They will set in motion these things by rejecting their past. How else is revolution fomented? And in *Fathers and Sons*, Turgenev brings natural themes to his characters to create a multilayered format of storytelling.

Bazarov, ever the scientist, expresses his contempt for the natural world ironically. As a student of medicine, he has had to master nature, and when he invokes nature upon itself, it is as an expert. When asked about Arkady's father's accomplishments as a landowner, Bazarov offers this assessment: "The cattle are inferior, the horses are broken down; the buildings aren't up to much, and the workmen look confirmed loafers; while the superintendent is either a fool or a knave, I haven't quite found out yet."[38]

When Arkady asks him directly if he believes that nature itself is nonsense, while gazing off dreamily into "varicolored fields, in the beautiful soft light of the sinking sun" Bazarov sums up neatly his views, not just on nature, but on everything: "Nature's not a temple, but a workshop, and man's the workman in it."[39] In that one sentence Bazarov has succinctly expressed his views of modern young people. To him they must seem out of step with all that is important, willing to abandon the critical context within which he believes everything exists and interacts.

If Bazarove is nature's antichrist, then Nikolai, and to a lesser extent Vassily Ivanovitch, Bazarov's father, are nature's champions. Nature dominates and befuddles Nickolai. Nature also has a hand in controlling his emotions. While under his favorite arbor in his garden, Nikolai is despairing of Bazarov's renunciation of poetry. He wonders how someone can have no feeling for art and poetry, which he directly equates with nature. The entire scene is saturated in nature as it builds: the sun behind a small copse of aspens (which Bazarov earlier disparaged); swallows flying high; even a peasant on a white nag is considered part of the flora and fauna.

In this intense moment, Nikolai begins to daydream. He remembers his wife, not as she was when she was dead, but as she was when she was a lithe, interesting girl. Without realizing it he has begun comparing his current paramour, Fenitchka, the mother of their 6-month old baby, to his deceased wife. He paces his garden, looks up at the stars, and cries causeless tears. Even amidst this intensely personal moment, he despairs that Bazarov would laugh at him, could he only see. When his dry and sarcastic brother, Pavel, discovers him in this state, he too is moved to emotion, though not in such a liberating fashion as Nikolai.[40]

In his essay "*Fathers and Sons*: The Novel as Idyll," James H. Justus reinforces the intense level of nature that Turgenev achieves. About the above scene he writes: "Here is more than scene painting. Couched in ever more religious terms than the references to most religion itself, this episode is Turgenev's most explicit use of nature as a symbolic system embodying the deepest values of the Fathers."[41]

That is to say that the natural world of the fathers is being challenged. Throughout this scene nature is played as counterpoint to all that is explicable firmament, all that is Bazarov. Nature is invoked as if Sylvanus himself were orchestrating from on high. The sun, the stars, the night, the wind, lazily humming bees, swarms of midges all conspire in a potent cocktail that forces Nikoai to admit: "How beautiful, my God!"[42]

In the death of Bazarov, Turgenev offers a final glimpse of nature asserting preeminence over all else. Bitter after his rejection by Odintsova, he returns home for the six weeks remaining before his studies resume, and ends up helping his father practice medicine. When a patient dies of typhus, Bazarov attends the autopsy, and cuts himself. Infected immediately, Bazarov begins to die.

Nature, in all forms, is having the last say over Bazarov's life. When he earlier mocked nature ("Nature, too [is nonsense], in the sense that you understand it."[43]), Bazarov levied an affront to the natural world, which is juxtaposed against his nihilism within the novel. But nature cannot be stopped anymore than it can be denied, and Turgenev's final comment on the state of Russia's youth movement is cemented when Bazarov finally dies, delusional, saying "There's a forest here."[44]

If Turgenev intended to cast nature as an omniscient presence which dominated all character, he succeeded. Bazarov as the nihilistic medical student dies of an infection, a natural thing that even he cannot control. That the hero would die in this fashion must not go unnoticed. But has the character of nature incited change, or was change a function of nature?

Nature is this book's religion, its God. It surrounds all, controls all. The characters are all but secondary players to its will. By identifying the fathers so closely with the solidness of the land, Turgenev accomplishes several things: he neatly summarizes Russia's agrarian past, juxtaposes old ways against the new, and shows, by Bazarov's death, that not even a nihilist can escape nature's omnipotence. Bazarov may have played his part by advancing the seedling of change while he lived, but in death his true purpose is revealed. Nature is evolutionary, and Turgenev brings to light all its immutable forces, while casting it throughout his characters and settings as the one constant in life.

The Second Short Critical Paper:
"Believing in Faith: Thematic Continuum in a
Short Story Collection"

Authors often impose a theme across a collection of short stories, sometimes because the theme was planned from the start, sometimes because they discovered it among certain of their works in hindsight. Either way, a unifying theme invests a collection with a cumulative dramatic power greater than the sum of its stories.

In *The Times Are Never So Bad*, Andre Dubus creates a crisis in faith—Catholicism, in this case—and uses it as a unifying theme for his collection. The theme of this collection might be stated as: Catholicism's inherent flaws lead believers inexorably to more pain and suffering—but it is pain and suffering that they would have experienced anyway, even if they had not been Catholic.

The collection opens with "A Pretty Girl," a story of domestic abuse, predation, and misogyny. Dubus portrays the helplessness of Polly, the heroine, as a direct result of her Catholicism. Polly's ex-boyfriend stalks her: after they broke up, he broke into her apartment and raped her. Then, Dubus inserts a quiet scene showing Polly ritually preparing herself for Mass. As she dresses, the rote actions she has performed each Sunday of her life soothe her. By contrasting this ritual with the horror of Polly's existence, Dubus demonstrates the unreal relationship of the scene to the rest of the story, and the incongruous place Catholicism holds in her life.[45]

In the end, Polly does exactly the opposite of what her faith demands. With the aid of her father (who supplies her with a gun), she kills her tormentor. Dubus doesn't explicitly condemn the Catholicism; he allows its archaic limitations to indict themselves.

In the Hemingway-esque "Bless Me, Father," Dubus continues not only the theme of Catholic impotence, but the structure of centering the story around a single event, or moment, which reveals the theme. A college girl discovers her father's infidelity and confronts him. In a clear and direct exchange of dialogue, the father abuses not only the Catholic sacrament of confession, but his own trust and authority over his daughter. About going to confession the daughter asks:

> "Do you still believe in it?"
> "Sure. Don't you?"
> "Of course I do."
> "Are you still a virgin?"[46]

At that moment we understand the father's ruthlessness and his contempt for his daughter's beliefs. The subversion of the father-daughter relationship demonstrates the emptiness the Church offers people with real problems. The daughter trusts her father absolutely. When her father violates that trust, the daughter falls back on dogma. But in the face of the father's secular cynicism, dogma is impotent.

"The Captain" is ostensibly about a father and son hunting trip. Yet Dubus ritualizes everything, from the hunting trip itself (Mass) to the making of a camp breakfast (symbolizing the Eucharist):

> Three hunters came out of the trees and stood at the table to his left.
> "They use spatulas," Phil said.
> "True enough. But I will turn the eggs. How they come out is in the hands of the Lord."
> "Bless us o Lord in this thy omelet."[47]

In "Sorrowful Mysteries" Dubus casts the social injustice of a falsely accused black man's impending execution as a Passion Play. The young Catholic Gerry dreams he sees the black man nailed to the cross, the suffering Christ.[48]

The final story in this collection is the most forceful. In "A Father's Story," Dubus creates the character of Luke Ripley, a man who has compartmentalized his conflict about his Catholicism. Ripley's wife has left him, yet he remains devoutly Catholic. Ripley suggests that it is perhaps the ritual of Catholicism he is addicted to when he says: "...ritual allows those who cannot will themselves out of the secular to perform the spiritual."[49]

And so we see that Ripley has separated his family from his faith. Dubus shows this divide in earlier stories: Polly's preparations for Mass in "A Pretty Girl"; the father's ability to halt the incursion of religion in "Bless Me, Father"; even Gerry's Passion Play imagery in "Sorrowful Mysteries."

In "A Father's Story," Ripley's parish priest foreshadows the conflict when he tells Ripley: "Belief is believing in God; faith is believing that God believes in you."[50] This time the separation comes when Ripley's daughter strikes and kills a pedestrian while driving drunk. Her father covers up for her, wrecking her car to obscure the damage. And despite his devotion, Ripley never confesses his sin. In fact, he is adamant about not even considering it.

In a stunning ending, Dubus sums up the division between religious faith—Catholicism—and man's unrepentant acts, which sometimes must be performed against God in order to live in this world. This is the nexus that Dubus has been writing about throughout this collection of stories, and to illustrate the point, Ripley talks to God. God asks him if he would have willfully sinned for one of his sons and Ripley answers no. God asks him if he loves his sons less than his daughter. Ripley answers:

> ...it is not that I love them less, but that I could bear the pain of watching and knowing my sons' pain, could bear it with pride as they took the whip and nails. But You never had a daughter and, if You had, You could not have borne her passion.
> So, He says, you love her more than you love Me.
> I love her more than I love truth.
> Then you love in weakness, He says.
> As You love me....[51]

195

The irreverence of this exchange cannot be overstated. Coming at the very end of the last story of the book, it serves as the defining dramatic effect that unifies the collection. It relates the theme of conflict within Catholicism directly back to all the preceding stories.

In *The Times Are Never So Bad,* Andre Dubus shows how large themes can be masterfully handled. His technique is subtle; he avoids heavy-handed diatribes. Instead he highlights the problems with dogma—in this case, Catholicism. By allowing the real troubles of his characters to preside over their actions, then contrasting those actions with the duties of their faith, Dubus reveals his theme. Dubus's stories stand alone while simultaneously sharing a mounting, unspoken direction. This provides insight for authors considering a thematic approach to a collection of short stories.

Long Critical Paper:
"From Pip to Garp: A Look at the Literary Relationship
Between Charles Dickens and John Irving"

In his essay, "The King of the Novel," John Irving writes that *Great Expectations* was the book that made him understand that he wanted to be a novelist, to share with the reader what he felt.[52]

It's a sentiment I relate strongly to. What moved me as a young reader—what made me want to write—was not *Great Expectations*, by Charles Dickens, but *The World According to Garp*, by John Irving. After I finished reading *Garp*, I remember thinking something very close to what Irving expressed above.

There's more between Dickens and Irving than just inspiration. There's a thread of descent, not just in the novels *Great Expectations* and *The World According to Garp*, but in the authors themselves, in their lives, the themes they chose, and the characters they created. By looking at these two novels and these two authors—with a focus on the characters of Pip and Garp—one of literature's unique relationships will be revealed.

Pip and Garp are fatherless boys whose stories are chronicled in *Bildungsromans*. We'll discuss the roles of fatherless boys within the context of each novel—and each author—as well as how the stories and characters relate to each other: What important themes surround Pip and Garp? How did the personal experiences of each author manifest themselves in these novels? Both books are set in times of revolution: the Industrial for *Great Expectations*, and the Sexual for *The World According to Garp*. How did these revolutions affect Pip and Garp?

Both John Irving and Charles Dickens made ample use of their personal lives in their fiction. Understanding which autobiographical elements each author included—and which ones each omitted—illustrates how authors of different periods could share such a close relationship.

***

There's an old literary saw that goes, "Authors allow their works to speak for themselves." Relying solely on the work for a more profound understanding, however, might not be the best way to discover the author's intent. An examination of the autobiographical elements behind the inspiration sheds light on the writing—it connects the author to the reader. The city of Vienna is one such element in Irving's writing.

Vienna recurs as a setting throughout Irving's writing. His knowledge of Vienna is first-hand: he studied at the Institute for European Studies in Vienna in 1963.[53] How Irving uses Vienna in his fiction gives life to his stories. In Irving's writing, Vienna often takes the form of violence and decadence.[54] When Garp and his mother move to Vienna, Garp writes to his future wife, Helen, that Vienna felt dead.[55] The character of Charlotte—a prostitute dying of cancer—offers a good example of Irving's treatment of Vienna. After Garp's mother buys Charlotte for him, Charlotte becomes Garp's only friend, until she dies of cancer.

There's no evidence that Irving befriended a dying prostitute while in Vienna. But his attitude toward the city permeates *Garp*. As Charlotte dies, Garp sees only darkness, a place in the throes of decay.[56]

Irving remains dismissive, almost cavalier, when faced with questions linking his own experiences to those of his characters. In a talk to the Boston Center for Adult Education on October 18, 1996, Irving said that Vienna is not as important to him as to the critics.[57]

And yet there it is, over and over again: Vienna. In his memoir *The Imaginary Girlfriend*, Irving hints at what might lie behind the unflattering portrayals of Vienna in his stories. He and a friend (who was also studying at the Institute for European Studies), he said, didn't adore Vienna, a place he thought antagonistic to foreigners.[58] This suggests a basis for his dark portrayals of Vienna.

If Irving remains adamant about sidestepping the issue of autobiographical influences in his writing in general, he's gone out of his way to specifically deny links to Garp—and *Garp*. In a May, 1998, essay he wrote for *Saturday Night* magazine, Irving clearly defines his position vis-a-vis himself and his writing: "Whether a novel is autobiographical is besides the point," he argues. He goes on to reiterate the separation of the writer and the work several times throughout the essay: "…it is a novel about a novelist, although almost no reader of the book remembers it as such." When Irving asks himself what *The World According to Garp* is about, he finally settles on this: "It's a novel about being careful, and about that not being enough." He echoes that sentiment at the end of the essay when he says it's more about "a father's fears."[59] Listening to Irving through that piece is a little like listening to Mark Antony say he came to bury Caesar, not to praise him. If Irving wanted the work to stand on its own, he could have simply remained silent.

The question of autobiographical influence in *Garp* remains important because of what we *do* know of Irving: he's a novelist; he studied in Vienna; he's a protective father. These are all bases for characters and situations that appear in *Garp*. Of all the parallels Irving uses from his life in his writing, most astonishing may be that his biological father was a World War II flyer, shot down over Burma.[60] In *The World According to Garp*, Garp's father, Technical Sergeant Garp, was a ball turret gunner on a B-17E who died a slow, not unpleasant, death after receiving shrapnel wounds.

Is there basis for Irving's life in *Garp*? Irving says no. He even expresses this notion fictionally, through Helen Garp, after Garp's death. In an effort to fend off biographers, she advises people to focus on the writing, the products of the author, not the life of the writer.[61]

And who are we to question the author? Who knows better than the creator what the creation stands for? Yet question the author is exactly what we'll do. *The World According to Garp* remains, above all, a book about an orphan—not a Dickensian orphan, perhaps, but surely an orphan who reflects all the sensibilities, all the wry, twisting humor, all the guilt and struggle of *Great Expectations*' Pip.

***

There's no shortage of biographical information about Charles Dickens. Masters like Edgar Johnson and Peter Ackroyd provided us with links to all things Dickens, and we feel we almost know what he must have thought about every word he wrote. For the purposes of this paper, we'll limit our examination of Dickens's autobiographical influences to the context of Pip.

Philip Pirrip—"Pip"—embodies many recognizable characteristics in Dickens's writing. Oliver Twist became synonymous with the orphaned boy of the 19th century, while David Copperfield may most closely reflect how Dickens felt about his own childhood.[62] In writing *Great Expectations*, Dickens was motivated to seek out the deeper places of his childhood, going beyond even where he went in *David Copperfield*.[63] According-ing to Edgar Johnson, Dickens obfuscated many of the things he found impossible to talk about even with his own family, notably his father's incarceration in debtor's prison, and his time at the blacking warehouse. These shames recur as central themes in *Great Expectations*.[64]

In addition to those mentioned above, other experiences in Dickens's life found their way into *Great Expectations*. One well-known example is the origin of Miss Havisham. In his essay "The Genesis of a Novel: *Great Expectations*," Harry Stone relates the encounter that served as the inspiration for one of fiction's most memorable characters. Dickens (writing in his magazine "Household Words") tells of a woman in all white, a ghostly apparition.[65] Stone argues that Miss Havisham's character markers are already in place. Later, Dickens included an account of an-other bizarre woman in his periodical *Household Narrative*. Dickens wrote that this woman lived a hermitic life after her rejected suitor shot himself.[66]

Those must have been powerful experiences for Dickens. He draws Miss Havisham so vividly and so bizarrely that she seems unreal. But she's real—at least to Dickens. And he makes her real for us through Pip's experiences with her. We see her as Pip sees her, as she tells him about her aberrant wishes.[67]

But is Pip Dickens? Certainly not. Just as Miss Havisham as-sumes the character of the white woman from Dickens's childhood, Pip reflects the experiences that moved Dickens. When Estella torments Pip, or when Mrs. Joe assaults him with tar water, we don't believe Dickens experienced those things as precisely as he wrote them. But, based on what we know of Dickens's childhood, we can imagine what he went through. The events of Pip's life spring from the experiences of Dickens's own life. How he chose to use those experiences defined the writer he became.

The best-known of Dickens's childhood experiences took place in a blacking warehouse. With the family finances failing, Dickens's parents accepted an offer for Charles to go to work. At the age of twelve, Dickens was paid six shillings a week to plaster labels onto bottles of blacking.[68] The bitterness he felt about that episode demonstrated itself in letters he wrote more than 25 years later, which wistfully recall his descent and rejection.[69]

Pip echoes the tone in that quote many times throughout *Great Expectations*: he's sarcastic about his lot in life. This is how Dickens remembered his youth. Experiences like the blacking warehouse job shaped his writing later on. These words speak clearly to Dickens's motivation behind characters like Pip. That he views himself as an urchin links him to the likes of David, Oliver, and Pip. They are all Dickens. The source of Dickens's use again and again of the condition is shaped by this experience.[70]

***

Philip Pirrip and T.S. Garp share numerous character traits and occupy much of the same thematic literary territory within their respective novels—they're both true icons of literature. Simply uttering their names evokes an instant reaction. Like Pele in sports and Madonna in music, their single-name appeal transcends their genre. What is it about these characters that so captivates our imaginations?

That they're both fatherless—in Pip's case, a true orphan—isn't necessarily special. It's what each author does with that character setting that makes Pip and Garp unforgettable. Boys without fathers always arouse a special emotion in literature. Who will show the boy the narrow way?

Sociologists warn about the negative potential of fatherless boys. In his book *Real Boys*, William Pollack argues that absent fathers can be linked to many factors that place boys at risk, including many kinds of juvenile crimes.[71] This understanding can be used as a literary technique. The fatherless boy is at risk; the stakes are raised because of the impact he can have on society as a whole. By introducing the character of the fatherless boy, an author tells the reader that this is a situation that can go terribly wrong, with far-reaching consequences. *Great Expectations* and *The World According to Garp* use the dramatic potential of the fatherless/orphaned boy to keep us wondering: What's going to happen to Pip and Garp?

***

T.S. Garp isn't an orphan; he's got a mother who actively and intelligently raises him. But that doesn't reduce the impact of his father's absence. Garp knows how he was conceived, and what happened to his father.[72] How he deals with that knowledge forms an integral thread of the story.

John Irving doesn't populate *The World According to Garp* with traditional Dickensian orphans. Irving's "orphans" all have at least one parent. What connects them to Dickens's orphans is the desperation they feel because of their situation. It's what motivates them. Garp's mother Jenny came by her desperation when she felt the world around her limited her choices. Though she comes from an established family, Jenny made herself an orphan by rejecting all that her family expected of her: she dropped out of college, she shunned men, and she slashed a soldier who made an unwanted advance at her in a movie theater. Garp's father is another orphan—though it's probably wise to stop short of calling him Garp's father. Let's call him the man who gave Garp half his chromosomes.[73] Other single-parent characters include the woman T.S. Garp would eventually marry, Helen Holm,[74] and Duncan Garp's friend, Ralph.[75]

Irving portrays the character of Jenny Fields as the first feminist. Like many Irving characters, she's an example in the extreme. When she decided she wanted to have a baby, she saw nothing wrong with raping an airman who was in a coma. She claims not to like the sexual act, however she wanted a baby.[76] Can Garp's conception be interpreted as a desperate act? When considering the alternatives, it seems to be extreme.

Interpreting Irving's message on feminism through Jenny Fields remains tricky. Though it's Jenny who becomes famous, Irving spends more time showing Garp's frustration with his mother's fame. And both Garp and Jenny are assassinated, like political figures, by fringe characters who mutated from the feminist movement Jenny ignited.

Into Jenny Fields's world-view came Garp. But unlike Dickens, Irving doesn't cast a perilous life for his main character. Garp grows up in a place devoid of Mrs. Joes and Miss Havishams. In fact, Jenny's life becomes focused on one thing: raising Garp. To that end, she takes a job as a nurse at the prestigious Steering Academy, guaranteeing Garp a superior education. In *The World According to Garp*, there's no mystery surrounding Garp's benefactor.

The early chapters of *The World According to Garp* feature two T.S. Garps. The character of Garp doesn't utter his first word until page 55.[77] From that point on, the reader follows his development in the more or less traditional fashion of a linear narrative. Before page 55, Garp appears omnisciently, in the form of quotes, as if he wrote the book himself—or at least read the galleys and added these asides. When Garp's mother articulates her desire to eschew men from her life, the omniscient Garp appears.[78]

Kim McKay comments on this technique, calling it "double discourse." Irving, she says, "forms a type of dialogue…that of the biographer and that of the fiction writer." She goes on to say that "Garp is not a character created but a historical figure for study."[79]

These introspective addenda produce an effect that places Garp in the future: we know he's made it there in some form because he's writing about it. This gives us a parallel with Pip's narration in *Great Expectations*. When Pip tells us, "I never saw my father or my mother, and never saw any likeness of either of them (for their days were long before the days of photographs),"[80] he's telling us these things from somewhere in the future. Like Garp, he's historical.

This "double discourse" allows the reader to look to the future. It's effective because much of *The World According to Garp*'s early narrative thrust deals with Jenny Fields. Irving places a lot of weight on Jenny's character; the "double discourse" relieves some of that pressure by telling the reader that Garp is in the future, and that he's important. When he began writing *Garp*, Irving thought the book might be about Jenny Fields; he had difficulties discovering its beginning: "There was a time when Jenny threatened to take over the novel, when I wasn't at all sure if Garp or his mother was the main character; something of my in-decision remains."[81]

Jenny approaches the issue of Garp's fatherlessness the same way she approaches everything in her life: practically and logically. She be-comes a voracious reader, sits in on all the classes at Steering (so that she'll be able to guide Garp to the best ones), and eventually becomes a more famous writer than her son—a fact that causes some friction be-tween them.

Jenny Fields exemplifies the belief that logic and intelligence over-come tradition. The tradition is the family unit—married parents (of dif-ferent sexes), raising children. In *The World According to Garp*, John Irving seeks to change that "value." He surrounds Garp with a bizarre cast, including a transsexual former football player, a prostitute dying of cancer, a society of women who cut their tongues out, and lovers with lisps.

***

Dickens's Pip fits the scenario of the fatherless boy in trouble, and Dickens sets the stage with an ominous opening to *Great Expectations*. Pip engages in familial speculation, trying to divine what his parents looked like by the lettering on their tombstones:

> The shape of the letters on my father's (tombstone) gave me

an odd idea that he was a square, stout, dark man with curly black hair. From the character and turn of the inscription, "*Also, Georgiana Wife of the Above,*" I drew the childish conclusion that my mother was freckled and sickly.[82]

Pip's frank account suggests that he's accepted his orphan status. But it also suggests a level of ignorance on Pip's part, for what child would so nonchalantly cavort on his family's graves without feeling some kind of fear or emotion? The only terror he feels comes when the desperate convict Abel Magwitch appears, turns Pip upside down, and threatens to cut Pip's throat and eat him. That terror resounds so fully in Pip that he's able to commit larceny against his sister, Mrs. Joe, who's as able and eager to harm Pip as Magwitch.

Dickens immediately casts Pip in the role of a victim. We sympathize with his plight. This allows Dickens to create obstacles for Pip. Only through his struggles does Pip overcome the obstacles. And then Pip discovers that his conceptions about his benefactor are erroneous. Pip's greatest obstacle becomes himself. But it's through Pip that the action happens. In this story, Pip's the transitive verb.

For a role model Pip has Joe Gargery, his sister's husband. Joe, a slow-witted blacksmith, sympathizes with Pip because he, too, suffers the wrath of Mrs. Joe. But Joe can do little for Pip except to commiserate, teach him the trade of the blacksmith, and soothe his humiliations at the hands of Mrs. Joe. Joe's limitations are neatly summed up in the scene of Christmas dinner at the Gargerys. While the other guests are treated to a special feast, Pip is given "the scaly tips of...the fowls" and "those obscure corners of pork of which the pig, when living, had had the least reason to be vain."[83]

Pip continues, describing his uncle's place:

Joe's station and influence were something feebler (if possible) when there was company, than when there was none. But he always aided and comforted me when he could...by giving me gravy. There being plenty of gravy today, Joe spooned into my plate, at this point, about half a pint.[84]

Joe's performance at Christmas dinner becomes allegorical. Though he's got almost nothing, Joe gives Pip what he can—in this case, gravy. This scene echoes the earlier scene when Pip stole food from his sister to feed Magwitch. It's echoed again later when Magwitch becomes Pip's secret benefactor. In this glimpse of Dickens's world, the poor take care of their own.

Joe Gargery's only the first of Pip's benefactors. Benefactors are crucial to the development of the orphan in fiction. (A little later we'll compare Dickens's and Irving's use of benefactors.) Without Magwitch's financing, Pip can't become a gentleman—or at least discover the truth about himself while chasing that false expectation. It can even be argued that Mrs. Joe, in her own brutal way, qualifies as one of Pip's benefactors. Like Miss Havisham, Mrs. Joe has a twisted view of what it means to be benevolent. While Miss Havisham's mental illness manifests itself in the manipulations that eventually bring Pip and Estella together, Mrs. Joe believes she's doing Pip a favor by bringing him up "by hand," which is code for beating him at every opportunity she gets.

Amid all the turmoil of his upbringing, Pip displays a remarkably wry sense of humor. We understand that Pip narrates the story of Great Expectations from a time in the future; that is, it's a memoir. So when he makes cracks about Mrs. Joe's ugliness, we know that it's the grown-up Pip reflecting back on the memory: "I sometimes used to wonder whether it was possible she washed herself with a nutmeg-grater instead of soap."[85]

This sense of humor doesn't dull the accuracy and insight Pip perceives of his situation. The motivation for his sense of humor lies above the pain of his reality. Though Pip never comes out and says how he feels about being an orphan, we see his pain when Estella's cruelty brings him to tears. Pip is quite enamored of Estella, describing her as "pretty,"[86] and "beautiful and self-possessed."[87]

Though she's not an adult—she's close to Pip's age—Estella behaves like many of the adults in Pip's life: she's cruel. This reinforces the theme of adult cruelty so prevalent in Dickens's writing. She feeds Pip like a dog, leaving his food on the ground; Pip cries.[88] This delights Estella. When Pip leaves, she asks him:

> "Why don't you cry?"
> "Because I don't want to."
> "You do," said she. "You have been crying till you are half blind, and you are near crying again now."
> She laughed contemptuously, pushed me out, and locked the gate upon me.[89]

In the most articulate expression of his youth, Pip explains his feelings not as an orphan, but as a child:

> In the little world in which children have their existence whosoever brings them up, there is nothing so finely perceived and so finely felt as injustice. It may be only small injustice that the child can be exposed to; but the child is small, and its world is small…Within myself, I had sustained, from babyhood, a perpetual conflict with injustice.[90]

Dickens—through Pip—is talking about injustice. And for Pip, that injustice is the unfairness of life.

Pip's quest to become a gentleman forms the novel's structure. Beneath lies what we recognize as the classic Dickens indictment of the Industrial Revolution. Dickens—through Pip—shows what perils await the fatherless boy. He seems to say, *Look what's befallen this boy. What's to become of him?* Dickens spends the rest of the book answering that question. Even at the end, when Pip appears to have resolved his own questions, we know that Pip never really fulfilled his own great expectations.

***

Earlier in this paper, I made the point that orphans need benefactors. Within the fictive narrative, the character of an orphan needs an external impetus, or else the story stops moving; the orphan stagnates or spirals downward. *Great Expectations* and *The World According to Garp* provide benefactors for their orphans: Pip has Magwitch; Garp has his mother.

Neither Pip nor Garp can make it on his own. To continue their progress, they need others to sustain their momentum. Sometimes the source of this sustenance is indirect. Uncle Pumblechook, in a bizarre way, is responsible for Pip's eventual happiness (depending on which reading of *Great Expectations*'s ending you choose) by initiating the events that eventually bring Pip and Estella together.

Pip's true benefactor turns out to be Magwitch. After being transportated to Australia, Magwitch earns a measure of financial success. He never forgets the boy who returned kindness in the face of his assault, and he repays Pip by helping him achieve the one thing he truly desires: to become a gentleman. The discovery of Magwitch's kindness by Pip evokes at first a rejection of his benefactor:

The abhorrence in which I held the man, the dread that I had of him, the repugnance with which I shrank from him, could not have been exceeded if he had been some terrible beast.[91]

But then, Pip "forgets his own expectations,"[92] and tries to help Magwitch avoid capture. Pip traverses a wide range of emotions regarding his benefactor. When the benefactor is unknown, Pip feels free to assign an identity that conforms to his expectations. When the benefactor is revealed, Pip rejects the truth at first, then embraces it. T.S. Garp experiences similar peaks and valleys with his benefactor.

Unlike Pip, Garp knows his benefactor: it's his mother. And like Pip, Garp isn't happy about the arrangement; his mother has been his benefactor his entire life. He wants separation, as a writer and as a person. For his entire life, Jenny made Garp's choices: she chose the courses he took at school; she chose the sport of wrestling for him; she even pre-empted his plan to go to Europe and become a writer.[93]

Jenny's benevolence continues to intrude into Garp's life, even after he's married and has his own family. While Garp has become a writer, Jenny has become rich and famous *because* of her writing. Her financial support of his family infuriates Garp: For the first five years Garp and Helen were married, Jenny paid their bills.[94] Garp comes to terms with his mother's role in his life only after he publishes his first novel.

Pip and Garp suffer from bouts of indignation when faced with the realities of their benefactors. Because he believed something false, Pip reacts more passionately; Garp, on the other hand, smolders. For the fatherless boy, a benefactor is crucial to development, both realistically, and from the narrative point of view. Realistically, we see logical growth. Story-wise, we see progression.

Dickens and Irving knew this. They both understood what's important to a boy in that situation. That makes the role of a benefactor crucial in both novels.

***

John Irving's writing has been described by Pulitzer Prize-winner Robert Olen Butler as containing "flamboyant, even bizarre characters; unlikely and arresting plot twists."[95] Irving, in "The King of the Novel," calls Dickens's plots unlikely.[96] Listening to the echo of Robert Olen Butler call Irving's plots "unlikely" after hearing Irving describe Dickens's plots as "unlikely" is eerie. It's possible that Butler may be consciously or unconsciously reflecting what he read in Irving's essay "The King of the Novel"—if, in fact, he read it. More likely is that Butler—a teacher as well as a writer—recognized inherited elements within Irving's style, elements that harken directly back to Dickens's influence.

Great Expectations and *The World According to Garp* chronicle the journeys of fatherless boys to manhood. The way Pip and Garp overcome their fractured and missing families is a shared theme. For Pip, that means finding a way to lift himself out of his origins, and into the realm of gentlemanhood. For Garp, that means defining himself as a writer. Neither character can accomplish these goals without the inter-cession of unlikely benefactors. Both characters come of age against the backdrop of revolutions: Pip lives during the Industrial Revolution in England, a time during which little compassion is paid to orphaned boys; Garp comes of age during the Sexual Revolution, under the shadow of a mother described as the first feminist.

Dickens and Irving have a relationship; John Irving told us so in the opening of his essay, "The King of the Novel." Both authors used ele-ments of their own lives in forming the stories. And both expressed a vision of the world through the development of a single, dynamic charac-ter—the story within the story.

It's tempting to envision a passing of the baton here. But more likely the links between Pip and Garp, between *Great Expectations* and *The World According to Garp*, between Charles Dickens and John Irving, rest upon both men's sobering view of the world, best expressed in the last line of Irving's novel, the greatest fatalistic phrase of modern literature.[97]

Academic Reflection

A Reflection on Academic Reflection

On the surface, the following pieces seem to function solely for the benefit of the writer, allowing introspection at the moment of conception, a chance to revisit the process from beginning to end and connect the learning in context. But they offer much more. They are full of excellent ideas that I go back to again and again, not just as the author revisiting his work, but as a writer and a teacher, as someone who needs fresh ideas each time I create a course.

"The Third Party" is the process paper I wrote at the end of my graduate studies. On the surface it's a look back at the journey of a single writer through a challenging and vigorous program. But it's really about more than just a single writer. It highlights the entire community of a writer's life, how their forces shape, change, and influence the writer. And so what use is it to the reader? On one level, aspiring writers might recognize themselves in the story. They might see some of the hardships and successes of their own journey here.

"Art and Craft" documents the emergence of a teacher. The interesting part of my particular march toward teaching is when it came. It wasn't the result of any focused course of education, or any premeditated outline. It came as a requirement to engage the community in the learning I was experiencing at that moment. I led a creative writing workshop in Stowe, and though I went in without any understanding of what it meant to teach, to lead, I came out having discovered the elements needed for good teaching. More importantly, I discovered that those elements already lived inside me. Like so many other things about writing, the journey became the point.

Process Paper: "The Third Party"

There's no doubt; there never was. I'm a writer. It's the simplest, most elegant way to describe everything about me. Everything else funnels through the writing. *I'm a skier.* The first idea I sold to a magazine was for an article about a small ski area (I got the kill fee). *I'm an outdoorsman:* The first short story I sold was to an outdoors magazine, about a boy's first hunting trip. *I'm an innkeeper.* For two years I wrote a regular column for a local newspaper about innkeeping. Dress me in any fashion; underneath I'm true to myself. I'm a writer.

But how did I get here? Where am I from? What forces steered me along this path? Like all writers, the answer to the riddle of me is cumulative. I grow, I gather. I fill in the promise of myself with each experience along the way. I percolate. I gestate. I ruminate. In nature, the goldfish grows to fit the size of its pond. Writers differ little; we're all potential. We're cast in the beginning, not quite a blank piece of paper, but a piece of paper nonetheless. We're drawn to the promise of filling the lines on the paper with words, words that speak in our place, like Cyrano speaking his true love. We need that third party, the written word, to define ourselves, to tell our stories.

I first searched for that connection in the adult fiction found around my house. But it wasn't until high school, when I began exploring literature, that I found a place to slake my learning thirst. Before then, I'd created my own course of study, a course heavy on American writers such as Cooper, Poe, Melville, Twain, and Hemingway.

That course of study climaxed when I read *The World According to Garp*, by John Irving. Up to that point I'd been experimenting with writing: I used to rewrite the stories I read in the sports section of the *Boston Globe*. I thought mine were better. But reading *Garp* set me on fire. Irving's brashness blew me away. His story mastery overwhelmed me. For the first time I thought, *This is what I want to do.* Teachers in high school echoed those thoughts. One English teacher wrote in my yearbook, *"I'll always remember you as one of my most creative students.*

I'm sure your imagination will benefit you." As a student with a strong academic record, I should have aggressively pursued writing as an undergraduate.

So why didn't I?

The things that contribute to a lack of focus happened. When my parents divorced, I was ten years old. Without a strong male figure around to guide me, I drifted. By the time I reached high school, I was tall, athletic, and socially desirable. I loved it. I continued the behavior right through my undergraduate days at the University of Maine at Orono, and it led to four years of college without a degree. It led me back home, where I worked in the commercial fishing industry, and as a carpenter. Noble professions, yes; but it wasn't writing. Hindsight enlightens, and when I look back, it seems obvious where I chose unwisely. A small writing school would have been better for me. But as a boy who'd been starved for attention growing up, I couldn't let go of the excitement. Not until I got married.

Marriage led me back into writing. It was my wife, Chantal, who said, "You're a writer. You should write." We moved to France and I invented myself again, this time the way I wanted: as a writer. In France I found success. I began to publish fiction and non-fiction, short stories and articles, and though I had success with my short fiction, selling a novel eluded me. The Catch-22 of needing an agent to get a publisher to get an agent frustrated me. I wrote novels, then threw them away. Then I wrote more, and I saved them. But by the time we'd moved back to the States in 1998, I'd hit another wall: I couldn't continue to write as a hobby. It was too important to me. I had to go to work full-time when my wife left her job to stay home with the children.

Until we moved to Vermont and bought a bed and breakfast, I didn't write. But in Stowe, I found an outlet. The local paper loved my sardonic look at innkeeping, and I chronicled my adventures in a column called "Innsights." It proved to be the springboard to the next phase of my writing life, the one I'm in now.

When my brother-in-law went to graduate school at the age of 37, the idea that I could do the same struck me. *But why?* I asked myself. *Why pursue an MFA?* I wondered where a graduate degree in writing would lead me, how it would change me, how it would change my writing. My greatest frustrations as a writer had been inconsistency, lack of focus, and an inability to publish a novel. Would an MFA in Creative Writing change that?

I knew the answer to the question was that there was no answer. There would be no guarantees. But there would be something. Like any good story, there'd be a change. I might not know what waited for me at the other end of the experience, but it would be there, visible to me only after I'd changed in some way. That change would form the structure of my graduate studies in the Goddard program.

Knowing what I'd write about during my graduate studies was a subconscious fact. It lived in my bones, and it printed itself all over the writing I'd done in the years leading up to Goddard. It was a clarion theme, (*fathers and sons, fathers and sons*), but I didn't actively register it in my thinking. Like so many other things about the Goddard process, it was intuitive.

I journeyed back through my writing: my earliest works, the stories I began writing when my wife and I moved to France, my novels, my journals. All of these things were laced with a topic that repeated itself over and over: *Father and son, father and son, father and son.* But what about the father and son? What would I leave the community with when I was finished? The question wasn't—and still isn't—mine to answer. The work would be the gift, the change in me would be the thing that lasts. As a result of that growth, my subsequent writing would be left to the community. It had to be that way, I realized, because it was the only thing I had to give.

One of the great gifts that the Goddard program gave me was permission to (re)discover the writer I am. Much of the reading I'd done over the years reinforced the direction I'd taken with my writing. Hemingway's Nick Adams stories, in particular, grabbed me early on, and held me, influencing my writing. Consider this passage from "The Deer Men," the first short story I sold to a magazine:

> I can only say that outside of deer camp, I have never eaten as conspicuously or as gratefully. In the middle of the large plate was a large fried steak. It was surrounded by fried potatoes, fried eggs, strips of fried bacon, piles of brown beans gooed together with gobs of molasses, with large hunks of sweet bread— fried, of course.[98]

While the connection between the outdoors and outrageous eating has always existed (picnics, camping trip menus), the lesson is that I made that connection in my writing. I demonstrated literary descent from a major influence into my writing. There was a third party nexus that connected me to Hemingway, and that nexus was the outdoors, and fathers and sons, and writing. Other writers influenced me through that nexus as well. John Irving's *The World According to Garp* played a dominant role in how I thought about writing a novel. In my unpublished novel *A Regular Guy* I blended elements of Hemingway's toughness and Irving's character madness to create a syncopated adventure about a man who's convinced he's the only sane person on the planet. Here's an excerpt:

> One of the tenants of being insane is that you immediately become sedate upon entering the loony bin...for none of us could remember doing anything truly insane to get here in the first place. Of course, that topic led to others: maybe we're just too crazy to remember what funky thing we did to offend normal folk...It took Chauncy and me to turn them on to the third option: we're not crazy at all. "Do anything fucked up today?" Chauncy asked, joining me in line.[99]

At this point, my writing career resembled something that might be found between chaos and clarity. Swirling around the cosmos of my existence were all these elements: fathers and sons, influences like Irving's portrayal of life's madness and Hemingway's stripped down pain, a certain amount of writing ability, a passion for craft, and a love of literature. For these things to coalesce, I needed to take the next step.

I had no idea what this meant. My eyes saw no specific goal, like a Ph.D. program, or teaching. Well, maybe there was an interest in teaching. I'd taught my son when we homeschooled him, and I think I learned more than he did. But I considered myself a writer, and the most specific thought I had was that I'd be more qualified to sell my writing after an MFA in Creative Writing program. I thought I'd explore the issues surrounding fathers and sons through my writing, and that would represent my contribution to my community.

I expected rigor, I expected challenge, and I expected the need to dive deep beneath the surface of Shawn the Writer. But I didn't know the specific forms those expectations would take. Since Goddard is a low-residency program, I couldn't compare it to other, traditional graduate programs. I understood, however, the concept of independent study. I understood the value and responsibility of the kind of freedom Goddard offered. When I arrived at Goddard, I was hungry and thirsty for the kind of attention that had been missing in my literary life. I wanted to engage in thoughts and ideas unavailable to me outside the world of learning. I decided that the only limitations I'd tolerate would be the ones imposed on me by physical health and family obligations. Everything else would have to assume a holding pattern.

Soon after beginning the Goddard program, I realized that I'd be writing a short story collection, and that I'd be creating it as I traveled through my graduate studies. This was important to me, because I wanted my final creative thesis to represent the new writer in me, one who'd distance himself from the trepidations of the past, while preserving the elements (like the my inherent sense of structure and narrative) that made my writing strong and accessible in the first place. I aimed to keep the strengths as I launched into the program.

I grasped the concept of the reading list and annotations quickly. I immediately saw how the readings affected my writing, but more importantly I saw how I could manipulate the readings to address challenges I discovered in my writing. In that way, my annotations directed themselves. When I explored the relationship between character and plot in my writing, I sensed something missing. I found instruction in that aspect of my writing in one of the books from my first semester reading list, *A Man Finds His Way*. That ability took root quickly in me, guiding me through the annotations that followed. I learned to look more critically at my writing; I learned confidence. Having the confidence to challenge my own work, the motivations behind it, has been a huge addition to my writing.

As I said somewhere in my application packet, my work method is to start fast and maintain intensity. Once I understood the process, I worked it hard, and in turn it worked on me. That first semester produced a lot of critical writing: fourteen annotations and both short critical papers. In the short critical papers I discovered the depth beneath the writing. Both papers, while expanding my critical writing skills, released in me desire to delve into writing—my own, and the readings—and discover the movement within them.

The first short critical paper, called "The Character of Nature in *Fathers and Sons,*" opened portals for me to understand better 19th century Russian literature. Ivan Turgenev painted sweeping portraits of heartache between father and their children, and all the while Nature played an active role. It showed the real power of Nature in literature, how it could be used without inviting pathetic fallacy.

In my second short critical paper, I looked at how a theme was carried out through a short story collection. This directly related to the thoughts I had during my first semester about what shape my creative thesis would take. In "Thematic Continuum in a Short Story Collection" I explored Andre Dubus's collection *A Father's Story*. Several themes ran through these stories, but at their core was a crisis in faith, a dilemma faced by each protagonist that challenged their notions of self, and what was right. Dubus did this subtly, which is the way I chose to treat the themes in my collection.

Throughout my first two semesters, Richard Panek drew from me the ability to divine my own conclusions. Richard understood the importance of the process letter, and through that format he allowed me to explore the changes I brought upon myself. Toward the end of my second semester, in Packet 4, Richard commented on my work through the process letter:

> I can't tell you how much I get a kick out of hearing about your struggles and eventual insights. They're tremendously gratifying, and not just because I'm your advisor. They delight me in some deeply aesthetic way—like, Oh, yeah, this is what art is like, this is what art can accomplish, this is how art can change a life.[100]

Richard was referring to my understanding that we have to master rules in order to ignore them, or forget them. Only when we learn the rules well enough are we allowed to break them, to step beyond them in order to achieve something extraordinary. This reminded me of something my father used to say...or, rather, something he used to do. If he was fixing an engine, or working with power tools (he's a mechanic, electrician, and carpenter), and he did something unsafe, like stick his hand in a running engine, he'd always turn to me first and say, "Never do this." Then he'd go ahead and do it. And I understood what was happening. He knew the risks, he'd mastered the rules of the engine. But he was going to break them to do the job. Only because he knew so intimately the consequences of his actions, only because he knew the environment in which he worked, could he do that.

Richard trusted me to come to my own realizations, to work through the issues I faced in my writing, and to solve them. When I wrote the long critical paper during my second semester, Richard asked for a rewrite. Not, he said, because the paper wasn't well written. He wanted a rewrite because he felt I could demonstrate a "deeper execution," and I could "further the possibilities within your arguments."[101] This related directly to the issues I experienced in my creative writing. And my creative writing benefited quickly from the rewriting of the long critical paper.

The first draft of the long critical paper, "From Pip to Garp: A Look at the Literary Relationship Between Charles Dickens and John Irving," had too many thrust points. I'd uncovered a wealth of information about Irving and Dickens, and I needed to narrow things, as Richard had urged. It's hard to hack down something you find deeply moving, and that was the case with this paper. Its inspiration came from an essay that John Irving wrote called "The King of the Novel." In it, he extols the reasons why he believes that Charles Dickens is so great, and why he believes that *Great Expectations* has the greatest plot in the English language.[102] Anyone who's ever read one of Irving's complicated novels knows from where he got his inspiration.

For me, true revelation came from the opening line of this essay. When I read it, lots of things clicked together in my head, all at once, and a deep understating of myself as a writer and as a person swept over me. That's exactly how I felt when, at the age of twelve, I read *The World According to Garp*. I knew that all I wanted to do was write, and that I wanted to make people laugh and cry and be scared all at the same time, just like Irving.

This example illustrates a larger theme that's occurred throughout my Goddard experience: the triad of readings, creative and critical writing, and explaining. I've come to think of these three elements as a multi-dimensional, equilateral triangle. They occupy a space in me and are bound by an energy that pulls me together with them. The readings form the influence and reflection; the writing demonstrates the change; and the explaining shows how the two come together, thus setting in motion another cycle. To me, it's the perfect perpetual motion machine.

The stories began to pile up. Some fit naturally into my theme. Others were well-written, but didn't explore the place I sought. One such story was "Tara Gadofsky's Voice," which appeared in the Fall 2005 edition of *Pitkin in Progress*. The story was quirky and entertaining, but it didn't fit into the larger structure I was forming. To put it in musical terms, I was writing an album of music, not a collection of disparate songs. I was writing something inspired by the great albums of AOR—album oriented rock—era of music, which began with The Beatles' *Revolver*, and lasted roughly through the early 90's. I distinctly remember experiencing something close to an orgasm when I listened to Bruce Springsteen's *Born to Run*. Other albums that engendered similar responses were U2's *The Joshua Tree*, and Pete Townsend's *All the Best Cowboys Have Chinese Eyes*. These weren't collections of songs; they were larger stories. And that's what I aimed for with my short story collection: only the things that contributed to the overall theme would be included. Everything else, even if it was good, didn't go.

I have to be clear here and say that I'm not writing a novel-in-stories. What I'm creating is far more subtle, a mood, a feeling, an impression, something that makes the reader say (upon reflection), "Whoa." And I also must say that I didn't start out with something specific in mind. As I said above, what I'm creating is as much a feeling as it is a brick-and-mortar short story collection.

In my second and third semesters my reading became much more focused. I was reading short story collections almost exclusively. Works such as Carson McCullers' *The Ballad of the Sad Café*, Annie Proulx's *Close Range*, Chinua Achebe's *Girls at War*, Mary Swan's *The Deep*, Dan Chaon's *Among the Missing,* Sherwood Anderson's *Winesburg, Ohio*, David Quammen's *Blood Lines*, James Joyce's *Dubliners*, and Ernest Hemingway's *Islands in the Stream* all contributed master lessons to my writing.

By my third semester the time had come to apply this learning in a different way, and the result was so astonishing to me that it's not an overstatement to say it changed my life. What happened was the Teaching Practicum. As I said before, teaching was something that I'd only brushed against. And of all the tasks of the Goddard program, the

Teaching Practicum intimidated me the most. I'd been hosting the writing lab at the Community College of Vermont for a semester, but creating and implementing an entire curriculum on my own was something I had no experience with. So I approached it the way I approach everything that scares me: I dove in.

The luxury that I did have with the Practicum was being able to create the course I wanted to teach. For me, a general creative writing workshop would give me the most opportunity to attract a good crowd, and dabble in all the things I found exciting about writing. Being able to share all that I know would be my safety net, my comfort zone. I was lucky to have the help and support of my sponsoring institution, the Stowe Free Library. The space and the students were great, and I felt comfortable and prepared going into the workshop.

As I dealt with classroom issues, presented my material, and listened to my students, my own studies were never far from my mind. As it turned out, I received my first packet back just before my last workshop class. In the packet, my advisor, Sarah Schulman, thoroughly evaluated a short story I'd written. She urged me to rewrite it, but this time keep in mind the sequence/consequence method of asking myself "Does this follow?" I felt a bit muddled entering the class, and as I was teaching, I found myself standing in front of a blackboard and teaching the sequence/consequence method. I stopped for a moment, and when I realized everyone was waiting for me to continue, I put the chalk down. I told my class that the very thing I was teaching them was the very thing I needed to be doing in my own writing. It was a pivotal moment for me, because it showed the power and reward for teaching. When you teach, you never stop learning. That's something I want to have as a part of me, and it seems to be happening. In the fall, Community College of Vermont offered me a position as an English Composition teacher.

I entered my third semester with two major tasks before me. The first was to write the Teaching Essay. The second was to write enough stories to complete my final creative thesis. The Teaching Essay is another of those moments unique to Goddard. You begin it thinking, "I'll

create a narrative documenting what I did, how I did it, who I did it to...."
Or some such drivel. At least that's what happened to me. But when
you're done, you realize you've changed again, in an exciting and unexpected way.

That change for me was a discovery of my love for teaching, and an
articulation of an essential teaching philosophy. I stated both of these
things immediately in the essay, called "Art & Craft: A Creative Writing
Workshop." I used a quote by Confucius to lead off the essay: "Anyone
learning without thought is lost; Anyone thinking but not learning is in peril." I went on to say that before the first class of the workshop, I felt calm,
as if I knew I was where I belonged.

With my creative work, I still prohibited myself from consciously
thinking about a deliberate structure. But about halfway through the semester, I sensed something different happening. I began to articulate a
strong message about the consequences of father and son relationships.
Though I'd been in that area throughout my writing, in stories like "A Fully
Stocked Bar" I began to venture into a place I hadn't before: the present.

What's happening now? How are fathers and sons affected by it?
What was happening now was a war in a far-off land, for far-off reasons.
Lots of sons were dying, and lots of fathers were sending them away to
die. Along with "A Fully Stocked Bar" I wrote "God's Front Porch" and
"After George," all of which deal with the consequences of the current
conflict. War affects fathers and sons in a unique way: one causes war,
one fights wars, and we all suffer; the accounting is terrible. I asked myself how each character would feel in such situations, how they would
act, what they'd do next. The stories I created surprised me. Not war
stories, they were stories about the outcomes of war, the remainders, the
mess that goes forward in time.

But there was something else happening, something larger than the
stories I'd written. When I'd finished writing the last story of my third semester, I stepped back to take a breath and I saw something extraordinary and surprising: a collection had appeared. Independent of
any planning or deliberate forethought, the stories I'd written over three

semesters now shook themselves into a thematic order, a structure that showed an arc. A title even suggested itself: *Name the Boy.* Within the collection would be three parts, or divisions. Part One would be called "Nor'easters," after the storms that whipped the coast of the small fishing village where I grew up. The stories—"The Natural History of the Bear," " 62 Clam Alley," "Name the Boy," and "Cream Soda"—all take place in and around Green Harbor, my hometown. But, more importantly, they all invoke the boy's, or son's, point of view. They all use the ocean as a metaphor for our inability to control fate, and they all represent the hopelessness of childhood.

Part Two would be called "Troubles." As a boy growing up in a predominantly Irish Catholic enclave just south of Boston, I knew from an early age just what "the Troubles" represented. These troubles would symbolically invoke the kind of rebellion the other troubles failed to achieve. "Hemlocks," "Foolish Fire," "Barometers," and "Hands" would deal with the way grown sons separated themselves from their fathers. In the context of my short story collection, trouble would find fertile ground between fathers and sons.

And Part Three would be called "Wars." Wars of the heart and wars of conquest. At their core, all wars are about the same thing: control. "A Fully Stocked Bar," "God's Front Porch," and "After George" look at the results of war on fathers and sons.

Standing back and looking at the assembled stories surprised me; not just because there was something structural there, but because of the makeup of that structure. There are things inside me that I've been unable or unwilling to write about, things I've struggled with, namely my relationship with my own father. When my parents were married, life was bad. When they divorced, things got worse for me. I lost my sense of self, and at the worst time in a boy's life: adolescence. Those things represented the inner struggle that fuels my writing to this day. The writing I did during the last two years has flushed out the walls holding that energy back. At the outset, I was too afraid to actually wish for something this profound and affecting. I contented myself with the prospect of hard work and some kind of reward at the end, a piece of paper. But like everything else along the Goddard way, I came away with much more. I came away different.

The G4 residency and semester loomed enigmatic in my mind. Between the end of G3 and the G4 residency, I busied myself rewriting the stories from *Name the Boy*. I brought the manuscript to the G4 residency without any purpose except to share it with any of my interested friends. Isn't that just like a writer? Bringing a manuscript to the G4 residency, when everyone else is completely wrapped up their own projects, demonstrates the depth of self-absorption—especially in this writer—necessary to live in the place where the work is created: the heart of my writing. The ability to find that heart, to surrender myself to it, represents a major accomplishment for me in this course of study. Before Goddard, I didn't know where my writing came from, or why I wrote certain things. Now I've uncovered the knowledge of truth in myself, that place where not only my writing lives, but all great writing lives.

When my advisor, Nicola Morris, learned that I had my manuscript with me, she asked if she could read it. Her plan was this: after she read it, we'd meet and go over it; she'd give me her detailed response, and that meeting and response would constitute Packet 1. I understood this as a rare opportunity, and it thrilled me. Of course I dreaded the instant feedback, but after our meeting, I felt confident and relieved. I went home with energy and ideas and I set about revising and rewriting. I went home with a shape forming inside me.

That shape continued to change as I revised the manuscript of my creative thesis. I knew I was fortunate to have met with my advisor during the residency, but I treated myself harshly as I approached the revision. It took a week or so for Nicky's comments to sink in, and when they did, I was ready to write—or, in this case, rewrite.

One of the particular advantages of writing a short story collection is that each story can be dealt with individually. Later, the stories can be examined as a whole work. But initially, I had to deconstruct my collection and rethink many of the stories. One issue that pervaded my writing was voices of the narrators. Nicky didn't get a clear sense of distinction with each different story. She wanted me to grapple with voice, and how it affected the language of the story, the syntax. To that end she highlighted places where I succeeded with distinctive narrator voices.

To say I took this challenge to heart is an understatement. Even though I had arrived at the G4 residency with a fully-formed, book-length, thematically connected collection of short stories, I knew I could make it better. When it came to incorporating criticism into the improvement of my writing, I took my cues from another major influence, Flannery O'-Connor. In his introduction to the Farrar, Straus and Giroux edition of O'Connor's complete short stories, Robert Giroux commented on her willingness to revise to improve her writing:

> Flannery always had a flexible and objective view of her own writing, constantly revising, and in every case improving. The will to be a writer was adamant; nothing could resist it, not even her own sensibility about her own work. Cut, alter, try it again.[103]

That's the spirit I carried into the revision. Two stories---"62 Clam Alley" and "Foolish Fire"—were nearly completely rewritten. Others, like "Barometers," benefited from Nicky's admonition to tackle the narrator's voice. In some cases, the narrator's voice didn't match the syntax. I found that by changing the words the narrator was thinking, the story came alive. In other cases, secondary characters—especially women— were wooden and unbelievable. This was the case with "Hands." By giving the narrator's wife real life and a significant, believable role in the story, I saw how the story deepened, became more urgent.

I also changed the order of the stories. Here I considered what the reader needed. I stripped away the three-part structure I began with, and placed the stories depending on their tone and point of view. I began with the title story, "Name the Boy," because both Richard Panek (my second reader) and Nicky felt it was strong, and I closed with "The Natural History of the Bear," because it's such an emotionally draining story. In a way, the revision and the re-thinking of the story order went hand in hand. Once I accepted the fact that I'd be doing some heavy revising, new ways to think about the story order opened up to me.

When I mentioned above that the G4 semester felt enigmatic to me, I didn't mean the work I'd be doing on the final creative thesis. The culminating semester is unlike the first three; it's full of a different kind of creativity, a creativity that mirrors the writing and reading we do, but in a professional way. I'm speaking about the Transcripts and Narrative Descriptions and Course Equivalents—even the Process Paper. But as I got into this process, I realized something about my learning. This Goddard process is full of small places that return you to the consciousness of what you're learning. An example of this is the end of semester evaluations. As I traveled back through my semesters here, creating the course equivalencies and narrative descriptions, I reconnected to my learning in an unexpected way. By revisiting the things I'd experienced, the things I'd accomplished, a larger picture emerged. In many ways, it mirrored the way my short story collection coalesced. It was a case of something being obvious in hindsight: Duh, of course that's what you've been doing. That resonated with me. That was one of those "Whoa" moments around which life pivots. For the first time, I saw my shape as a writer.

One of the things that contributed to that shape is the Goddard community. This community changed me as much as anything else over the past two years, and that may have to do with the nature of the way we now think of community in our lives. Like everything else about Goddard, the community is cutting edge, it's non-traditional, it challenges the conventions we bring to the program. But as cliché as it sounds, that community connected with me, and I discovered how valuable it was to have friends—writers—with sympathetic ears and informative mouths. The warmth with which I was received by my fellow students was overwhelming. I asked for nothing; they gave me everything. They gave me their fears, their hopes, their trepidations, their feedback, and in return they asked for nothing, except a place to send it to, a place to connect them, as I needed to be connected. It changed the way I think of myself.

I've always been a "loner with a loner's point of view," as one friend described me. My mantra was Ernest Hemingway's acceptance speech for the Nobel Prize in Literature:

> Writing, at its best, is a lonely life. Organizations for writers palliate the writer's loneliness but I doubt if they improve his writing. He grows in public stature as he sheds his loneliness and often his work deteriorates. For he does his work alone and if he is a good enough writer he must face eternity, or the lack of it, each day.[104]

But now I know that's wrong; it was even wrong for Hemingway. He had all those things. He had Gertrude Stein and John Dos Passos and Ford Maddox Ford. He had community, a third party. And now I have it, too.

Teaching Essay: Art & Craft: A Creative Writing Workshop

Anyone learning without thought is lost;
Anyone thinking but not learning is in peril.
--Confucius

Introduction

I never had opening night jitters. As I slid the key into the lock of the Community Room at the Stowe Free Library on the first night of my writing workshop, I remember feeling calm. Not confident of success, but peaceful, secure in the knowledge that I was where I belonged, where I wanted to be.

I contribute that feeling to preparation. Was the hard work, reflection and anticipation enough? I'd find out in a few minutes—and over the course of the five-week workshop. But I was prepared. I had detailed plans for each class, a philosophy to guide the implementation of those plans, and an armload of material to back it up. I had tips from classmates and others with teaching experience. I had snacks. And, if all else failed, I had myself, my personality, my experience as a writer.

Beginnings

Two teaching experiences colored my expectations going into the Teaching Practicum: first as a ski instructor, and second as my son's teacher, when my wife and I homeschooled him. Though different in structure and execution, both experiences gave me a sense of what it meant to be entrusted with a student's hopes, to understand the notion of the learner's needs.

Teaching skiing involved direct methodology. The ski school gave me technique—the steps to follow with students. It didn't give me, the teacher, much confidence, and I remember being nervous as I faced my first class: a group of people who'd never skied. The head of the ski school, an Austrian named Hans, gave me some of his "method."

"Look, Shawn," Hans said in his thick Austrian accent. He pointed to a couple of tall, good-looking women in tight, one-piece ski outfits. "Zere are a couple of honeys in za class for you. Just tell zem to bend za knees. Ven dey bend za knees, za tits bounce. Ven za tits bounce, zey are skiing correctly."

Hans slapped me on the back, and left me to my class. What he said didn't give me much confidence, but I succeeded anyway. I taught them to ski by following the method that Hans and the other senior instructors showed me—not the sexist one mentioned above, but the legitimate PSIA (Professional Ski Instructors of America) technique. Things were broken down into small, easily mastered steps. As each step was completed, it was added to another step. After an hour, the students got it—they could turn and stop, just like it said in the book.

Homeschooling my son, Seamus, marked my ideas about teaching more profoundly. My wife and I knew we couldn't fight him about what he needed to learn, so we let him create his own experience. As long as he got the basics—math, science, reading, writing—he was free to do things his way.

An example: Seamus loves stories, but hates to read. So we let him listen to books on tape. He chose The Odyssey. But then he had to write about it, and his writing and comprehension improved rapidly. Science: same thing. Seamus found a whole planet of scientific learning outside his door. With our guidance, he related everything he learned to his own experiences. He completed a self-styled circle of learning.

Those are the two teaching and learning experiences I brought to my Teaching Practicum: method, and open. The method was the systematic, step-by-step way I taught hundreds of people to ski. Open was the way Seamus learned: naturally, organically, relevantly. His learning made sense to him because it came from him. Both have their place in teaching. It's the duty of the teacher to judiciously apply the right one at the right time.

For my workshop, I wanted something more for my students: to learn, yes, but to understand what they were learning—and why. And I wanted them to be their own teachers, to leave my workshop with a different, deeper understanding of themselves as writers. They should have not only a method—the toolbox—but also the ability to relate their writing to themselves in a way that allows for close self-examination. Like the old proverb that says, "Give a man a fish, feed him for a day. But teach a man to fish, and you feed him for a lifetime," I wanted my students to acquire the understanding behind the ability.

I wanted to teach them to fish.

Ideas

The inspiration for this class goes back to December, 2004. While at a gathering for local business people here in Stowe, I spent some time speaking to Charlotte Maison, the director of the Stowe Free Library. When she learned that I was student in Goddard's MFA in Creative Writing program, she suggested that I teach a writing class at the library. We talked about what the library had sponsored in the past, and based on that conversation, I decided that a general writing workshop would best serve the community.

I had a target audience in mind. Since the class would be comprehensive in approach, I guessed that most of the people who signed up for it would be working adults. With that in mind, I scheduled the workshop to run on five consecutive Wednesday nights in July and August, from 6 to 9 p.m. The time slot would serve a working person's needs, and the length—3 hours per session—would set a good pace, providing enough time for students to write, to relax, to learn, to talk about writing, to think about writing, and to prepare themselves for the real, non-writing world. Three hours gave the students the feeling of a mini-retreat, the same way that our residencies at Goddard give us the feeling of a writer's retreat.

Why was this important? I wasn't going to stand in front of the class and open my toolbox and say, "Okay, here's a metaphor. It goes here.

And here's a detail. Use it to operate a metaphor. Oh, and here's some structure, it fits like this. Have a nice day." I wasn't going to be formulaic. The way I taught the workshop would distinguish it from others.

Fall 2005 Residency

The residency fell between the preparation for, and the actual start of, the workshop. I deliberately scheduled the first class for Wednesday, July 6. I knew I'd be taking the Teaching Practicum Workshop during this residency. I'd also have the chance to speak to many classmates about their teaching experiences. Gleaning valuable information during the residency wouldn't allow me to go back and change the set-up for the workshop, but it would give me enough ideas and information to handle anything unexpected.

Other, less obvious reasons for the workshop's timing combined the non-traditional approach I'd be teaching with a spirit of reflection. Goddard residencies charge me with energy and euphoria. I wanted that feeling fresh inside me when I started this workshop. I planned to show —not tell—my students that there's another way to write, different from the way we've all been taught. Within the traditional structure of a workshop/classroom setting, I'd give my students the opportunity to tap into the things that I'd discovered while at Goddard.

Acknowledging my students as writers became my first task. When I arrived at Goddard, MFA-CW program director Paul Selig met with the G1's, and said, "Welcome to *your* Creative Writing program. You're in the right place." It was the first time anyone besides my wife validated the most important part of me. It gave me purpose and confidence; it gave me the desire to return that spirit of empowerment to the world around me.

I'd base the rest of the workshop on developing their faith and talent by recognizing them as writers, by radically changing the way they thought about their craft—and themselves. And by that change would their writing evolve, deepening, becoming more relevant.

In her book *The Right to Write*, Julia Cameron says, "To be truly human, we all have the right to make art. We all have the right to write."[105] That's the point around which successful writing turns. When students receive that "right to write," they shed the things that distract them, and they travel to unexpected places. My class would nurture that concept.

The Class

It's one thing to plan a creative writing workshop; it's quite another to do it. And it's still another to succeed. I think success depends on surprise. Much like a great story shows a character changing unexpectedly but justifiably, so too must success itself be defined by an element of surprise. The teacher must anticipate that, but when it happens, he should still marvel at its occurrence.

In many ways, teaching is like prayer. Praying for something isn't the object of prayer; prayer itself is the goal. It's the praying—the teaching—that we (as teachers) show our students. By giving them that technique, we're giving them the ability to teach themselves, so that their learning may continue throughout their lives. It's something that's already inside them, a talent they possess. We're just lighting the path.

My experiences as a teacher—and as a writer—colored the way I'd teach this writing workshop. As a teacher, I'd learned these lessons:

1. Make it fun.
2. Make it interesting.
3. Get the students involved.
4. Let them think that they're learning, not that you're teaching.
5. Listen.

As a writer, I'd learned many things, most of them the hard way. I'd learned how to publish stories by first learning how not to publish them. I'd learned how to score a regular column in a newspaper by being persistent and waiting for one editor to die off and be replaced by another. But most of all—and this is the thing I'd bring to my class—I'd learned that to write you must be dedicated to yourself as a writer. You must think as a writer every day. That dedication, that confidence, revealed itself in my life as a daily mantra I used before writing: "You are a good writer," I'd tell myself. "You are a very good writer. You are a great writer." Over and over I'd repeat that, until every cell in my body was pointing in the same direction. And then I wrote.

And that's how the workshop began. The students—I ended up with 9—came in and sat in a circle of chairs. I briefly introduced the class to them, and then we launched into a writing exercise. I asked everyone to write a biographical paragraph about themselves, and I had them write it in the third person POV. When they were finished, they passed what they'd written to the person on their left. Then, each student read aloud their neighbor's bio.

This was a great opening exercise for a couple of reasons. First, it got people writing. It was a lesson I'd learn over and over during the workshop: when they're writing, students are happy, and they're learning. Second, it was fun for them. By introducing a neighbor, they got some insight about someone else's writing style, as well as learning a little about each other. That made them more comfortable in the class.

From the beginning I was emphatic about what was going to happen in this workshop: I wasn't going to teach. They were going to learn. It was *their* workshop, and in the Class Overview handout I gave them, that's what I said in the first line: "Hello, and welcome to *your* creative writing workshop!" I told them that my focus for the workshop was "you and your writing." I wanted them to discover the relationship between themselves and their writing, between the art and the craft.

But I had to create a place for that discovery to occur. That's where the Workshop Philosophy took over. The essentials of my Workshop Philosophy were: Safety (as in trust), Confidentiality (what happens in workshop, stays in workshop), No Censorship, No Judgment, Belief in the Creative, and Letting Go. These would be the only structures to guide us.

That first night, we came to a rhythm that would establish itself for the rest of the workshop. I'd introduce a topic, such as Truth in Writing. Then we'd do a writing exercise. Then we'd read some of what we just wrote. Then we'd discuss how we felt about what happened to our writing, and the way we think about our writing.

I found it important to keep the momentum going. Tempting though it was to linger on a subject, we had to press on, or risk losing our focus. We had a lot to cover, and my challenge became not one of having too little material, but of having too much, and missing some important topics.

My students were both varied and homogenous. They were all women. They were all my age (which is to say middle-aged) or older. These weren't new writers, embarking on their writing lives. These were writers of some experience and talent. It's important to note this because different students have different needs. But they also shared many of the same needs, and that's where I'd focus my attention.

I'll try to mention a few of my students when relevant, and I'll start with Sara. Sara came to the class with a lot of experience writing—she'd even thought about making a life as a writer. She told me that when she retired, in a few years, she was going to seriously pursue her fiction writing. At the end of the first class, Sara approached me and said, "I'm not sure this class is right for me. I've got lots of experience writing. I've taken writing classes at the New School. This seems a bit below me."

I told her the decision was hers to make. I told her to think about what I'd said about the difference between this writing class and others, about how we'd be trying non-traditional ways of writing, how we'd be learning about who we are as writers as a way of unlocking our talents. She seemed skeptical, and I honestly didn't believe I'd see her again.

Before the class ended, I gave them an assignment: create a detail. Focus on one small thing in a scene, write about it, let the writing bloom without knowing where you're going, and see where it takes you. The next class came, and in walked Sara with a big smile on her face. "I can't believe what happened," she said. "I started writing this detail the way you told us—you know, I figured I'd give it a try, what the heck—and this story came out. This story I never knew about just came gushing out." By risking a little, she gained a lot, something she'll never forget.

Other students experienced something similar. Theresa, a shy poet, produced a breathtaking detail about what she saw during a walk in the woods. Louisa, a former teacher and writer for over six decades, also produced an unexpected passage. It was clear that I'd struck a vein with the detail exercises. But why?

We began by asking ourselves, "What kind of writer am I?" We explored some of the techniques offered by Natalie Goldberg in *Wild Mind*. Foremost among these were the Rules of Writing Practice.[106] Applied in a controlled setting (the workshop), the Rules of Writing Practice demonstrated results instantly. When given ten minutes to freewrite, writers always surprise themselves. The students began to see the origins of their writing. They were learning about themselves.

These exercises, these questions, were important because the students needed to be comfortable with the knowledge that they existed within their writing. Once they trusted themselves, amazing bits of writing began to emerge. I say "bits" because that's what they were: small passages we built upon. I saw that learning—to be effective—must come from the heart of the student. They had to buy the system before they'd buy the product, and *they* were the system. This approach wasn't for everybody, and I lost one student after the first night. She emailed me and said that she was just too busy, but when my wife saw her a few weeks later, the student said, "It was too personal, I was uncomfortable with that." The teacher can't be everything to everybody; that's not his job. But the teacher must show his students that if they trust themselves, they'll succeed—and that success will be measured as change.

One of my goals involved making in-class writing more than just freewrites. I wanted the exercises to be germane to the topic we were discussing the way we're organic to our own writing. One of these assignments didn't work so well. It was "Writing Between Two Passages," where the student tries to write bridging narrative or dialogue between two dissimilar passages. It flopped. The students told me they just didn't get it, though they all made decent attempts. I'll try that exercise again sometime, but I'll approach it differently. I'll have the students create their own dissimilar passages to bridge, that way they'll be closer and more comfortable to the writing.

The students asked to workshop some of their writing during the class, and this proved fruitful. They shared works in progress, got productive feedback, and explored different revising techniques. One thing that helped them came from an article by Frank Conroy called "The Writer's Workshop." In it, he reveals the area where writer and reader overlap.[107] Understanding this "zone" helped shape the way the students thought about their writing while they're writing—not afterwards. We also learned that stories—and really good writing—don't come from plots, they come from the small places inside us. Along with thinking differently about writing, I wanted to show them, over the course of the workshop, how a story is built, from the small to the large. How it occurs organically, intuitively, and that we, the writers, are just there to help it along with some craft.

By the last class they were ready for Narrative Arc, the place where they could put their writing together. And while I stood in front of a blackboard, showing them how a narrative arc works as we invented a story based on sequence/consequence and the positive choice of the character, something unexpected and very cool happened.

As a student, I'd just received a packet back from my advisor, Sarah Schulman. She did a thorough critique of my story "If Hands Could Taste Like Whiskey." She felt the story needed a serious rewrite, and she ended her letter to me by telling me to "stick to the principles of events having consequences as a way of moving the story forward." As I extolled this very advice to my class, it hit me: I was teaching what I needed to be doing in my own writing. I was the teacher. I was the learner. I'd never stop being the learner, no matter how great a teacher I might become. There would always be *so much yet to learn*.

The moment transformed me.

I stood there, slack jawed, for about a minute, until I realized the room was filled with dead air. Instead of mumbling apologies and moving things along, I put the chalk down and told the class what just happened, how what I was teaching them was what I needed to be doing in my own writing, and how I'd just realized all this while standing here, teaching. The class loved it; the experience connected us. I saw things falling into place on their faces. It was a watershed moment for me as a teacher, as a student, as a writer. It showed me that teaching and learning and who I am will always be entwined, and that being honest with my students will always work as a positive force in the classroom.

Observer's Report

My observer was Scott Atkins, a local writer, and a graduate of the University of Virginia's MFA in Writing program. When we spoke afterwards, some of the things he said surprised me.

In the report he mentions that the first 20 minutes of the class were spent discussing how the learning affects the students as writers. Scott asked if this was a "Goddard thing." I explained to him the importance of the Process Letter in the Goddard approach, how that's the place where the learning is demonstrated. I wanted something similar for my workshop students, so I initiated a discussion at the start of each session about their lives as writers, how they were incorporating the things they were learning into their writing. Scott told me he was impressed with the technique.

Scott also mentioned the way I invoked the previous week's lessons at the start of class as a way of connecting the subjects. This was important for me to hear because the whole workshop was connected, building up to the final session, where we'd create a story together, using all the things we'd learned.

The most important thing I took from the Observer's Report was trust in myself. I was nervous about having someone watch me—especially someone as accomplished as Scott. I handled it by trusting my teaching style and myself. What would I change? I might be a little more

forceful, a little more directed with the class, guiding them more purpose-
fully through the subjects. We didn't cover as much ground as I'd originally planned.

Conclusions

I feel a little guilty, as though I learned more, I changed more, than
my students did. I know that's not true. I know they felt the same things
I felt in the class. That's why the class was a success. In her evaluation,
one of my students wrote that she found her voice as a writer. Bingo.
She found her voice. She changed. That was my goal.

That doesn't mean there weren't places for me to improve my teaching technique. We didn't get to cover all the subjects I wanted. When we
hit a good groove in class, my habit was to linger in the moment a little
too long. I thought if the students were learning so much, why not explore things further? I see now I should have been more succinct. That
would have given the students the learning they needed and the feeling—that feeling of involvement and success—they craved.

I'd also change the way I approached the lecturing portions of the
class. I felt nervous about this part, and I tended to race through the material. I need to give the lectures substance. There are times when it's
necessary to give information. For those times, I need to add color,
depth. For example, I could relate a personal anecdote about my own
experience with the material, and how I succeeded—or failed—with it.

This teaching experience has solidified my thoughts about how and
why teaching succeeds. Students aren't all the same. Real learning depends on understanding that an exchange occurs in the classroom. I've
also seen again how important it is to involve the student in the teaching.
When I homeschooled my son, he responded positively when he was
allowed to participate in the creation and implementation of his curriculum. When the students in my workshop were asked for their ideas
about the subjects we looked at, they became more active, more involved, and more successful in their learning.

I wanted my students to get both the method, and the feeling, that understanding of who they were as writers. So while we covered the classics of creative writing—journalling, image, metaphor, character, setting, plot—we did it in a way that deepened the student's understanding of why these things were happening in their writing. With that knowledge, the students can not only write well, but know why they're writing well, and teach themselves again and again what they need to learn.

They'll be able to fish.

Part Three:
Creative Nonfiction

Creative Writing: The Word

In the beginning was the word, and the word was good—and it was enough. Then came the various classifications and sub-genres, muddying the water, until what used to be referred to as fiction and nonfiction became an unintelligible tower of writing types, from Military Sci-Fi to Journalistic Fiction. Now, what used to be called writing is assigned a specific moniker in the name of making it more consumable. What's a writer to do?

My technique has never been to write to a particular market. I write what I know, what I've experienced, what I believe to be true. Then I run around like a fool, trying to find a place to market what I've written. If publishing is your goal, my system is not the one to adopt. To make things more confusing, I've never pursued one form of writing over another and stuck with it. I've written novels, short stories, articles, newspaper columns, magazine fillers, blogs, letters to the editor, interviews, clandestine notes to Karen F. in 11th grade English class, academic treatises, and translations. A good representation of it all is in this book.

My scattergun approach to writing reflects not an inability to focus, but a love for all writing. And I'm willing to suffer the consequences of that, because I'm not willing to suffer the consequences of denying myself my true identity. So when I call the third part of this book Creative Nonfiction, I'm not caving into the demands of pablum-weary publishers, editors and readers; I'm just giving that section of writing its appropriate name.

This section of writing comprises most of the forays I've made into the nonfiction world. About the only thing not in here is the column I used to write for a Japanese language hockey magazine called The Edge. What is in here is a good cross section of what a writer does to sustain and promote himself. The first piece in this section is called "The Feral Father," and it originally appeared in Backpacker Magazine in September, 2004. It's a good piece, representative of the lightness and humor I'm capable of in my writing, and it paid me four hundred dollars. I was pretty proud of that payday. But thinking back on it, I'm not sure why I didn't pursue that line of freelance writing. I think it had to do with houses and kids.

The two columns I wrote for the Stowe Reporter are in here, too. That newspaper and its publisher, Biddle Duke, have played a significant role in my development as a writer. The first column I wrote, "InnSights," allowed me to flex my writing muscles, which had been dormant from the time we returned from Montreal in 1998 (when I went to work for FedEx) until 2001. By the time the column ended, I had moved on to a place that would eventually lead to Goddard College and its MFA in Creative Writing program in 2004. In "An Author's Road," I chronicle the life of a book, in this case my creative thesis, as it travels from concept to publication. In a way the columns book-end that phase of my writing life, the before and the after.

The middle of that phase comprises much of the writing done at Goddard (which was featured in the previous section), the literary criticism and academic writing. If they're done right, these writings incite further thought and discussion, rather than offering something dogmatic and final. So are they all creative? In the sense that I created them, yes. And are they all nonfiction? Hell no. There's as much fiction in nonfiction as there is nonfiction in fiction. After all, these are just words, and they're hardly enough.

Freelancing: Backpacker Magazine

Making up the nonfiction of "The Feral Father"

I can't overstate the significance of the publication of this story. And beyond the effect it had on me as a writer, it's useful to examine within the context set forth in the introduction to Part Three of this book. It's a nonfiction article, but is it true? Is it nonfiction? Does nonfiction have to be true? The answer is: it depends.

What it mostly depends on (and I hate to shatter everyone's idealistic dreams, but here I go) are the editorial needs of the magazine. If a magazine clearly states that they want only first person true-life accounts, then this story wouldn't make it. What Backpacker Magazine was looking for was a humorous piece at the end of each issue. It had to tie in closely to the theme of the magazine, which was the outdoors in general, hiking and camping specifically (note the use of the word "camping" in the second sentence of the story). This story did all those things. But is it true? And if it's not true, is it fiction? And if it's fiction, do the editors know I duped them?

As soon as you read the story, you'll know it's not true, that it's genre is probably best expressed as "embellished and amalgamated memoir." It's more about capturing a feeling than it is about documenting a true event. I never went on a specific trip with my father into the wilds of northern Maine in February. But I've been there, with him, in the woods, in the winter, many, many times. And all those time left me with small images, like pieces of a quilt, that I sewed together to create a narrative, a story that has a recognizable shape to the reader. That's where the craft comes in: the ability to create something, to imagine and then to build.

"The Feral Father"[108]

from Backpacker Magazine
September, 1994

My father is a genuine shunner of civilization. His idea of a restful weekend is to stuff all of his camping gear into a vehicle and head north until he runs out of gas. Since he drives a prehistoric 4WD equipped with ocean-sized gas tanks, he usually manages to reach the Jo-Mary Lakes region in north-central Maine before the fuel gauge needle hovers above the E. He then gets out and hikes farther north still, until the sun sets. He likes to do this in mid-February, when the cold is painful.

In years past, I was often approached by my father before these little sojourns. "It's not the companionship I'm looking for," he'd usually say. "I just want someone younger to walk in front of me and break trail."

Once, as a near-blizzard was raging outside, and assuming our trip would be called off, I curled up in front of the fireplace. That's when the Great White Thing appeared, half frozen from the short walk from his car to the front door. "It's a good time to leave," he pronounced, dragging me out. "There's no traffic on the road, and the woods'll be pristine in the morning."

There was no traffic on the road because there was no road to be seen. Snow smothered the world, and I had no clue where we were going. I knew our destination was someplace in northern Maine that didn't have a name. Baseball-sized snowflakes spread out from the headlights, and the silence created by the falling snow was unnerving. Dad was unfazed. I was hypnotized by the whiteness falling all around.

When we reached our destination, of course it was beautiful. We spent two days trudging around on snowshoes, shivering and eating strips of freeze-dried beef. Dad doesn't believe in consuming anything that doesn't look like the beast from whence it came, and since the neighbors no longer tolerate him drying beef out on the front lawn, he settles for the packaged stuff.

Soon after that fateful trip, I moved to France where there's a population density of 268.4 people per square mile. I stand a better chance of bumping into the Pope than the Yetis of northern Maine my father was always tracking. I'm content with Dad's letters, which sound as if they were written by some 17th-century wilderness explorer. A sampling:

"Went for an overnight in early February. Came upon a fresh deer kill and was menaced by viscous [sic] coydogs, which are pestilent and plague my nights with their infernal howling. It was 5 below zero (that's Fahrenheit, son) when we went to sleep, a fierce gale loosed in the pines… In the morning I had to revive Peter (camping buddy victim) by pounding vigorously upon his chest… He took in a little brandy and will probably keep seven or eight of his toes. *Haw!!!*"

Occasionally I get back home for a visit. The most recent was last June, and I should have known something was amiss when I awoke in Dad's 4WD. We were already deep into Maine, headed for Piscataquis County. I could think of only one thing, or maybe I should say a zillion things: blackflies.

Dad had a mystery bug repellent that worked quite well, although I was afraid to ask what it was. Along the trail we came across several almost bloodless hikers who'd forgotten their DEET. Dad gave them a little of his bug concoction, to which one immediately blurted "Gross," after sniffing the brew. "This smells like panther piss." Dad winked at me and smiled. "Close," he said to the hiker.

Whatever the stuff was, it wore off around lunchtime, and the biting frenzy began in earnest. Dad didn't notice. He was too busy studying the cloud of flies encircling his head. "Protein snacks," Dad explained as he snapped at the bugs.

Today in France it was beautiful, and I went for a hike along one of the well-worn, well-marked trails. I passed people picnicking, eating with silverware, and sipping wine, and for a minute, for a brief minute, I wished I were with Dad, lost in the middle of a place nobody had yet bothered to name, plagued by the howling of "viscous" coydogs.

Journalism: The Stowe Reporter

The Importance of InnSights

In the spring of 2001, I was desperate. The autumn before, my wife and I had bought a bed and breakfast in Stowe, Vermont. I transferred my job with FedEx from Boston to Burlington, and we moved north. But the moment I walked into the FedEx station in Williston, I knew I'd made a mistake. But what could I do? We needed the income and the health benefits that employment with FedEx provided. It helped us get the loan to buy the inn. But the job required me to work from 7 in the morning to 7 at night, not including the 35-minute drive each way from Stowe to Williston. It meant that I never saw my sons, aged six and four at the time. And I could offer almost no help to my wife in the operation of the inn. I quickly learned that driving for FedEx in suburban Boston was vastly different from driving in rural Vermont: weather, delays, and an intransient culture at the FedEx location knocked me off balance. To make things worse, I suffered a debilitating back injury at work, and my employer blamed me for it. I spent nearly three months that winter re-covering from it.

By the time the snow melted and my ski season had been ruined, I knew I had to get away from FedEx. But how? Not much had changed from the fall: we still needed the money and health insurance. I felt trapped and desperate. How could I have ended up here? How could the guy who used to live in France and write novels and short stories end up in a delivery vehicle stuck in a ditch on the side of a mountain? What happened?

That spring I saw an ad in the local paper, the Stowe *Reporter*, for a reporter position. I applied for the job, but only half-heartedly. But that application led to contact with the paper's editor, who encouraged me to pitch him a proposal for a regular column at the paper. Being a writer and living at an inn, I naturally came up with a column revolving around those two things: the true life of a small innkeeper, what he has to go through to make it work, how unglamorous it really is. It was well-received, but when that editor left the paper, the idea was shelved. Then the publisher, Biddle Duke, came across the proposal. He thought it was a great idea, and he asked me to start writing the column. I called it InnSights, and it saved my writing career.

Without going too deeply into the "making lemons from lemonade" cliché, the column allowed me to really focus my creative need on what was happening in my life. That it happened to be an interesting subject was a bonus. Plus, I got paid: twenty dollars per column. The money functioned more as validation for me, but it put some beer money in my pocket, and it made me feel like a real writer again. More importantly, Biddle liked my writing. That summer he published eight of my columns (the *Reporter* is a weekly paper), and I was suddenly known around town as the writing innkeeper. The validation was exhilarating, and it turned my thoughts to pursuing my writing further. Maybe my writing—the relentless urge to create—could be used to change my life. Three years later that happened: I was accepted into Goddard College's MFA in Creative Writing program, and Biddle Duke wrote one of my letters of recommendation.

But of all the success I had with the column, the thing I liked most about it was the tag line that came at the end of each piece. It neatly encapsulated what was happening in my life, and reflected where I was going: *Shawn Kerivan runs and owns an inn in Stowe with his wife Chantal, but he drives a FedEx truck to make ends meet.*

I've chosen some of those columns to represent that progression I experienced as both a writer and an innkeeper. They're not all my favorites; rather, they show the emergence of my style, my voice. In these columns can be seen my slightly sardonic way of examining life, the voice and tone that has become my calling card in both fiction and non-fiction. Here it's nascent, raw, and growing. Here it's going from lemons to lemonade.

Column title: "Friday Night at the Inn"
Original title: "Friday Night at the Inn"
Publication date: Spring, 2001

It was a Friday night like any other mid-winter Friday night in the innkeeping business in Stowe: we had all just sat down to dinner, crossed ourselves, thanked the Big Guy, and were about to dig in when...

The phone rang first. Though Thursday nights are usually reserved for endless hours of phone ringing and room booking, there is always a last minute barrage of desperate skiers looking for accommodations. No sooner had my wife dispatched that wave of New Yorkers to their cozy digs than the bell on the front door jingled. Keeping a small inn, I was quickly learning, was akin to some twisted Pavlovian experiment devised to test your tolerance to the jingling of bells. I can only say that it is a good thing that bell-wearing cows don't wander by my door, else we'd be buried in sirloins.

By the time we had made it half way through the meal and my wife still hadn't returned from checking in the guests and showing them to their room, we began to worry. This could only mean one thing: the new arrivals were interesting folks and my wife was chatting them up, which is one of the reasons we got into the innkeeping business in the first place. I went looking for her and found her down in the basement scowling at one of the heaters.

I should explain that in the small basement under the inn there were no less than four different heaters: two for hot water, one forced hot water for heating the rooms, and one to heat the hot tub. Leading to and from these heaters was an array of plumbing, a head scratching jungle of copper and cast iron.

"There's no heat in room six," she informed me. "But," she continued, "there is heat in five, two and three. Nothing in four."

"Whose in six?" I asked.

"Those young guys that are with their friends in room five."

"Four?"

"They won't be here till 11 or so."

"What about one?"

"That gets heat from the hot air on the other side of the house."

For a moment my eyes narrowed. Was my wife making an oblong reference to me and my proclivity for pontification? She was inscrutable. I moved on.

"Here's what we do," I said. "Tell the guys in six to spend some quality time with their pals in five. Sell them on the heat in five and the lack thereof in six. Tell them I'm working on it, it'll take me two, three beers tops to figure it out. The people in two and three might experience a slight chilliness. This will be temporary. Might want to give them a heads up. I'll get right on it."

My wife now looked at me dubiously. Would she buy it? She had to. Plumbers were sixty-five bucks an hour, ninety an hour in Stowe.

Five beers later I was on the phone with the heating company. It was 9:30 p.m. and ninety bucks an hour was starting to look like a bargain. I was missing a hockey game and thus far had succeeded only in knocking out the heat to room two.

The heating company sent Don over, a nice, careful guy who really didn't know what he was up against. He kept asking if he could use the phone so that he could speak with Kevin, whom I assumed knew what Don was up against. About 11 o'clock, after succeeding only in dismembering several circulators, he told me Kevin was coming over.

Great. 180 bucks an hour, no hockey game, and I was out of beer. Kevin finally arrived and told me that they needed to replace a part that they didn't have. What Kevin did, though, was rig a by-pass so that at least all the rooms would have heat overnight. I went up to tell the guys in five that half of them could go back into six, but nobody answered the door. I didn't blame them.

By the time I got to bed it was nearly time to get up and make coffee for the skiers. Thank God for the snow. Just another Friday night at the Inn.

Column title: "The Wonderful View from my Window"
Original title: "Wanderings"
Publication date: June 7, 2001

It was one of those fat Vermont mornings that make you wonder what clocks are for. Dollops of mist hung in lacquered sheets over Cady Hill and the promise of rain, spring rain, soft and cool and sweet, stung the air. These are what I call the coffee commercial times, when I fill my mug, take a deep whiff of bean vapor, and check to see if Juan Valdez is hiding around the next corner.

The inn is half full and I'm worried about the guests in Room One. Three girls from Quebec came down for Stowe's version of a pub-crawl: Margaritas at Miguel's, Rolling Rocks at the Rusty Nail, and Mudslides at the Matterhorn. I know because one of them told me last night at 11:30 when she asked me to open a bottle of wine for them. By the time I got back with the corkscrew, she was snoozing in the lobby. Mid-morning and still no signs of activity. I just want to make sure they are out before the charwoman goes in there (we already ran their credit card).

Outside, above, and all around, work continues on the venerable old place. The metal roof has been well received, and now the water comes off it at breakneck speed. Which, we hope, will lead to a decrease in the number of buckets needed to catch the interior drips. The new decks are getting nailed together finally. I go out and survey the quality of the work and think, I could build these myself if I wanted. I just don't have the time. I could, you know.

That reminds me: I just refurbished the boys' room downstairs and I need to deal with the recurring water problems. Insidious, calculating, unpredictable, water finds its way into the basement despite my best efforts. I'm currently considering a giant umbrella with the inn's name emblazoned on it, but I don't think that will fly with the zoning board.

Then there's the breakfast room, the focal point of every inn. When the inn is full, the competition for the two small tables in front of the windows is keen. Guests, previously unknown to one another, now jockey for table position. To secure prime seating, savvy lodgers will sometimes send a scout ahead. Many mornings we'll arrive to find Englishmen, Dutchmen, and mortified Long Islanders squaring off for prime croissant space. What we need is more window seating...another brilliant deduction by Your Innkeeper.

Speaking of window seating, one of the prime spots to eat breakfast has been...embellished. Starlings have built a nest in the eve above one of the window tables. Scratching and frantic chirping emanate from the ceiling from early morning to late evening. I was so concerned about this bothering the guests that I formulated a plan to "remove" them. But much to my amazement, people just love watching the parent bird fly up with a beak full of worms. They sip their coffee and eat their cantaloupe wedges and it absolutely delights them. OK, OK, the starlings live. But as soon as they move out, I'm cementing shut their nest.

Oh I've got ideas. Lots of ideas, lots of coffee, and lots of time to watch the mist drift across the river.

Original title: "Water, water everywhere"
Column title: "Water, water everywhere"
Publication date: June 14, 2001

Quick—think of Stowe. Tell me the first thing that comes to mind. Skiing. (Duh). Snow. Hiking, biking, fine dining. What about water? It's there, but it's probably down on the list, and it probably falls under the heading of "Scotch and water" or "spa at Topnotch." That's not the kind of water I'm thinking about.

Of all the things we thought we'd have to deal with when we became innkeepers, my wife and I never dreamed that water would figure so prominently in our lives. Having made our way to Stowe via Montreal and central Maine, we were prepared for snow. We actually prayed for it. We just forgot that snow, when it warms up, becomes water—and not the stuff you can splash in a rocks glass filled with Mr. Walker.

There was, for openers, the hot tub. Upon seeing the hot tub for the first time, I remarked "That thing would look good filled with concrete, flooded, and frozen to mimic a hockey rink." Then I climbed in. Bubbling hot water took my breath away and melted away the tension accrued from a day spent in Williston. My toes tingled and a permanent smile creased my mouth. The hot tub was cool.

Until we tried to clean the filter. Our hot tub was not one of these new, self-contained deals. This beast was systematic, with its own gas heater and a pump stolen from a nuclear power plant somewhere. The filter was taller than my six year-old son, Seamus, and when it had to be cleaned we took it to the car wash. That messy job done, everything was reassembled, the switch was flicked, and we went to bed. The next morning the hot tub was empty.

After much detection, apprehension, and consternation, we discov-ered that the filter housing had not been secured tightly enough, and when the beast began to circulate, the water had simply squirted out all over the basement floor, flooding the place. Happily, there was a drain in the basement floor. Unhappily, we had to refill the hot tub to the tune of 400 gallons. Next time we had to clean that filter, I went down there and tightened the filter housing with my teeth.

As winter went directly to summer, the icy shroud around the inn let loose rather quickly. Given no choice, water began doing Houdini things, running uphill, jumping gaps, refusing to evaporate—doing anything it could to infiltrate our building. The first line of defense was sandbags.

Then came the wet-vac…till we burned out the motor. Finally we had to move the boys out of their basement bedroom and up into the suite. When they began disassembling their new bedroom (as only little boys can do), I tried reminding them that they were staying in $150 a night digs, but that was like trying to talk dogs off a meat wagon.

With the advent of 80 degree April days, our thoughts turned to the pool. Specifically, what do we do with that big blue square out in the back yard? We knew we had to get it going—it was in all our brochures and on our website. New Yorkers would expect a pool when they got here.

"Fill it with concrete, paint a red line across the middle, run a zambonie over it." That was my advice. I tend to turn holes filled with water into hockey games.

But that wouldn't do in June. So we went down there and pulled the cover off.

Our pool was a biologist's cornucopia. In addition to the scores of bugs living there were at least a half dozen frogs. And there were tadpoles. Thousands and thousands of tadpoles. Maybe millions. "Bazillions," my four year-old son, Brendan, added. I was dumbfounded. Then I had a brilliant idea.

"Listen, honey," I told my wife. "We'll just run a 220 volt line down here, throw it into the pool, then bring the whole thing to a boil. We'll skim everything that floats to the top and bring it down to the Isle de France for their daily special."

What else could I do? I'm not a pool guy. Pool guys wear lots of gold. Pool guys have big round bellies, deep tans, and gray curly chest hair. They stand poolside with a drink in one hand while skimming and daydreaming about their mutual funds.

I still don't know what I'm going to do about all this water. When I close my eyes, visions of sump pumps fill my head. Artesian wells spring to mind. Anything to control all the water around here. I think I'll pray for a drought—until next winter, when I'll surely pray for snow.

Original title: "Zen and the Art of Innkeeping"
Column title: "Zen and the Art of Innkeeping"
Publication date: July 26, 2001

At the crossroads of the journey stands the innkeeper. Situated somewhere between the dull edge of twilight and the sharp refrain of dawn, the innkeeper breeches the two worlds of the traveler: the world of the unknown, and the world of the familiar. Offered is the promise of a warm bed. Implied is the prospect of sincere conversation. Given is that, and more. It's got to be the raison d'être of innkeeping, because it sure isn't the money.

It should not be surprising that there is an element of spirituality to this way we have chosen. Not religion, for that is too organized for what I mean. Rather, a lightness, a reverence for place and time, an acknowledgment of a higher power. And by higher power I mean that place at the end of Mountain Road, the Mecca that draws the pilgrims to our back yard. In the wake of that promise comes the innkeepers, giving the traveler a home and a little bit of time away from their journey so that they may better appreciate, enjoy, and absorb it.

I sometimes refer to this feeling as my innkeeper mojo. Innkeeper mojo is the thing that makes me pull my car over to the side of the road when I see a group of cyclists loaded down with saddle bags on Route 100. Brightly colored, helmeted, bedecked in stretch pants, they're true road warriors. Maps and water bottles occupy the center of their circle as I approach.

True, the first words out of my mouth are, "Do you have a place to stay yet?" But truer still is the spectrum of reasons why I offer them lodging. Their stories surround them like an aura. The easy way their feet grip the road tells me that we are kindred spirits, for what innkeeper isn't also a traveler? We are as interesting as the people we welcome. We know it, but we let the light shine on our guests. It is their moment, and we are happy to share it.

Innkeeper mojo is the thing that comes between other innkeepers when they are sharing. This camaraderie is a very strange thing to become accustomed to, for it seems to contradict logic. But peek under the surface and you'll see it again: the spirit of this place that throws us all uniquely together. Our backyards are mutual and our goals are fairly common. That is why it is not unusual to see innkeepers co-mingling, exchanging ideas—and stories, of course.

Innkeeper mojo is also that thing that rips at me each morning as I drive out of town. I didn't come up here to leave every day, I tell myself. I can see it in the faces of the others that share the road with me. But that is the way it is, for now. Besides, when it gets bad during my workday, I can just look up and see the other side of the Mountain, and then I feel it all come back to me. On weekends we see one another and we understand, because innkeeper mojo transcends innkeeping, just as spirituality transcends religion. We laugh and exchange derogatory tales of commuting and then we quiet down and watch the sun dip below the lush green expanse of our lives.

The patron saint of innkeepers is St. Julian the Hospitaller. His full title is the patron saint of ferrymen, innkeepers, and circus performers. It's not surprising that a medieval Frenchman who relentlessly battled the Saracens during the Crusades should have been assigned such a motley collection to look after. All that traipsing around gave him ample opportunity to experience those positioned "along the way."

That position, that station along the roadside, is what the innkeeper gives. It cannot be stated as pancakes and sausage, or a swimming pool, or even a warm welcome. The innkeeper, much like the writer, transmits. The innkeeper is a conduit for what this place is. We can only hope that a small part of that feeling—call it mojo or call it spirit—is passed along. If we accomplish that, we've done our job.

Original title: "Tire Kickers"
Column title: "Kicking Tires with the Inn Crowd"
Publication date: August 9, 2001

There are many businesses which invite browsing. These business-es, most of them of the retail variety, have many different items for sale, and browsing is actually part of the selling strategy. The idea is to get the shopper in the front door for one thing, then let them discover many other things to buy once they are inside. Many endeavors are launched on this theory. Innkeeping is not one of them.

Before exploring this phenomenon, I'd like to set it up a little with some comparative background. Like the old George Carlin comedy rou-tine about the differences between baseball and football being so radical, so too does there seem to be a wild dichotomy between winter visitors and summer visitors to our region. It can be like night and day.

When the snow flies, winter people lock and load. They set their sights north, they pack up, and they drive. Their approach to their activi-ty is direct and involves very little of what can be called leisure. The exe-cution of their plans begins on Thursday night, when innkeepers are so-licited by telephone for room availability. Skis are strapped to car roofs, woollies are folded into suitcases, and I-89 is filled with powder pilgrims on Friday nights.

These folks are up early on Saturday mornings looking for breakfast. I've often found them wandering around as early as 6 a.m., just staring out at the snow. They take coffee, muffins, croissants, as many carbo-hydrates as you can give them, then they are out the door, robust and bright eyed and smiling. They are the manifestation of energy in the hu-man body. By five they are back in the hot tub, but not to unwind, for now they are formulating plans for dinner. Everything with winter people is calculated, planned, direct. They are a football coach's dream.

The summer traveler suffers from no such restrictions. Summer people are generated from a more languid place, and are blessed with a more languid pace. They are usually not restricted to any one activity when they arrive here, and they have more time than a weekend to do what they want to do. Summer visitors have blurred their boundaries, loosened any constraints, and put on their sandals. You see a lot of toes in the summer up here.

With the shackles of conformity lying in a smoking heap, the summer traveler drifts more than drives. There's a vast peripheral intake they possess that is missing from winter folk. Their field of view is enormous, their urge to browse is insatiable. For retailers, this is a boon. For innkeepers, this can be frustrating.

Here's how the scenario plays out: a car pulls up on a Tuesday evening, usually in the middle of dinner. No one gets out of the car. Two figures can be seen inside, engaged in obvious discussion. Finally someone gets out. Sometimes a man, sometimes a woman, sometimes the driver, sometimes the passenger. Do we have a room available? Private bath? What are your rates? May I see the room? Several rooms are shown, emphasis is placed on the property and the view and the pool and the comfort of the rooms. There is polite grunting, thoughtful mmmm-hmmming. Then comes the inn browser's inevitable line: "I have to go speak to my wife/husband/life partner."

The looker, the person who actually comes in to see the rooms, is usually happy with what they've seen and the value of the place. They become your pro forma sales representative when they go out to talk to the person that did not come in, for it is that person that is holding things up. Sometimes they come back in and book a room. Sometimes there is gesticulating by your sales rep, animated discussion out in the parking lot, fingers run through hair. Then they take off.

In the trade, these people are identified as tire kickers. We've been trying to find a way to prevent this from happening on any kind of a regular basis. One idea is to actually charge a fee for showing prospective lodgers the rooms. Sort of like a mini sightseeing tour, an intra-inn showing charge. Another idea is to actually require any and all persons inter-ested in renting a room to come in and view it—no hanging back shyly in the car while honing your veto power.

It's a summer phenomenon that thankfully doesn't occur all that of-ten. But those are the things you end up obsessing over. Why did they leave? What could I have done differently? That angst is quickly re-placed when that other kind of traveler shows up. Those are the folks that come in off the road dog-tired, go for a dip in the pool, and retire for the evening. They're also the ones who are easy to forget, because they're too easy to remember. Besides, they're probably skiers.

Original title: "Paying Guests"
Column title: "Figuring Out Your Family Values"
Publication date: September 6, 2001

There comes a time in every innkeeper's tenure when someone—a close relative, a distant cousin, an estranged spouse—shows up on your doorstep expecting lodging for nothing and their breakfast for free. When you set up shop in a place as lovely and alluring as Stowe, it's in-evitable. Like all things in life—and here I'm thinking of the half-hour sit-com—these occasions usually stem from a basic misunderstanding, a failure to communicate.

Zooming out for a moment, we see that this problem is endemic not only to the innkeeper, but to all small business people. The attorney who hangs out a shingle soon discovers the hidden legal problems of friends and family. The butcher is surprised to find out just how many vegetari-ans will come out of the closet for a pound of really nice German bologna. And, of course, the masseur who studies all those years to achieve just the right touch finds out how many aching backs dangle from the family tree.

Innkeeping is not immune from this affliction. In many ways, the innkeeper suffers more than other entrepreneurs, because the job of an innkeeper, by definition, is to give so much of oneself, to give so much intrinsic value, that when discounts—familial and otherwise—are expected, the stress of the internal dissension can be monumental. The obvious answer is to adopt a hard line, to take the cue from our nationally historical isolationist past and to adopt a one-price policy: you stay, you pay.

Here's the problem with that solution: we just can't do it. We love meeting and greeting people. We welcome them into our home, for crying out loud. We don't punch a clock. No matter how irritated I am when someone drags me out of bed in the middle of the night, I'm always gracious as I explain that no, I don't have any champagne iced down, and by the way, it's 2:30 in the morning. When we start talking about family, we get all mushy.

Add familiarity to that equation, and things become muddled. After much consternation and observation, discussion and meditation, I think I've reached a middle ground. Anyone with opposing or differing views, ideas, or intuitions are encouraged to share them. Here's the deal: your mom stays for free. Everything else is negotiable.

Let's talk about family and mom. First, a definition. I suggest a list. Sit down with your spouse/partner/innkeeping advisor and define who is and who isn't family. When the smoke clears, take a deep breath and hash out a final list. These are the people who stay for free no matter what. If the bank forecloses on their house Christmas week, you set up cots for them in the living room. If a fire ravages their pad right before the Antique Car Show, tents pop up on your property. These are the people you go to the wall for.

Try and keep this list short. So far, only my mother, my father, and long deceased members of my family have qualified for this list. By long deceased I mean people that never saw the light of the 20th century. This eliminates many gray areas and possible conflicts, such as Great Uncle Wilbur, who survived a power outage in the hospital. For a guideline, try the following: only people who gave birth to you, and people who cleaned up after you regularly as a child, should be allowed this accreditation, which I call Level 1 Status. This status is accorded the people who really loved you because they had no choice. As a child you were awful and you smelled badly, but they believed in you and loved you anyway. People like these deserve the red carpet, ad infinitum. Put them in the nice suite whenever possible.

Level 2 Status goes to brothers and sisters and hockey buddies from college. The theory behind this is that these are the people who love you up to a point, that point being anything that might land them in jail. They're true, but not maniacal. Level 2 Status means that during Christmas week, February vacation, and the entire month of August, you're full, no matter when they call. If these people insist on being up here during one of these peak times, refer them to a major hotel chain or campground.

Finally, we come to Level 3 Status. These are the people that I call the Knots, because they seem to come out of the woodwork when you apply the stain. Where were they when I was painting the inn? When these people call, you'll hear things like, "You remember me...I was that guy that sat behind you in study hall in eighth grade...." These folks get a discount on the mud-season price, but that's it. In other words, nothin' from nothin' leaves nothin'.

The inherent problem with the above guidelines is this: there is always a time when your mom wants to come up when the inn is full. No matter how strict you are, or how motivated you are by the goals of your endeavor as an innkeeper, you are going to have to make that tough decision. And when you are trading income for family, just remember this: there is a direct correlation between face wiping and free rooms during August. Your mother said so.

Original title: "Innkeeping in the New World"
Column title: "Innkeeping in the New World"

Publication date: September 20, 2001

Like many of the columnists here at the *Stowe Reporter*, I had penned a completely different arrangement of words before the tragic events of September 11, 2001, changed the world. It may have been breezy, it may have been funny, and it may even have contained that germ of Zen insight I feel is so necessary to innkeeping and life. To be truthful, I can't remember, because I haven't looked at it since Draft #1. Right now, things like innkeeper's tales seem brutally inconsequential.

I'm not sure if there is an American among us who wasn't touched by this unspeakable terrorist act. If you weren't affected directly, you'll be affected indirectly. Surely, we all changed, and September 11, 2001, will take its grim place among the pantheon of dates that changed our history, alongside December 7, 1941, and November 22, 1963. Even here, at our small roadside inn, we have felt the echo of the blasts in so many ways.

The most blatant result is cancellations. As of this writing, we have only suffered a few. Two were from visitors who would be flying in to Burlington. They expressed fear not only of potential security breaches, but also of the ability to arrive here on their original schedules, given the instant state of flux our domestic carriers were thrown into. I could sympathize instantly. I work for an airline, albeit one that flies boxes instead of folks, and for two days last week, tens of thousands of us stood idly, bravely smiling, the frustration mounting.

The first time I picked up the phone and had to deal with someone on the other end wishing to cancel, I didn't handle it well. I mumbled, bumbled, and stuttered, and by the time I had hung up the phone, I was awash in a cold sweat, as if a ghost had just visited me. I took a breather and tried to come up with a plan. I figured there'd be more of this ahead of us, and while we would ultimately respect the wishes of people in this difficult time, we also strongly believed that it is of paramount importance to "carry on," as our British brothers say.

The next time someone called up to cancel, I replied, "What can I do to change your mind?" This comment caught this woman off guard, and the result was a long and cathartic conversation. In the end she did cancel her stay, but we both felt so much better for our conversation. We were able to bridge a treacherous gap that has grown instantly within the American psyche, a gap that was the real intent of the gutless terrorists on that Tuesday morning. Just by our mutual expressions of honesty and the connection that resulted, we both felt better. We both felt blessed, and she promised to call back when the dust settled. Whether she does or not is not our focus. We're happy we made a friend, which is why we got into this business in the first place.

The next part of my story deals with the night of Tuesday, September 11, 2001. That day was the eighth anniversary of our marriage, and we had planned a night out featuring dinner at—where else—one of Stowe's incredible eateries. By 9:30 or so that morning, both Chantal and I realized that our plans would be marred. About an hour later we understood that we would never think of that day the same way again. As with other tremendous shocks, the first thing the body does is shut down all sensory perception. We both knew that we couldn't *not* celebrate our anniversary. Besides, we were both punch drunk from the unbelievable images we had witnessed all day, and the future of my company was anybody's guess at that point. We're still in love, so we went out to eat.

The mood at a candlelit restaurant is always muted, but that night seemed especially melancholy. Looking back, with the benefit of a week's perspective, it was, perhaps, best that we went out that night. The deepness and completeness of the horror had not set in. For a few hours, our little community of Stowe worked its magic on us, and we were able to disengage our brains, if not our hearts. The people eating at the table beside us had a similar experience. After finishing her desert, the woman sitting close to me let out a long sigh, then said, "I didn't think I was going to get through this, but I'm glad we came."

That's when I truly realized how special this place is, and how lucky we all are to live here. Not because we are insulated from the kinds of losses incurred last Tuesday—certainly none of us escaped untouched in some way. But because here at Stowe we live in—and share—such a magical place. Therapeutic is the word that comes to my mind. I'll travel to the Mountain many times in the upcoming days. I'll need its strength. I'll try and tell that to the folks that don't think they can make it up here to visit us. Then I'll let them make their own decisions. And I know that we will all arrive at a better place, because in Stowe, we're halfway there. God bless America.

Original title: "Horse Latitudes"
Column title: "New Attitudes for Horse Latitudes"
Publication date: October 18, 2001

As the last leaf reluctantly surrenders its final bit of unearthly luminescence and the hordes recede slowly down the interstate in search of something to carry them through the gray urban winter, we can all unclench those perma-smiles, loosen our belts a notch, and enjoy the bounty. Though we are fortunate to live in a place whose natural beauty sustains us for most months out of the year, seasons inevitably change, and there are a few selected months when everything gears down. In the innkeeping business, these breaks in the action are euphemistically referred to as "value season." In my personal lexicon, I refer to this down time as the Horse Latitudes.

The times I'm thinking of run generally from the end of October through Christmas, and then from sugaring season to somewhere around the middle of May. Like astronauts emerging from their re-acclimation chambers after a long flight in space, during these times we find ourselves gasping with the renewed sensation of gravity. Then realization spreads, and we see the time as a transition that must be endured until the next wave breaks.

These "transition months" offer us opportunity to reflect, to recharge our batteries, and most of all, to panic. Just as we panic when hungry/thirsty/exhausted travelers arrive on our doorsteps *en masse*, so too do we find ourselves twitching with bewilderment as the Horse Latitudes drag on. What to do?

One of the more popular pastimes is hiring a carpenter to tackle an impossible renovation around the old place. By impossible renovation I mean an improvement that involves renting a crane, or pouring a concrete foundation. Something, in other words, that will require a professional to separate you from your money. By my calculations, there are a total of three carpenters between the Connecticut River Valley and Lake Champlain, and two of them have retired to the small Pacific atolls they bought, *grace a nous*. So great is the demand for these tradesmen that should you be lucky enough to secure the services of one of them, you will most likely find yourself sharing him with someone else. During the lulls in the seasonal action around here, we all have the same bright idea: Let's add a deck/wing/widow's walk to the place!

If you wait until the last minute to begin a major construction project, the aforementioned panic blooms exponentially. Of course, tardiness in the decision-making department can be overcome by waving gobs of money around. But be warned: that approach risks impugning quality, as contractors try to serve us all by doubling up on jobs. It's advisable to have your builder firmly committed well before the last tracks are cut into Mt. Mansfield, or before Stowe is transformed into Little Bavaria. If you're adding a new roof to the place, for example, you'll want work to begin soon enough to warrant the shoveling of snow off the old roof. That way you can feel good about seeing the project finished before the summer crowds arrive.

Having the opportunity to get together with other innkeepers during thumb-twiddling season confirmed our suspicions: we were all trying to get our projects completed during the lull, and we were all sharing the same builder. This imparted a new twist to our coexistence, creating a polite tension that hadn't been there before. While many of the inns around Stowe are sufficiently unique as to preclude direct competition, as soon as remodeling season kicks in, all bets are off.

We saw the doldrums as a two-pronged problem: we needed major work done around the inn. This would be pricey, we knew, which led to the second part of the problem: how could we defray the cost of this work while still getting heads-in-beds?

My brilliant solution is to organize workshops and have all the participants stay here at the inn. How would that get the work done, you ask? That's the brilliant part. The workshops will literally be *work*shops, featuring power tools, paint brushes, and pressure treated lumber. The name of the seminar will be "Fixing Up An Old Inn." Full Continental breakfast included. With yours truly as foreman and chief animator, the program will stress meeting deadlines, coming in under budget, and attention to detail in all phases of carpentry, electrical wiring, and that old standby of ancient inns, plumbing. Call now for availability.

By the way, for those that don't know, the Horse Latitudes is an area of the Atlantic Ocean between 30 and 35 degrees of latitude that features high barometric pressure and little wind. Early European mariners would be tooling along on their way to the New World when suddenly they would find themselves becalmed. In an effort to overcome their lack of forward progress and avoid a mutiny, they would jettison ballasts, including horses. While I haven't seen anyone around here forcing horses out onto the street, the principle holds true that during slowdowns you have to be forward thinking.

For now that seems tolerable. Given the level of congenital traffic failure we experienced recently the calm is much appreciated. But the wise ones are already waking up to the sound of hammers rapping and diesels idling. The leaves may be the only things falling now, but the skies will soon be blanched with the white stuff, and nobody really wants to look at unfinished projects at Christmas, do they?

Original title: "The Skiing Inn"
Column title: "Fulfilling the Skier's Need for Sharing the Experience"
Publication date: January 24, 2002

In this world, there are some things that have a symbiotic relation-ship, things that just go together: Lennon and McCartney, filet mignon and an '82 Chateau LaFite-Rothschild, Hemingway and adventure. To that list you can add skiing and inns.

By no means is this meant to slight the amenities offered by some of the finer resorts and hotels that are found around world class ski areas like Stowe. Many folks prefer the all-inclusive options, the convenience and choice they offer. But when you stand in the parking lot at the foot of Mt. Mansfield and gaze up at the famous Front Four, the tradition, the oneness, the pure and uncomplicated wildness of the ski experience here invade you.

What does an inn have to offer the powder pilgrims that travel here to pay homage to this spectacular place? Very little, and therein lies the point.

I must confess that skiing is a glue in my life, a common thread that has woven itself throughout, influencing turns and weighing on decisions. It is sinewy and strong and flexible, and it has as much to do with who I am, what I do, and how I got here, as anything else I can think of. I met my wife while we were both ski instructors. We both had a passion for the sport, and skiing has managed to insert itself into our lives right up to our decision to become innkeepers.

The pureness of the skiing spirit has always driven us, has always bound us, and we had a strong vision of what kind of innkeepers we wanted to be. We wanted to have a place that doesn't get in the way of the skier. That doesn't mean that we line'em up on cots in the back hall-way and kick'em out before breakfast. What we were searching for was that comfortable, homey feeling. We wanted to partake of that warm, satisfied glow all skiers have as they sit back and remember that near perfect run they had earlier that day.

That spirit has ruled many of our decisions as innkeepers. It has served not only as an identifying marker, but also as an external manifestation of what kind of lodger you'll even consider. That means that sometimes you lose a little business because folks are looking for something a little different. What we've tried to achieve is something that we think closely approximates our shared dreams, something that reflects the great love we have for skiing in particular, and the outdoors in general. We can't give people everything; we're far too small to offer much more than coziness and ourselves. Today I even talked someone out of booking several rooms with us. To have satisfied their needs, we would have needed three more buildings and far too many hours in front of the planning commission. They were looking for something else, and that's okay. Fortunately there are plenty of great places in Stowe that had what they were looking for, and I was able to steer him in the right direction.

When people come back to us after a day of skiing, they are absolutely aglow with excitement. The Mountain has given them all they need, all that is important to them. We are there when they come home, we trade skiing stories and compare all the different places we've been. Being ourselves as innkeepers has taken a little practice, but we've found our niche. This has been fully evidenced every weekend this winter.

Despite an economy that is supposed to be on its knees, combined with the psychological effects of a war, the faithful are getting in their cars and coming up to ski. In fact, they're tripping over each other. The meteorological peculiarities of this winter—especially coming in the heels of last year's monster snows—need not be retold. Perhaps a contributing factor to this year's enthusiasm is an echo effect from last year.

What that means for us is not as limiting as it sounds. Far from being simply single season folks, we can't wait to get the mountain bikers, and the hikers, and all the other travelers who love to visit this place.

Snow and skiing do not engender a spirit of exclusivity. Rather, they are the reality of a certain combination of things that transcend weather and geography. They are part of a larger spirit, a spirit of humanism that we are so lucky to tap into as innkeepers.

Same as it ever was—and maybe that's the reason. Maybe for skiers all it takes is a great mountain, a little snow, some cold air, and blue skies. Just as innkeepers live for hospitality, so do their lodgers live for that pure, uncomplicated adventure that comes with a ski weekend. As long as they keep coming up the road with that childlike look of excitement across their faces, we'll be here with a place for them to hang their skis and put their feet up.

Original title: "The Innkeeper as Caricature"
Column title: "Personal Growth: An Innkeeper Evolves to Caricature"
Publication date: February 7, 2002

It didn't happen all at once; these things are, by definition, evolutionary in speed. Nor did it give off any signs that might have been recognizable, a warning to alert me to what lay around the next bend. What is was, I'm learning, was inexorable. What it is, I'm trying to say, is my slow descent—or ascent—into a caricature of myself as innkeeper.

From the distance of time, I can tell you only how I suspect it happened. I'm more of a titular innkeeper, I must confess. I deal with all the testosterone-laced issues, like electricity, wood splitting, and anything involving a circular saw. It is my wife, my much better half, who deals with the vascular goings-on, like money, food, and everything else that doesn't involve a circular saw. Freed from so much responsibility, I am able to build fires in the fireplace and stare at the flames for hours, or take slow walking tours of the property with my hands in my pockets.

It dawned on me last weekend, when we had a crowd from Harvard staying with us. A brilliant lot they were, oozing with brains, yet I watched in amazement as they struggled to execute a left hand turn into our driveway. After a crying jag and some quick hand signals, they docked without further incident, then discovered that it was the middle of winter up here. They disembarked and found themselves confronting the innkeeper, who at the time was wielding an ax and conducting a seminar on colorful language out in front of the inn. Knotty wood does it every time.

Nevertheless, without the proper context in which to place my blaze red Irish face and razor-sharp ax, this gang of asphalt and neon denizens looked aghast to see me. I immediately understood their concerns, and I smiled, and tipped my hat, and said, "Welcome to Stowe. If you've got any wood that needs splitting, you're just in time." I playfully brandished my ax, which repelled them collectively the way bright lights clear out the pub after last call. I knew then it would be a fun weekend.

But what really surprised me was my deadpanned—dare I say laconic?—verbiage. Where did that come from? I asked myself. It happened again, later, while one of our guests watched me methodically lay the fire. While none among us can deny that a little bit of performance doesn't slip in while being closely watched, I tried to concentrate on my work, even as I embellished the crumbling of newspapers. When I was finished, I stepped back and admired my handiwork, a truly flammable concoction of newspapers, kindling, and selected dry quarters of wood, all of it begging for a little ignition.

"Are you going to light it now?" my guest asked demurely.

"Well, I'm not going to frame it," I replied. She thought that was funny.

And that's when it hit me. That's when I realized that I was no longer a Dad, a writer, a courier, a jack of all trades and master of none. I had become a character built for the amusement of flatlanders. I was becoming part of the local color that brings folks up here in the first place. Let's face it, if this place were full of cynical suburbanites, no amount of vertical drop would keep them coming.

I thought about this for a moment. I could suddenly recall other witticisms I had been producing lately. In November we had some folks up who remarked that lots of people were wearing blaze orange while hiking and biking in the woods. When I explained to them it was hunting season, and that people were just being safe, they were shocked. They wanted to know if they would be mistaken for deer and shot at if they went for a hike that afternoon.

"Not unless you grow a rack of antlers and a white tail," I told them.

That solidified the full circle for me. When we arrived here, our own similarly innocent questions were met with replies that combined the edge of disdain with just enough humor to make you wonder. Questions like "Where's the dump?" were met with answers like "At the end of Dump Road." And now here I was, returning the favor, so to speak.

The whole thing made me smile, for that is one of the enjoyable benefits of innkeeping. You become more than just a person handing out room keys, or a toilet scrubber. You animate, enliven, and entertain. You advise, console, and conject. And when you begin to inject your personality into things, to color your canvas with the freedom that comes from the comfort of home, then you start to move beyond innkeeper and into the realm of "local color."

Meanwhile, my guest was waiting for me to light the fire. I struck a match, tossed it into the fireplace, and smiled at the dramatic "whoosh" of the blaze.

"Wow," she said. "I guess you know what you're doing."

"Either that or I just like playing with matches," I answered.

Original title: "TV, or not TV"
Column title: TV, or not TV"
Publication date: February 21, 2002

TV, or not TV, that is the question: Whether 'tis nobler in the mind to suffer the slings and arrows of the cell phone generation, or to take arms

271

against a sea of satellite dishes and wires, and, by opposing, lose business. To cable TV, to wire rooms with phones—who knows what to do?

While I'm sure the Bard never dreamed his prose would be co-opted to express the frustrations of so pedestrian a pursuit as innkeeping, so too am I sure that he was never confronted with the Byzantine choices innkeepers face when it comes to choosing which technologies you wish to include in your establishment for the convenience and comfort of your guests: Cream or sugar? Oatmeal or eggs? Color cable television or a chair out on the back deck?

Small innkeepers approach the television question with a wide range of emotions, from trepidation to ambivalence to animosity. Because so much of what you do in this métier is a reflection of your personal philosophy, you can't hide your decisions. What you put into your inn says not only what kind of person you are, but what kind of traveler you cater to. With that in mind, we beg the television question.

Though considered still a babe by the standards of the grizzled and savvy veterans of innkeeping in these parts, our inn has already confronted the heinous television question enough for me to wince at the mere mention of the word. What we have decided is that cable television in the rooms is viewed by the gentle traveler in the same light as the pool and air-conditioning: you need to have it on the sign out front to get them in the door, but once they are here, they could care less about any of it. In fact, I'm thinking of replacing our pool with a giant picture of a pool that I can unroll out on the back lawn whenever someone pulls in the driveway.

With the electronic arrival of the Olympics these past two weeks, the question has again come to the fore. Last week we had to break the news to some stunned snowmobilers that the tiny black and white telly in their room only picked up one and a half channels, neither of which televised the commercials that squash network coverage of the Olympics, nor the Games themselves. Luckily they were amenable to viewing the Games at one of our town's pubs. But the situation got me going again on the cable television question.

In the name of research I called an innkeeper friend who has satellite television. The response I got, while refreshing, was eye opening. Apparently, the TV question is a no-win situation. I was told tales of customers unfulfilled by their cathode ray offerings. If ESPN was offered, someone would undoubtedly complain that they didn't carry ESPN2. And here's the real kicker: the satellite system doesn't offer the network that carries the Olympics, so we're not alone in our stock of customers wanting biathlon with breakfast, hockey in the hot tub, and figure skating by the fire.

What it comes down to is this: Who are you? What do you want? I've used this space to say this before, and I'll say it again, we really love this thing called innkeeping, and we do it because of the people. And the kind of folks that stay with us share more than a love of all the beauty that Stowe has to offer. They are willing to risk a little bit of themselves, just as we are, in the hopes that they will take away something that you can't save on film. Part of that is this place, and its dinky black and white televisions.

When I was a boy, my parents used to take my brother and me up to Twin Mountain, New Hampshire, snowmobiling. As big a thrill as that was, the most fun we had was late at night, watching the tiny black and white television that came with the cabin. We would stay up just to watch the late local news, listening to the newscasters talk about all those northern New Hampshire things that sounded as exotic as Ecuador to us.

There's still a little bit of that in those old black and white televisions we have in our rooms. I like to imagine somebody sitting in Room 2 on the edge of the bed trying to tune in Channel 22 so they can get the late weather report. I imagine them bathed in the fuzzy gray light, squinting, cursing in sotto voce, cajoling the set, holding the antenna at just the right declination, until the weatherman comes into focus long enough to utter that magical word: "Snow."

I can't sell that kind of experience on our website. Nor can I hang it on the sign our front (all my square inches are used up). I can only hope that when I book a room and that questions arises, that maybe they'll remember why they chose a cozy little inn in the first place. And maybe when they get here, they'll take one look around and forget.

Original title: "Terroir and Two-stroke Nirvana"
Column title: "Terroir and Two-stroke Nirvana"
Publication date: May 16, 2002

In France, "terroir" is a big deal. Terroir describes everything about the particular area in which a vineyard is located: the microclimate, the topography, orientation, and the soil itself. So focused on terroir are some people that grape variety is almost an afterthought. Recent local mechanical events ignited this French memory of mine.

As we pilot this inn through the swells and swales of one season and another, a certain philosophy emerges, asserting itself the same way that terroir defines the kind of wine that can be produced in a certain area. So absolute is the power of terroir that the same grapes grown under similar conditions in other parts of the world yield startlingly differ-ent wines. The same truth holds for innkeepers.

The philosophy I speak about is the feeling we as innkeepers get in this place at this time doing this thing. I have accepted that there will be triumphs and tragedies, and I do so while keeping my specific sight fo-cused on the horizon, and my peripheral sight focused on everything else. It's the kind of stoicism that keeps the decks steady underfoot. Unfortunately, a rash of mechanical frustrations has conspired to colorize my vocabulary and test my ratchet memory.

Last weekend, amidst an inn full of guests, the oven gasped its last breath when the door refused to close. That meant that in order to bake bread we either had to find another stove, or raise the temperature of the kitchen to 400 degrees. Luckily, both my father and my brother were visiting, and when it comes to fixing, they shame me. Alas, no matter how long the three of us lay on the kitchen floor grunting and poking, we

274

could not fix that door. We resigned ourselves to cooking al fresco—gas grill and open pit—until we could decide the stove's fate. That was just the beginning of the trials.

As days lengthen, so does grass, turning a young man's thoughts lightly to those of mowing. Modern mowing is achieved in three stages: riding tractor, for the multiple acres; push mower, for the crucial front lawn; and power trimmer, for that fresh barbered look. Since the front lawn is what everybody sees, I decided to disinter the push mower.

I won't lie and say I didn't know the flywheel on the push mower was kaput. It happened last September, at the end of mowing season, and I remember clearly my reaction then: I'll fix this thing in the spring. So last week found me diligently applying my talents in the field of small engine repair. Here's where philosophy comes in.

I have no talent for small engine repair. But, I reason, a mower is a small mechanical device that was logically designed to accomplish certain things, notably, spin a sharp blade two inches off the ground. I also reason that I am intelligent and thoughtful, and by applying my calm logic to the problem of the mower, I would achieve Briggs & Stratton nirvana. I quickly removed the flywheel housing, wrapped the new pull cord, replaced everything, and attempted to start the mower.

That's when I remembered I had only ten percent of my right arm to work with. So I called Chantal, and she tried to start the mower, but succeeded only in straining her rotator cuff. Shelving that problem, I turned to the riding mower. It could be pressed into service up front and combined with the trimmer to achieve grassy presentability. But when I turned the key in the ignition, a dead battery foiled my philosophy and me once again. True, the battery could be jump-started, but that was not possible right away. I turned to the trimmer.

Our gas powered trimmer is a beauty, and it has a certain something that neither of the other two small engines had going for it, something I was counting on to save the philosophical day for me: newness. It was less than a year old and still shiny and as I added fuel I hoped it would reward me with the ear splitting sound of a two-stroke music. I primed the fuel into the engine, laid the beast on the ground and braced it with my right foot, and with my left hand yanked the starter cord.

On the third tug the trimmer buzzed to life with its distinctive, high-pitched drone. I picked it up quickly and regulated the throttle. Then I raised it triumphantly over my head, dancing a jig (or maybe it was a reel) and shouting "Wooo hooo!" I waved to Chantal and pranced around, annihilating anything green that had the misfortune of appearing before me. When I had adequately marred the yard, I calmed down and reflected on this small victory. My terroir and my philosophy were seam-lessly blending into one, and it felt pretty good.

Original title: "Gentle Traveler"
Column title: "Ode—or Owed—to the Gentle Traveler"
Publication date: May 30, 2002

There are times when I sit down to write these words and something entirely removed from the thoughts in my head makes it onto the page. I'm not lying when I tell you that when I began typing (38 words ago) something completely different was poised in my head, begging to make the quick run from brain to pen. For this phenomenon you may thank Gentle Traveler.

I have referred to Gentle Traveler in this space many times before. Gentle Traveler is the moon and the sun and the caprice of the stars. Gentle Traveler is at once demanding and accommodating. To put it in baseball lingo, Gentle Traveler is a big league curve ball, so beautiful to behold, so hard to hit. Gentle Traveler is to the innkeeper what the muse is to the artist: inspiration, motivation, frustration.

Gentle Traveler came to us in multiples this weekend. They were a group, several families traveling together, and there was nothing gentle about them. They invaded us and took us over. We heard them before we saw them, a low rumble punctuated with shrill chirps. There were sixteen of them, and they made us wish Stowe hosted a biker week.

Our first inkling of trouble came when the door to the kitchen burst open and several small children tumbled in. They immediately began grabbing anything and everything their fingers could close around, as if this were the first venue in which they could test their opposable thumbs. I firmly but gently herded them out, pointing out the private sign on the door and telling them that this part of the property was off limits.

After checking in, the group receded from the lobby and I could see them pouring outside, attacking the hammock, hanging off the hot tub. Wildlife fled before their advance, and the leaves on the trees tried to twist themselves back into their buds. Our peace was fleeting; they soon returned and now they needed dinner reservations. A rundown of Stowe's 60 restaurants was given, details were relayed to the group by an emissary, discussions were held, arms were waved, shoulders were shrugged, more questions were asked.

And there were special requests. Someone was having a birthday, and they wanted a cake. Could we help? Of course. We picked up the Cake Phone, which has a direct connection to Cake Lady, and what followed was a scene from an Abbott and Costello movie: Could Cake Lady supply a cake? Yes. Ah, but could she produce this cake in the form of a dinosaur? We waited...Yes, it could be done. A velociraptor? Eyes were rolled. But yes, it was possible. Now the request changed. Not a dinosaur...a Power Ranger. The blue guy. Cake Lady said yes.

While all this was going on, I thought perhaps we were trying too hard. These people were getting high season effort for the value season rate. To be fair to our Gentle Travelers, they were quiet gracious, thanking us and inviting us to the birthday party on Monday. I looked skeptical. I didn't see how we were going to avoid this group's party in our small inn. But they weren't finished.

When we went to clean the rooms we were greeted with destruction. The rooms themselves weren't so bad, but the common room and sitting area were trashed. Pizza boxes were strewn, plants overturned, books scattered, personal belongings abandoned, and mud obscured the floor. It looked as if a goat herder had overnighted his animals in the space. To top it off, the lock on the door to Room 4 was broken. I sent Chantal in through the bathroom window and it would have been funny had it not been a sunny Sunday afternoon. Abracadabra, I'm a locksmith.

To survive the darkness, this situation required a look at the bright side. At no time did I fear for my safety, or the safety of my family. I also had no concerns at all that the bike rental shop they invaded on Sunday afternoon would ever forget them. And it gave me great pleasure to bask in the knowledge that come Monday they would head home, full of fond memories.

Gentle Traveler can surprise you like a lover. But Gentle Traveler can also push you a bit off your balance, force you to adapt and impro-vise. Though we all love to have those low maintenance guests who check in, make their own beds, then tell you what a lovely time they had, it's the other kind which forge your identity. They are the big league curve balls that you'd love to sit on and hammer out of the ball park. But sometimes it's better to lay down a bunt. After all, Gentle Traveler should be kept off balance, too.

Original title: "Innkeeping in Paradise"
Column title: "Innkeeping in Paradise"
Publication date: June 13, 2002

How many of you have a job where this can happen: A customer walks in to your establishment, looks at your T-shirt, smiles, and begins singing "Cheeseburger in paradise, Heaven on earth is an onion slice, not too particular, not too precise, I'm just a cheeseburger in paradise."

There aren't too many bad things you can say about a business transaction based on a Jimmy Buffett song. There are no accounting firms misleading investors. There are no unethical leaders spouting utopian slogans. And there are no lines loaded with angry customers all demanding service for impossible issues. On the surface, it sounds like a win-win situation. But like any other endeavor, innkeeping has its "moments."

The above described incident is true. I was wearing my "Jimmy Buffett Domino College" T-shirt when a guest checked in. He took one look at me, bedecked in my bright yellow Teva sandals, my parrot head top wear, and my peeling sunburn, and knew he had made a connection. His kids thought he was out of his mind, but I get the feeling that they might have reached that conclusion long before they checked into our place.

Welcome to summer in Stowe. In the past, I have used this space to lament the capriciousness of the summer traveler. They stagger into town, not really sure why they are here, and around dinner time, begin making the rounds of the "Vacancy" places. They are not really sure what they want. A suite? Yes, but does it have a big living room? A pool? But there are so many stairs to get down there. Air conditioning? Absolutely. But those are window units...don't you have central air. (This is Vermont—take a guess.)

If you are able to nurse them past all the superficial objections, price is always an issue. No matter what the price, it is always too much. "What does that include?" is inevitably the question. "You mean besides breakfast, use of the hot tub, the pool, exercise equipment, the invaluable company and conversation of my wife in the morning, the peaceful views across the river to the mist-draped hillside where the deer feed languidly, the playful meanderings of the woodchuck family, whose lives have been spared for your amusement, and all the ice you can stuff into your gin and tonics?"

That's what I want to say...sometimes. Often our "tire kickers" can be quite charming and polite and as gracious with us as we are with them. Delivery is everything, and we don't mind playing "20 Questions" with most folks. But sometimes the road wears people down, and they don't know why they ended up in Stowe. They're looking for something that we don't have—and by "we" I mean all of us. They are looking for some kind of chain food store, some kind of standardized experience that won't scare them, or force them out of their comfort zone.

Flexibility becomes important. For every potential lodger who comes in humming "Margaritaville," three others come in humming "Taps." There is very little you can do about the tough sells. In fact, we have evolved a way for dealing with them: we encourage them to leave. It's a matter of economics. One fussy customer on a Tuesday night is not nearly as viable as filling that last empty room on a Thursday or Saturday night. While every penny counts, so too does quality, and the presence of quality cannot be overstated. What is quality? Quality is a condition of being from which all else flows. As it relates to innkeeping, quality can be directly tied to success, both in the long and short term.

As innkeepers, we would rather have one really positive guest in lieu of three or four that are just settling for what we have. One really positive guest will eventually come back, or tell someone else, and that is what quality is all about. In this town and in this business, service is at a premium. Truth in service will establish quality, and that will translate into success. It's a good paradigm for these times, when so much of what we believe to be true is co-opted in the name of profit. For us, it's not something new, just the way we live our lives.

The summer season so far has been as surprising this year as it was last year. When we didn't know we were in a recession, our lack of experience and lack of business teamed up to befuddle us. With another year under our belt—and with all the confidence accrued subsequently—we can more accurately anticipate our business and hone our skills and expectations. And when someone comes in and begins singing a chorus of Jimmy Buffett, that will be our gravy, and we'll just enjoy it and sing along.

Original title: "Everybody's Dream"
Column title: "Running an Inn is Everybody's Dream, Right"
Publication date: August 8, 2002

Sometimes our life perspective is achieved only through the triangulation of travel itself. I suppose it is what a lot of summer folks are looking for when they throw the game plan out the window and just head north with nothing more than a map and the memory of a little place they stayed at years ago. The realignment that they seek comes from viewing themselves from a different angle. It can be therapeutic or cathartic, revelatory or confusing. Innkeepers are not immune from it, either.

The event around which I orbited last weekend was my 20th high school reunion. For me it would be the first reunion I attended, having been *ex patria* for the others. These things, as many of you will attest, tend to take on a life of their own as the date approaches, and on the ride down to the town of my matriculation I was trying to devise ways to couch what it is I really do.

Armed with the evidence of my past—reprints of published stories and articles, brochures from the inn, pictures of the family, receipts, a well stamped passport—I bravely stepped back in time to the crucible of my adulthood. What happened was not unexpected, but nice anyway. I can now safely say that running an inn is not a real mainstream thing to do. Turns out that it's also what a lot of the people I grew up with would like to be doing: "It's always been my dream to do that." Of course I tried to dissuade them.

It's not the competition I fear. Rather it was out of a sense duty to old friends that I framed my ebullient assessment of innkeeping with the harsh realities of the job. For example, many people were blissfully unaware that the room had to be cleaned between guests. When that was explained away with the wave of a hand, I gave more details.

281

"No, you don't understand," I said. "You have to clean everything. And one of the subsets of everything is the toilet. Think about it." Thoughtful gazes turned sour as personal experiences were grafted onto potential duties while I nodded and emphatically raised my eyebrows.

Most of the time that was enough to cause pause, but if it wasn't, I could call upon a plethora of perplexities: basic wiring, roof shoveling, dinner time tire kickers, high maintenance guests, water and gravity, the phone, plumbing, plumbing, plumbing. When I thought I had gone far enough, I switched gears to dreamy and began waxing rhapsodic about the quality of life that all of us, not just the innkeepers, enjoy up here, which usually lead to one of the great innkeeping paradoxes.

While dropping off some film for developing the other day I saw a friend in the parking lot. We got to talking about vacations and about how all you have to do when you live in Stowe is open up your back door and you are on vacation. It was a subject that came up during the reunion, and to a certain extent it is true. The reality, however, is slightly different, and that's where the paradox is born.

As innkeepers we continually sing the virtues of this place and time. It's tune written long before we came, and one certain to be chorused long after we are gone. Through it all the land will endure. That spirit of transience was what I tried to convey to my old friends last weekend. Just as the traveler passes through our lives in 24 hour intervals, so too do we pass through the time of this geography and meteorology, renting a tiny fraction of its final reality. Sometimes that thought was clouded by beer and smoke and pleasant confab. But sometimes I would find someone staring intensely out across the harbor as I spoke, their reality briefly suspended by an old friend who deigned to change their perspective.

I don't yearn to trade places with anyone. And to paraphrase an old fishing idiom, the worst day in Stowe is still better than the best day almost anywhere else. But the nature of the business is almost defined as passing, in one direction or another. I was pleased to have achieved a certain measure of uniqueness among so many wildly creative and successfully unique classmates. To my amazement, nobody seemed really surprised by my news, which says a lot about how well my friends knew me, and maybe how little I knew myself.

With my outlook freshly re-minted I returned home, exhausted and talked out, but with enthusiasm and peace freely mingling. Though it was not a crisis of faith that gave me new views on what we do, the results were similar. So if you see me humming away while buying up all the drain cleaner, you might attribute it to the recent sale of a manuscript, or a large booking for a critical weekend at the inn. Or you just might remember that sometimes we all need a little adjustment of the focal plane to realize that we're on the right track.

If necessity is the mother of invention, then invention is the result of communal effort. Every successful person needs someone else standing behind them, someone to support them, someone to at least tell them how great they are. Throughout much of my writing career here in Vermont, my major domo has been the Stowe Reporter. And when I needed a place to promote my new book, the Reporter stepped up and gave me ink and paper and circulation.

As I went through the perambulations of trying to pre-sell copies of a short story collection that didn't exist yet, I turned myself into a P.T. Barnum character, a literary huckster, inventing myriad ways to promote myself and my unborn book. One of the first things I did was to email Biddle Duke, publisher of the Stowe Reporter. I explained to him what was going on, that I was looking for a forum, and I proposed several things that involved the newspaper. First I suggested advertising. I imagined a big corner of the paper devoted to some minimalist ad that suggested true literary genius lurking in the village of Stowe. Biddle didn't like that idea; he didn't want to see me spend money on something that might not generate real sales. Next I proposed an interview in one of the regular features called Ten Questions. He thought that was okay, but it would be a one-shot deal, and not the kind of exposure I really needed. How about another column? I proposed a semi-regular column chronicling the trajectory of the process I was going through with the publication of the book. It would be creative and expository, a narrative that gave the reader insight into my experience, while gently promoting me and the book. And so An Author's Road was born.

As you may have guessed, these kinds of things end up being cathartic. By writing about the thing I was enduring, I gained the kind of awareness that leads to enlightenment. It was a process akin to the Goddard experience, where the journey becomes the point of the experience. Writing the columns for An Author's Road did more than promote my book. It did more than record a moment in time. It brought me to a fuller understanding of my place in the writing world, it brought me closer to knowing myself as a person and a writer. Through the reflection, through the frustration, I grew. Being able to see that growth allowed me to give greater context not only to the book, but to me as a writer. So here, in order of publication, are the columns of An Author's Road.

An Author's Road: The Columns

September 28, 2006:
"The Genesis of Book"

The story I was going to tell was the story of how my book came to life. It should be easy, right? Just think back to that first morning, when I sat down with my pipe and my tea, gazing out across the river where the mist hung low. Or maybe I could tell how I hunched over my old Royal typewriter, a burned out cigar clenched between my teeth, glass of bourbon by my side, banging away into the night. But I can tell you none of that, because there's no beginning to writing a book. And worse, there seems to be no end. Like life, books happen, unfolding in surprising ways, growing like children, stretching through the writer like time.

The story I can tell is a writer's story, for in that story is embedded the story of the book, its conception, its writing, its imminent publication. That story—the relationship of the writer to the work—represents the inner workings of any piece of writing: there is no story, only character. Only characters, with their decisions, actions, and reactions, make stories. If you're writing about a red wall, then whatever happens to the red wall becomes the story, because the red wall is the character. If you're using the red wall as a symbol, then you're the character, and whatever you do, whatever happens to you becomes the story. So it is with the story of the writing of the book. The book is the result of the actions of the character, and that character is the writer—in this case, me. But at some point, something happened, and that's where the story of this book begins.

So we'll pick a point: six months after I moved up here with my family to become innkeepers, our first spring after our first winter in Stowe, and I was miserable. I was working full-time for FedEx Express, gone before sunrise, rarely home in the light, completely detached from the reason I came here. And worse, I wasn't writing. After scratching out a writing career that included dozens of short story publishing credits, hockey writing, publishing a novel—two novels—on line, I was flat. Not blocked, just empty. Thinking I could finally turn my attention to the inn, I informed FedEx I'd only be available in the mornings. But what I really turned my attention to was writing.

I wrote a story about being an innkeeper. More of an article. I sent it to the Stowe Reporter, and to my surprise, they jumped on it. They really liked it. They wanted more. Huh, I thought. Maybe there was something here. I called the column Innsights, and for the next fifteen months, there was something. On a bi-weekly level there were install-ments in the pains of trying to get a little inn off the ground. But there was something bigger going on, a meta-story, a plot arc comprising not just the inn, but the innkeepers, their guests, and the writing.

When Innsights ended, I almost thought I was back where I started. I almost thought, "Well, here we go again." I was doing everything I had to do, nothing I wanted to do. I started writing another novel, but I got stuck halfway through it. I hated the story, hated the characters, and I kept trying to kill them off. I tried to drown one guy, but an air pocket in the broken hull of a lobster boat saved him. I backed a bulldozer over another character, but he slid between the tracks. The characters of that failed novel existed to mock me. But then I heard something else com-ing from them: they were calling out for help. The guy I tried to drown told me not to take it so hard, and to try and do something else with my writing.

But what? I wasn't a journalist, and I couldn't get my fiction through the slush piles of New York for anyone to look at. And then something happened that caught my attention. My brother-in-law, the same age as me, went to graduate school. If he could, why couldn't I? And in a flash, the MFA in Creative Writing rose from the ashes of my writing mess and spread its wings. All prose writers harbor this secret fantasy. Earning an MFA opened all kinds of opportunities, both creative—the MFA qualifies your work to editors—and practical. Because it's a terminal degree, and teaching forms a significant part of the degree requirement, opportunities in the education field would become available. Teaching. Writing. Teaching writing. I was drunk on the thought. And there was more. To graduate, you had to produce a complete work, be that a screenplay, a novel—or a short story collection.

I started thinking about what I'd write even before I'd talked about the whole thing with my wife. I knew it would be a short story collection, and like the early stages of the formation of our solar system, I began to see the individual planets taking shape. And that's where the story of this book begins. But first, I had to get into graduate school. Or maybe I should say, first I had to figure out a way to pay for graduate school. It didn't worry me. Money, to a writer, is just another character to manage.

October 12, 2006:
"A Collection is Born"

Where does a writer look for a graduate writing program? Ignorance helped me stay local in my search. First, I looked up the road, to UVM. But they offered only a Master's of English, not an MFA. Their application process looked traditional, a little impersonal, reminiscent of my time at another large school, the University of Maine. I pictured myself hustling from my job to the school, spending even more time away from the inn. The thought made me frown.

So I looked again, and I discovered Goddard College, on the same road as the one that led to UVM, but in the opposite direction. Two things convinced me to apply to Goddard. First, their MFA in Creative Writing program was highly regarded within the writing world, known for turning out accomplished writers. They had distinguished alumni (David Mamet, Walter Mosely), but what appealed to me was their philosophy. Their commitment to diversity—diversity of not just students, but of thinking—addressed something lacking in my writing. Second, Goddard pioneered the low-residency program, where students attend classes and workshops during an intensive nine-day period at the beginning of the semester, then return home to complete their work. For someone like me, it was perfect.

Once accepted into the program, I had to figure out what I was going to write. In *Mystery and Manners*, Flannery O'Connor said "Anybody who has survived his childhood has enough information about life to last him the rest of his days." As I considered what I'd be writing over two years of graduate school, that sentiment crystallized within me. Sometimes it felt like I hadn't survived childhood at all.

Through years of freelance writing, I'd developed into a capable professional, able to handle creative nonfiction as well as fiction. But I knew I lacked something, the very thing that had sabotaged my ill-fated novel, the thing that kept me wedded to the slush piles. In my heart of writer's hearts, I knew its name. It's what almost every writer wrestles with in the name of art: self. I knew I had to creatively engage my past, not to exorcise any demons, but to return to the place where my writing was born. Only through that self-evaluation would I be able to tap the truth of my writing.

There's a section on the application to Goddard College's MFA in Creative Writing program that asks you to articulate what you hope to gain from your graduate school experience, and how your work will enrich the community. I knew I'd be working on a short story collection, but how it affected the community eluded me. Like many tasks a writer doesn't understand, I filed it away, and trusted that my process—that mysterious way writers metabolize life into fiction—would sort it out.

As it buried itself within me, that question began to nourish my writing. Choosing a subject is not generally on an author's laundry list before sitting down to write; nor is choosing a story. Usually, the story chooses the writer, becoming so insistent that we find ourselves writing just to shut the muse up. I immediately began seeing—and hearing—characters. They were the voices from my past, but they weren't my past. They were some synthesis that not only managed to avoid plagia-rizing the truth, but to transcend it. They were the things I knew.

The first story I wrote that first semester, "The Natural History of the Bear," would become the final story in the collection called *Name the Boy*. In a way, it's the signature story of the collection, still the most deeply affecting for me, and it set the tone for the rest of my writing. I followed that story very quickly with a story bearing the working title "Red Sox Story." Looking back, I can see the tragedy these two stories played out on each other, two fraternal twins with only enough resources to sup-port one. One would have to go, and it would be up to the loser to demonstrate why the winner survived. In the end, "Red Sox Story" was more of a groove than a story, an emotional thrust of dark purple bruises. It highlighted all the successful traits of its brother.

"The Natural History of the Bear" came out almost fully formed. Like all my stories, it went through myriad polishes and rewrites, but the changes were always cosmetic, more tinkering than overhauling. It's a story about a boy's fears and a family's dysfunction, and how terrible things can happen with nobody to blame—a theme that eventually per-meated the entire collection. With the death of "Red Sox Story" I could see the direction my writing would take during my graduate studies.

But the most important lesson that first story taught me was about theme. In my entrance essay for Goddard, I wrote about the father and son relationship, how important it was not only for boys and their fathers, but for society as a whole. I felt that relationship had been treacherously destabilized in our modern world, and the topics of my writing would ex-plore those consequences. "The Natural History of the Bear" demon-strated that my art could be applied in real terms. I was on my way, but first I had to survive two years as a full-time graduate student.

October 27, 2006:

"Finding Balance in Craft"

I've written several novels, and published a couple of them online in the late 90s, when online publishing was going to be the wave of the future. Instead of great surfing, the tide went out. But like many unpleasant experiences, something good came of it: I returned to the form that truly inspired me, the short story. Sometimes it takes a tragedy—like no one reading your novels—to find your way. Until that happens, the urge to write a novel, become famous and tap into what we're told is one of the seminal American dreams is overpowering.

I remember wanting to be a successful novelist so badly that I once deconstructed John Grisham's novel *The Firm*. Page by page, scene by scene, I wore out the paperback edition, summarizing, analyzing, looking for something constant, the way a scientist searches through a microscope, the way an astronomer searches the stars. When I finished pulling that mega best seller apart, I almost screamed.

There was nothing there.

I thought I was crazy. I must have missed something. With apologies to Mr. Grisham, I couldn't find anything that made sense to me. The characters were briefly drawn, almost caricatures. The novel was plot-derived. The style of writing was superficially engaging. Yet I thoroughly enjoyed reading the book. It hooked me, and I read it in a day or two. Why couldn't I write like that? Of course I could write like that, but it was too painful for me, because it wasn't me. Money and sales don't define success for a writer. Only when the artist can look into his heart and render that on the page in a way that moves others will he begin to understand what makes his writing successful and satisfying. The experiences with Grisham and my novels played an important part in my development, because they committed me to short fiction even before I knew it.

Writing a short story collection for a creative thesis is almost ideal. During each semester, I was able to write three to five new stories and get detailed feedback on them from my advisor. Since short stories are complete dramatic actions, the lessons I learned were concentrated and applicable across other genres. This gave me the direction with which I could aim my larger theme, that of the father and son relationship. It also allowed me to create a diverse reading list. For example, studying Chekhov is a must for a short story writer; but that led to discovering other Russian authors, like Ivan Tugenev, whose novel *Fathers and Sons* not only provided lessons on how to approach characters in a specific relationship, but also provided me with examples of how to use nature as a character. The use of nature as a character was important to my collection because the setting for most of the stories—a small fishing village—played as large a role as any of the people.

As my collection came together, I still didn't think of it that way, as something whole. Inside, I had something driving me, the desire to reveal the complex relationships of boys to their fathers in the new world. As we've evolved over the past sixty years, our society's family dynamic has changed radically. When I was ten years old in 1975, my parents divorced. I was the first person I knew with divorced parents. I wanted to explore this fictionally, through the point of view of the father and son relationship. And by doing so, I wanted to explore me, as a person, as a writer, as a father, and as a son. I wanted to disinter the voices that had lived within me all these years.

The best way to explain my mindset during the creation of the collection that would ultimately become *Name the Boy* is to return to Flannery O'Connor, who has been instrumental in my literary development. Of the matter that inspires your writing she said, "When you write a story…your beliefs will be the light by which you see, but they will not be what you see and they will not be a substitute for seeing." O'Connor's point was that while we are all in what we write, we need to find the craft to express it.

Discovering that craft was what Goddard was all about. I accumulated stories throughout my first two semesters. I wrote and rewrote, I sacrificed my little literary darlings for the sake of the story. I developed excruciating neck pain. But I still didn't see a collection coming together. And the most important thing I learned during that first year might have had nothing to do with craft. It had to do with trust, acquiring a patience that would allow me to stay focused and secure in the belief that the collection would come in its own time. I had to balance the requirements of the degree program with the impetuosity of my creative mistress.

At the beginning of the third semester, one of those requirements loomed: the teaching component. It was a large part of the MFA program, and not only did I have very little experience teaching, but I was unsure about how it would work into my writing. After all, what did teaching and writing a short story collection have to do with each other?

November 9, 2006:
"The Second Epiphany"

I had run into a wall, and her name was Sarah Schulman. For the first time in thirteen years—since I'd gotten a rejection slip from a publisher calling the story I'd submitted "too pedantic"—somebody didn't love my writing. Sarah was my second advisor at Goddard, and she wasn't buying the fiction I was selling. It's not that my previous advisor, Richard Panek, fawned over my writing; but his method of instruction was to cut subtly and deeply, allowing me to understand what I needed from the inside out. Sarah was more direct.

Of the first story I submitted to her, she said, "Shawn, this story is a real mess." My mouth dried and my carotid artery began to twitch. A mess? What was she talking about? I'd sent her a complex, layered story called "If Hands Could Taste Like Whiskey," about a dysfunctional family of adults just about to explode. I'd worked on the story for months, restructuring it, swabbing it with strokes of inspiration, then cutting and crafting with eye-aching effort. Had she read the story I sent her? My whole collection was suddenly in danger of being blown away.

She had read it, and her comments ranged from "Cut, cut, cut," to "This has to go." It was a proper thrashing, and I deserved it. I'd been growing tremendously as a writer, but now I needed to shed a little skin. It was going to take a jump in level, and Sarah's direct, succinct approach was going to take me there. I needed to understand that my writing wasn't just about me, about my needs. It had to be believable, it had to make sense, and Sarah—who is Goddard's designated Master Class in Fiction teacher—knew what I needed.

Falling in the middle of my fictional challenges was the Teaching Practicum. Because the MFA in Creative Writing is a terminal degree, students are required to conceive, implement and reflect on a teaching experience. Because it's a Goddard MFA, there wasn't a captive undergraduate audience to instruct; I had to teach in my community, and I had to do it all. Well, maybe not everything. Thanks to Charlotte Maison, I only had to worry about the academic stuff; she activated her publicity mechanism and in no time I had a class full of eager writers.

At first the teaching intimidated me. But when I realized that the hard work was in the preparation, and the joy was in the sharing with the students, I had the first of many epiphanies. The second epiphany was the one that changed me as a writer, the one that saw me burst forth and make the leap that would enable me to pull together this huge project I'd envisioned, this short story collection that was in danger of collapsing.

The second epiphany came during the final class of the creative writing workshop I taught at the Stowe Free Library. I was teaching the "perspiration" part of writing, the part where the writer has to get over his greatness and get to work. I was standing at the board, showing the students the Sequence/Consequence method that Sarah had shown me. In my head, though, I was miles away. My thoughts swirled with confusion about the direction my writing was taking. I struggled to find the place to break through. What was I missing? Sarah made the same comments about my writing over and over: "Consequence." And "What happens next?" Good writing has to make sense. Great writing has to make art out of chaos.

And then it hit me: I was teaching the very thing I needed to be doing in my writing. The teaching and the writing and the learning were all part of one big circle, and that's what I'd been missing. Not until I saw in my student's writing the same issues I struggled with did my puzzle come together. Standing in front of that class, I understood that it wasn't enough to show off my creative skills; the story had to mean something, to go somewhere. It had to be recognizable to someone who wasn't me.

That revelation informed not only the story I was struggling with, but the stories that were in the embryonic stages of creation, as well as the collection as a whole. For the first time I could see the larger theme I'd been skirting around. By applying the things I'd learned working with Sarah, I'd tapped into something bigger, a force I didn't fully understand yet, but something I could use to develop myself and my writing on a larger scale. And that's what I'd need to publish my book.

By my last semester I had the tools. I had the stories and the theme united in something that resembled a collection. I felt strong; I felt confident. I felt I was ready to not only present this manuscript to my advisor and second reader, I thought I was ready to begin submitting it to publishers. But was I ready? Had I learned the lessons I needed? I could only wait and see.

November 23, 2006:
"From Fantasy to Reality"

I had a secret fantasy. It was to have my creative thesis, *Name the Boy,* published by a national press before my graduation from Goddard's MFA in Creative Writing program. I imagined myself walking to the podium to accept my diploma, and speaking dramatic words to the gathering: "My creative thesis has been accepted for publication…"

It didn't happen quite that way. I began submitting my manuscript to publishers last spring. It's worth noting that the submission process for fiction begins in murky waters and gets progressively gloomy. Divining what publishers want is like, well, divining. There are many guides listing all the publishing houses and what their needs are—except the needs they list are rarely the needs they need. Then there's the Internet. The Web might be an author's best resource, because it allows a narrowing of subject matter in a compressed time frame.

From the research I'd done, I knew that my fiction was more likely to be accepted by a regional publisher. My short stories were almost all set in the place I grew up, Green Harbor, Massachusetts. Most revolved around the two dominant themes from my childhood: drinking and lobstering. It didn't seem likely that an urban press, or a small Midwestern press, would find much value in that subject matter. So I focused on publishers in New England. As I did this, I realized that a few of the stories I'd written would not make it into the collection. They deviated from the overall theme I'd strived for: the father and son relationship. As good as they were, they had to go. (To read one of the stories that was published but didn't make it into my collection, go to **http://web.goddard.e-du/pitkin/2005 spring/tara.htm** and read "Tara Gadomsky's Voice" in the Spring 2005 edition of Pitkin in Progress.)

I submitted *Name the Boy* to two publishers. The first was a larger, university press, with a well-known imprint that published many books similar in tone and style to mine. Except to say thanks, but it wasn't what they were looking for, I don't know why they didn't accept my collection for publication. Perhaps there was a level of erudition missing. Perhaps they just didn't want to venture anything on a collection of unpublished short stories.

I was going about this backwards. Usually, a writer crafts stories, then thoughtfully places them in various periodicals. Then, when all the stories had been published, the writer begins shopping them around as a collection. The main selling point for the publisher is that the stories have been previously published, accrediting them. With previously published work comes less risk. There were two reasons I didn't want to do it that way. First, I'd been down that road before with many of my stories.

Publication in a periodical is no guarantee that someone will snap up the collection. And placing all those stories takes time, lots of time. I figured two years. Two years and hundreds of dollars of postage. The second reason I didn't go this route was the thematic treatment I'd given my collection. I was confident of the collection's strength as a whole, and I wanted to give it a chance to succeed as it had succeeded as a creative thesis.

The second house I submitted my collection to was the Dan River Press. Dan River is a subsidiary of the Conservatory of American Letters, and one of their stated goals is to publish what has not yet been published. Right away I understood that this might be a place for my attention. Next I checked out their book list. My collection seemed like it would fit into the lineup. Then I went to the author's submission guidelines.

The guidelines issued a challenge: "Don't submit until you have a personal marketing plan." That was followed by this gem: "Tell me how we're going to sell enough books to make publication possible." The rest of the guidelines flowed in that same vein. Yes, content was the point, but it didn't matter to this publisher how good the writing was if it didn't have the potential to sell enough copies to break even. Dan River was a small press, and it didn't plan on going out of business for philosophical reasons.

Something about that tone appealed to the tough little Irish kid who grew up the son of a lobster fisherman. The challenge drew me in, and I found myself creating a document most anathema to writers: a marketing plan. Funnily enough, it felt natural to me, a part of the whole process. If I could create a short story collection, why couldn't I create a plan to sell that collection? Besides, it represented a chance for me to learn something new: the other side of publishing. If I could learn a little about selling books, I might be better positioned for future book publishing opportunities.

Dan River Press accepted *Name the Boy* for publication a week after I graduated, denying my fantasy. But I quickly seized on my new job:

book- seller. I began to enact my marketing plan. But besides accumulating advanced sales of my book, what did that really entail? It didn't matter. I was going to be published. I'd soon be able to link my MFA with a published work by a nationally recognized press, and that was the key to landing university-level teaching jobs. But before all that, I had to learn what "impending publication" really meant.

December 7, 2006:
"An Oxymoron Comes to Life"

Now that I'd succeeded in selling my short story collection to a publisher, I found myself with a new task: selling my book to readers. In the marketing plan I'd created, family and friends would form the backbone of my initial sales. Not only would they be the backbone, they'd be the muscle, nervous system, eyes, ears and nose of my sales. The contract that Dan River Press sent me was unusual. It called for the author to reach a specific dollar figure in pre-sales within a four-month window before publication was initiated. Based on the retail price, all I needed to do was bring an oxymoron to life and pre-sell about 190 softcovers of a book that was not yet published. In my mind, filled with excitement and puppy love, I thought I could do that blindfolded with one hand tied behind my back.

The first part of the marketing plan required me to supply the publisher with a master list of names and addresses of people who would not only buy a copy of my book, but who would pre-order a copy. The publisher would then mail those people an order form attached to a promotional piece, and they'd order the book. But as I was about to learn, there was a big difference between pre-ordering a book and buying it.

There were three problems with the publisher's promotional mailing. First, it looked like a piece of junk mail. The envelope was plain and undistinguished, with an address label and a generic looking return address. There was nothing on the outside to alert the recipient that this had anything to do with my book or me. Second, the promotional piece inside lacked any verve. It was a plain, typed announcement, and you had to look hard to see my name. The bottom portion was an order form that could be filled out and mailed in. That leads to the third problem: the Internet. There was no way of ordering the book online. When I asked the publisher about this, he said people could send him an email with their credit card number if they wanted to order the book. But as a small business owner who depends on the Internet for substantial sales, I knew that was not a secure way of doing business.

So I launched my own website. It was easy and effective, and I found a way to allow people to order a copy of the book and pay for it securely online. I was suddenly marketing me, a proposition not entirely comforting to someone more accustomed to observation and reflection. But for this book to succeed, for this dream to gain form, I had to do it. The publisher's mailing generated very few sales—and this was something that was sent to people who knew me, people who were related to me. I didn't panic; I got creative.

The next thing I did was send emails. After the first small wave of orders came in and I saw I was off the pace needed to satisfy my sales goal, I began contacting people via email. Out of 40 emails sent, I received 15 book orders. Compared with about 15 orders from the 200 or so people on the mailing list, it proved a far more effective method of selling. Then my wife came up with a great idea: postcards. They were cheap, and I could design them myself online. We sent them to people on the mailing list who should have been an automatic sale, but hadn't yet ordered: uncles, cousins, friends.

After a couple of months of this—including two weekends of working the phones—the publisher contacted me and said sales didn't look good. I told him that sales through my website were good. That surprised him. And that's when I realized I knew more about marketing my book than my publisher. That's when I realized that I controlled my own fate, that serendipity wasn't going to plop me down on Oprah's couch. This wasn't self-publishing, but neither was it all in the publisher's hands. I'd never be able to complain that my publisher made promises, then abandoned me. There were no promises. I was breaking new trail.

Sales reached a certain point, then stopped. People wanted to know when the book was coming out. People also wanted to buy the book: "Tell me when the book's published and I'll buy a copy." That was a line I heard dozens of times. I decided to make up the shortfall in sales by buying author's copies from the publisher. I get a substantial discount, plus I receive the royalty. Then I could sell the book at readings, or at the library, or on the Gondola climbing Mt. Mansfield. We reached the sales goal, and the book was going to print.

Just before Thanksgiving, the publisher promised me galley proofs, one of the final steps before publication. I'd learned a lot from the experience of pre-selling my book, but it wasn't something I wanted to make a habit of doing. Though I was now better equipped to deal with the business end of writing a book—and more knowledgeable about what works and what doesn't—I felt far from the creative process, and I struggled with my own writing. I've written exactly one new short story in the last year. And, I reminded myself, the book wasn't published yet. There were still the galley's to deal with. I still didn't have a book in my hands. I still had work to do.

December 21, 2006
"Waiting for Approval"

For the next few hundred words, I'm going to talk about something I know nothing about: the printing, or production, process of the book business. Up to now I've related the creative process, the selling process, and the marketing process. There was a measure of participation from me in each of these steps. But once the text is set in type, there's really nothing left to do but wait for the galley proofs.

I've spent a lot of time over the past few weeks explaining to people what galley proofs are. That's a neat trick, because I've never seen galley proofs before. And the reason I've been talking so much about them is because many people—especially the ones who pre-ordered a copy of **Name the Boy**—are beginning to ask me when it will become available. I've been telling them, "Soon...I hope."

The truth is that I just don't know. Throughout this whole experience I've been groping my way along. But now, I'm blinder than ever. What happened was this: the publisher initiated the production process, which resulted in galley proofs. I got the first set of galley proofs over the Thanksgiving holiday. In layman's terms, galleys are a test run of the printed book. The manuscript is translated into typeface, and a trial copy is printed. The margins of the galleys are extra large, allowing corrections to be written in during proofreading. These are what the publisher sent to me.

This much I knew about what to expect: the galleys wouldn't be perfect. Last summer, when I graduated, one of my advisors told the story of receiving the galley proofs for his first book. He was horrified to discover a typo on the first line of the first page. With that in mind, I carefully proofread through my first set of galleys. With one glaring exception, they weren't too bad. But that exception threw me into a dither. The last two pages of the final story in the collection were missing. Gone. As if they'd never existed.

I tried to calm down. There must be an explanation. So I returned the galleys to the publisher with my corrections, devoting much of my reaction to the missing pages at the end of the book. And then I waited. And while I waited, I began to realize that the book would not be ready before Christmas, as originally scheduled. And it probably wouldn't be ready for New Year's. Maybe for Elvis's birthday, but even that looked iffy.

While the publisher and I exchanged letters and sent the galleys back and forth (this time the galleys included that two missing pages from the end of the book), I found myself answering questions about the delivery date of the book. The publisher had originally promised the book by Christmas, and many people pre-ordered the book as a gift. Luckily for me, most people were understanding when I explained the situation. It didn't lessen the disappointment on their part or mine, but it at least gave them an idea of what to expect. And right now, I don't know what to expect. I'm waiting for what I hope will be the final set of galleys that I can sign, return to the publisher, and get the book printed and delivered.

The prevailing feeling right now is one of anticlimax. The first high came with the completion of the writing. Next came the thrill of being accepted for publication. The long process of pre-selling drained a lot of love from me. It was a holding pattern that moved me further and further away from the creative side of things. Getting the galleys should have been another high point, but it led only to more detours. Will the book make it to print? Of course it will, just as it will eventually snow in Stowe this winter. But the waiting is excruciating.

April 12, 2007:
"A Book is Born"

Let's see, where were we? Oh, yes, I remember: we were waiting. Waiting for the publisher to do whatever it is publishers do after the galleys of a book are proofed, waiting for the snow to arrive, waiting for the book to be published. Well, the waiting is over. Two boxes of books arrived on my doorstep last week. Now it's official.

The publishing process that was so enigmatic to me remains that way. I spent the winter mostly clueless about the progress of the book and when it would be published, just as I was mostly clueless about when and if we'd get the snow we crave. People stopped asking about it, sensing my bristling attitude. What could I tell them? I simply didn't know.

Okay, I knew something, but I didn't want to share it. The first thing that happened after the galleys were vetted and ready to go was that the

303

publisher lost the front cover artwork. More letters and emails back and forth. More waiting. When the front cover issues were resolved, somewhere around the end of January, we started in on the back cover. We'd missed our projected release date of Elvis's birthday, and Ash Wednesday wasn't looking good.

The publisher wanted a head shot of the author. The author, begging humility, didn't want a head shot for the back cover. Plus, the author didn't have a head shot, and would have to find someone to take the photos. The publisher wanted blurbs for the back cover, words of praise. Yet only four other people on the planet had yet read the book. So blurbs were begged. And then, when it all looked like it was coming together, the publisher sent the proof of the cover, which is very similar to the galleys of the text.

The layout looked fine, and I actually thought the author's photo was nice—I have to thank the publisher for pushing me on that point. But there were a couple of miscues in the blurbs and author's bio. I quickly checked the copy of what I sent, and it appeared that the publisher had changed a couple of things, specifically the capitalization of certain letters.

I know, I know: some of you are rolling your eyeballs and saying, "Only a writer—or an English major—could get riled about that. But we're talking about something permanent here, not a paper that can be corrected and turned back in. I read the proof of the back cover again. The author's bio read: "Shawn Kerivan holds an MFA in creative writing from Goddard college." Neither the "c" nor the "w" in creative writing were capitalized, nor was the "c" in Goddard College. Major gaff. I quickly reached for my diploma to check the spelling on it. There it was: MFA in Creative Writing from Goddard College. Emails were exchanged, and I received this cryptic note from the publisher: "the only course capitalized is a language course, college is arguable."

Hmmm. What the heck did that mean? I glanced up at the calendar. Ash Wednesday had come and gone, and I was forced to invoke my Lenten sacrifice: not getting ticked off at my publisher. St. Patrick's Day loomed, and spring skiing was in the air. I got the publisher to capitulate on the "c" in College, but not the creative writing. I wavered, and then someone asked me when the book was coming out. I fell. The nature of my MFA would have to be lower case. A perfect fit for my humility, but unsatisfying.

By now I could smell the fresh ink drying on acid free paper. And then my college roommate, the poet John Summerfield, published his book of poetry, *I, Suwannee.* Finally the publisher told me that the book had gone to press, which sounded good, much better than "college is arguable." I was told to expect books within the week. Two weeks later, they arrived. Somebody asked me how it felt to finally be published, to finally have books to hold. I told them that given the process, it felt like the prodigal son had returned. Time to slaughter the fatted calf.

And now that I've scaled that mountain, I stand at the edge of the slope, my skis peeking over the edge, nothing but knee-deep powder before me. There'll be readings, and signings, and lots of selling, but like turns in the snow they'll all have their own reward. So look for me, I'll be around—I'll be the one with the bagful of books called *Name the Boy.*

BLG 101: Intro to Blogging

Instructor: Shawn Kerivan

Meeting Times: Right Now

What's a blog? Hard to say, because my Microsoft Word 2003 spellchecker still underlines the word in red every time I type it, telling me it's misspelled. The spellchecker suggests I try bog, blot, bloc, blot, blob, or blow instead. I have to admit that even when I began writing a blog I wasn't completely sure what it was. To me, it was just an online place to write, another outlet for my creativity. As I was putting this book together, I realized that there may be readers who still aren't familiar with the form, so here's the best dictionary definition I could come up with:

blog |bläg| |blag| (*n*)

A Web site on which an individual or group of users produces an ongoing narrative : *Most of his work colleagues were unaware of his blog until recently.*

(v) (**blogged**, **blogging**) [intrans.]

To add new material to or regularly update a blog.

DERIVATIVES: **blogger** *(n)*

ORIGIN a shortening of **weblog** .

Shortening of weblog? But what's a weblog? The problem with new words coming into our language is that here, in the United States, we don't have the equivalent of the *Academie Francaise*, as they do in France, the organization that regulates words, among other things. Though the effectiveness of the *Academie* in preventing all sorts of un-French words from entering the language is debatable, it would be nice to have a final authority to turn to here in America for these matters.

Alas, we're left to deal with these things ourselves, and guys like me who actually practice the new art are on the front line, forced to define it.

And so the confusion over words like blog. The proliferation of political bloggers didn't help matters, especially when people began taking them seriously. There should be a rule that says readers shouldn't take anything seriously that they read on the Web. It's too easy to look good on the Internet without having put the time in to guarantee truth, quality, or anything else we hold dear when it comes to our words. That doesn't mean there aren't legitimate sources of information out there; it just means that it's easier to create a blog or any other kind of Web document than it is to have something physically printed.

So it is for my blogs. I started out with a blog about the inn, called Innkeeping Insights in Stowe. It was for purely commercial reasons. I linked the blog to our website, hoping that people checking us out on the Web would enjoy reading a little about the place they were thinking of staying at. It would give them a little inside information about their innkeepers. It does that, but it does more, too. It entertains. I'm constantly surprised by the number of guests who tell me (while they're checking in) that they read my blog all the time. They really latch on to it, and they often want to talk about something I wrote, but which I've now forgotten about. It's become more important than I imagined.

The second blog is called The Innkeeper's Husband, and I began writing it to promote my next book by the same name. After I wrote the columns for An Author's Road I realized that I shouldn't wait to promote my next book. Even though I was in the process of creating it, I documented that progress in the blog. I linked the blog to Innkeeping Innsights in Stowe, and it also generated interest among guests. Though I posted new pieces of writing to this blog less frequently, it still served as an important outlet for me.

I've selected some entries from both blogs so that you, gentle reader, may see not only how a writer diversifies himself, but also so that you might better understand the form and function of a blog. I hope you discover that the blog entries are very much like short newspaper columns, with quick, succinct themes, sort of a get in/get out format for writing. And, of course, I hope you enjoy them.

Innkeeping Insights in Stowe: The Blogs

Saturday, October 09, 2004
A Work In Progress

To describe what it is like to own an old inn in Vermont is like trying to describe what it is like to be happily married. From the outside, all appears quaint, cute, and happy. But there is a lot of work that goes on behind the scenes to make things work. A lot of innovation and creativity. A lot of compromise.

Compromise? With a building? Oh, yeah. The building that is the Auberge is 170 years old. It has outlasted four or five generations of cagey Vermonters, and it will probably outlast me. That's not to say that I don't wield certain advantages, mostly in the form of power tools. But the building has an inertia which transcends anything I can throw at it. The building has patience.

The door to my basement is not regulation. It is only 65 inches high. I am 72 inches high. So there is some yellow tape warning me to duck before I pass through the doorway. Most of the time I remember to duck, but because I am Irish I sometimes lose my temper, and when that happens, the doorway brings me back to earth. Now, I'm not saying that there is a conscious effort on the part of the Auberge to moderate me...after all, it was probably the Auberge--in the form of a renegade plug or a leaking faucet--which set me off in the first place. But the fact remains that this old place has a habit of laying down the law when need be.

This is because there is always something that needs to be done around here. That's where the comparison to marriage comes into play. It's not the big things that I do around here that make it work. It's the little things. Regular seasonal maintenance is more important than can be adequately described. Sure, a new heating system is nice, but it doesn't rent us any rooms. The little things are what make people--and old inns like the Auberge--happy.

So when you come up for a visit and you see an eclectic old place like ours, remember this: it's a work in progress. Oh, and be careful where you step, there might be a cagey old Vermonter crawling around the shadows, rewiring or caulking or trying to find out where the mouse gets in.

Wednesday, March 09, 2005
The Innkeeper's Family

Funny things happen to you while you're innkeeping. Sometimes funny means "ha-ha." Sometimes funny means introspective. As the month of March roared in with blowing and drifting snows, my life as an innkeeper came to a screeching halt for a few days. My mother was un-expectedly hospitalized, and I had to rush down to Boston for a couple of days to be with her as she underwent open heart surgery.

My wife and I have worked hard to get here. We've set goals that included our whole family--we didn't just end up in Vermont for us. We considered how innkeeping would affect our children, our extended fami-lies, our friends. Sometimes this journey has felt like a hand over hand struggle. Sometimes it's been like a sweet run down Mt. Mansfield's Nosedive. But when your mother--otherwise perfectly healthy--becomes so ill so quickly, you're forced to pause, to reflect, to reorient yourself.

I drove down to Boston through a vicious snowstorm. Route 89 through New Hampshire resembled a nasty ski run more than an inter-state highway. But I found comfort in the knowledge that I'd be with my mother through a difficult time. It was midweek, and we only had a few rooms out at the inn.

The good news is that everybody made it through just fine. Mom came through the surgery like a champ, and her prognosis is excellent. But the whole episode stopped me, forcing me to contemplate some things. We make choices in our lives that lead us down unexpected roads. We have to ask, What am I doing? Why am I here? Is this the right path? If we are unprepared to deal with these questions, we may find ourselves in a confusing place. As David Byrne once sang, "You may find yourself in a beautiful house/With a beautiful wife/And you may ask yourself/How did I get here?" If you can't answer that question, it might be time to reevaluate.

Our level of innkeeping at the Auberge de Stowe allows us to be a family. That was our driving force when considering places to buy. We are active parents, we get to spend lots of time with our sons. We're also blessed with an ability to see most of our extended family fairly often. That's the spirit we try to share with our guests. We try to involve them a little with the lives of their innkeepers. My mom may not know this, but there were lots of strangers praying for her. Strangers who became family for a few days at the Auberge.

Saturday, May 14, 2005
Your Internet Dating Destination

I don't know why I didn't think of it before.

This weekend we had a guest who came to meet her Internet, um, potential boyfriend. I'm sorry that I don't have the jargon down, but I'm new to all this. Since I don't date over the Internet, I'm not really sure where this might lead. But as an innkeeper I can see the potential in this. As an innkeeper I can see the potential is just about everything. As a writer I see the tragedy of it all.

When this guest arrived, her "friend" from Morrisville dropped her off. Chantal and I wondered what her situation was--why wasn't her "friend" staying? And why wasn't she staying with her "friend"? But, after you've kept the inn for a while, you shrug these things off, filing it in the "I've seen just about everything" folder. As usually happens, breakfast enabled conversation.

It turns out that our guest met her "friend" (Is it okay if I lose the quotations? They remind me of Dr. Evil.) in a church sponsored chat room, and she traveled to Vermont to meet him. I thought, "This has potential."

We're the perfect place for this. Our rooms are clean and comfortable, and Internet friends can get rooms across the hall from each other. Or they can rent two adjoining rooms that share a bathroom. What better way to get to know someone than to share a bathroom with them? Think of it: Do they leave the cap off the toothpaste? Do they leave the seat up? Are they a two flusher? Towels bunched up on the floor? Do they greedily take the last sheet of two-ply without refilling? Are they at least gracious enough to attempt deodorization, or do they leave it to you to call in the Haz-Mat team?

The evaluation extends beyond the john. How are their table manners? Do they hold their utensils like a character from Cooper's Last of the Mohicans? Do they shower the table with bits of food ejected from their mouths? How's their hot tub etiquette? Do they at least wait for the jets to turn on before adding their own bubbles? These questions all become marketing points in my sales material. The question is, How do I sell this? I can't possibly surf through all the chat rooms where friends meet. And when Internet people want to find a place to meet, how do they initiate a search?

This sounds like a lot of work to me, and I didn't become an innkeeper to work. I became an innkeeper to observe my guests and write a book about it.

In the meantime, if you know of any Internet friends that would like a nice, safe place to check out each other's bathroom manners, direct them to us.

Saturday, September 18, 2005
Desk Jobs

312

There's nothing worse than answering a potential guest's inquiries with bumbling bits of incoherent noise. It happened to me while at the front desk the other day. I couldn't locate the rates for Christmas week, and I had a mental breakdown. Instead of calmly flipping through the reservation book, I panicked, and began throwing papers randomly into the air, hyperventilating, and gnashing my teeth. I was also trying to fend off two kids, a dog, and a seedy looking character who had drifted in off the street and was asking me if I'd charge him less for a room if he didn't use any toilet paper. The point I'm getting to is that a clean, well-lighted space defines success in both innkeeping and writing.

I understand that desk space is as much about personal expression as it is about practical accessibility, but I've found certain truths immutable. I'd like to share both of my desk spaces with you, the one a use for writing, and the one used for innkeeping.

A big, honking, plastic computer colossus dominates the writer's desk. This is a real tragedy. There's nothing electronic about writing, and for the way I use the computer, I'd be as well served by a typewriter. The good news: this computer's not hooked up to the Internet. I stripped everything, save MS Word, from it, so it's a turbo file manager that lets me write. Around the plastic temple lies a variety of items meant to enhance the writing experience: a clear, plastic ruler (for back scratching), maps (for dreaming: topo maps of the area, maps of Montreal and France, and Boston, all places I've lived), several layers of books (Shakespeare, Cooper, Melville, Joyce, Hemingway and Cormac McCarthy), a nice pen the approximate shape of a Mont Blanc fountain pen, a good six inches of legal pads (duh), some kind of sports stick, like a golf club, baseball bat, hockey stick, or hurley (I have a Ping 2 iron; it's useless to me on the golf course, but it works wonderfully at my desk), a harmonica (for the really painful times), a huge cross section of grammar, usage, and style manuals, as well as the American Heritage Dictionary, Third Edition, red pencils (nobody's that good), and something from my kids. I have a drawing of a Medieval castle under siege, complete with

Old French expletives captured in dialogue balloons. That keeps it real, a reminder that it's not all about me.

The innkeeper's desk differs vastly. Telephone and reservation book occupy center stage. Next to them is the credit card machine, or, as we call it, Giver of Life. Scattered around the telephone and reservation book lies a vast array of loose papers: some are reservation slips, past and present; some are small notes, reminders to call someone back or leave extra towels in a room. There's also a doorbell mounted on a plaque of wood that says: "We're Here! Please Ring The Bell!" Next to that is a clear plastic squirt bottle with the word "Dog" written on it.

Our goal is to present our guests not with some contrived image when they enter the lobby; it's to give them the feeling that real people live here, real, eccentric people, just like them. Like the writer's desk, which reflects the idiosyncrasies of the writer, the innkeeper's desk reflects the kind of inn this is. You can check out the front desk when you come, but don't expect to see the writer's desk unless you bring some really good single malt with you.

Friday, December 23, 2005
End of the Year Lisps

The potential energy at the little inn is nearing the breaking point. With the place booked solid through the New Year, we're entering one of our busiest stretches of the year. And for the first time, we've done some major improvements that should make a huge difference. Foremost among those improvements was the replacement of the 40 year old boiler that serviced the guest rooms heating system. Normally not a fan of throwing 40 year old things away, we made an exception this year, and we added a heating zone out in the back room, along with brand new windows, making the place downright balmy. More importantly, it saves energy, and as long as we continue to suffer astronomical fuel prices, every little bit helps.

All this has to do with things an innkeeper doesn't want to hear. When you add guests to the inn, you add stress, stress on systems, like heating and hot water, stress on the hot tub, stress on the innkeepers. And when you add stress, things break down. With that in mind, I thought I'd share some of the things that guests have said to me. They're in no order of severity or shock, just what comes to mind at the outset of another calendar year. As you read these, remember the spirit in which they were spoken: out of the blue, usually with me in my jammies and a cup of coffee in my hand, or late at night, with a glass of bourbon in my hand.

* There's no (hot water/heat/electricity/high-speed internet access/ boot warmers/masseuse on staff/heated towel dispenser...you pick'em).

* I tried to fix the toilet, but...(use your imagination here).

* We need new sheets.

* Could you throw this away? (Imagine being handed a variety of bad smelling things: diapers, ashtrays, plastic bags filled with offal.)

* Um, I don't know how to say this, but...

* Do you have any rolling papers?

* Is the hot tub supposed to foam like that?

* What's that swimming in the pool?

* Have you seen my kids?

* Have you seen my car?

* Have you seen my husband?

* Did you you say we could or couldn't wear street clothes in the hot tub?

* Do you have a plunger?

* Could I borrow some paint remover?

* Can an iron be un-melted from a carpet?

* Are you the Innkeeper that writes?

Yeah, that's me. So be careful. You might end up in my blog. Or, better yet, you might end up in my upcoming book: The Innkeeper's Husband.

Saturday, January 28, 2006
How To Get Things Fixed

Running a small inn on a budget forces creativity. And when I say creativity, I mean desperation. Desperation as in, "I don't have money to fix that." In the old place that houses the Auberge de Stowe, there's lots that can, and does, go wrong. Pipes freeze. Circuit breakers pop. The hot tub foams over. And for the most part, I, the innkeeper's husband, can handle it. But for some things, I'm just plain ignorant.

That's where youth comes in.

And when I say youth, I mean the Internet, or computers, or whatever requires drinking a can of Red Bull to understand. Don't get me wrong; I'm not afraid to tackle my own computer woes. I'm just clueless, and I usually end up doing something really bad. Compare that to my forays into plumbing, which I always conquer, but which end up instructing my sons in the fine art cussin' as much as anything else.

This week we've got a large group staying with us, a ski club from an Ivy League school. We took this booking with trepidation: gaggles of twenty year olds aren't our target audience. But it was too good to pass up. Of course, when they arrived, they all whipped out their laptop computers and demanded to know if we had wireless. They needed to sit down right away and begin emailing each other: "Dude, we're here!" "I know, dude, I'm sitting beside you!"

But as they walked in, our Internet connection crashed. This was good news. I smiled and told Chantal that among one of these brilliant youth must be a computer geek--er, I mean, talented computer scientist. Now it was the guests who were desperate, and sure enough, one emerged. I think he was a sophomore, and he already had his own consulting business. Anyway, I brought him into the office, and he asked if he could start fiddling with wires. I cracked open a beer and said, "Knock yourself out."

A few hours later, before I went to bed, I went looking for him. He wasn't in the office. I found him out by the fireplace, with seven or eight of his friends. They were all sitting or sprawled out on the floor with their computers in their laps. The glow from the screens bathed their faces in foolish fire. But they were smarter than me. They got my Internet back up and working, and the wireless service, too.

They grunted absently when I wished them goodnight. But I didn't mind. I was thankful for their services. I was also trying to think of how I could get a plumber's club up here for a ski vacation, that way when the pipes in room one bust, they'd be as motivated to fix them as my Ivy Leaguers were motivated to fix the Internet service.

When you own an inn, these are the kinds of things you think about.

Sunday, June 11, 2006
The Second Law of Thermodynamics

So much for free time on my hands.

For a long time I'd looked forward to this spring with luscious antici-pation. Finally I'd be able to tear my head away from my studies and reacquaint myself with my surroundings. I'd go fishing with my sons, ride the lawn mower in the sun, drink a beer in the hammock. Be an innkeep-er.

That didn't happen--at least not yet. What did happen was a sched-uling explosion. When May rolled around, I suddenly realized that I was going to be as busy as I'd been the previous two years. It was that damn second law of thermodynamics again: systems becoming more compli-cated. The first thing that overtook me was the work remaining to wrap up my graduate degree. At Goddard, unlike other schools, you're re-sponsible for managing your own paper work. That means instead of a small slip of paper with a bunch of letter grades, we get a full narrative transcript, describing in detail the work of the past two years. It also meant I had to deal with drafts and revisions. Then I had to create my Final Product Binder, the tome which housed all this spit and polish writing. The work piled up on the edge of my desk like grains of salt filling the bottom of an hourglass.

And then there was my short story writing workshop at the Stowe Free Library. I'd conveniently ignored it, and with only a few weeks till its scheduled start, I needed to dive into detailed preparations. I'd prepared a detailed outline of the course when I made the proposal, now I had to fill in all the theoretical blanks with bricks and mortar. Leading a workshop may only occupy two hours a night on Thursdays, but the preparation goes on throughout the week.

Oh, I almost forgot. Baseball. I'm involved in baseball at all levels the way plumbers are involved with water flow. Besides being a fan and dedicating myself to watching as much on television as I can, I'm on the board of Stowe Youth Baseball, and I'm in charge of coordinating the Rookie Ball and T-Ball programs. While this mostly means organizing the parents who actually coach the kids, it's still a lot of running around, answering phone calls and emails. And then there are my sons. Both boys are in Little League, but on different teams. That means a different game every night of the week. Since the beginning of May I've stood on every Little League field in Lamoille County, in driving rain laced with snowflakes, smothering humidity saturated with the smell of manure, and twilight pregnant with clouds of black flies from Hell.

Did I mention the inn? Air conditioners need to be installed, paint needs to be scraped, pools need to be opened, reservations need to be taken, woodchucks need to be banished, lawns need to be mowed, guests need to be entertained, and, at some point, it needs to stop raining around here. Twice the river in the back has been up to its banks, something unheard of at this time of year. I even found a couple of trout up on my lawn who told me they got out of the river because they were just plain exhausted from swimming against the raging current. I didn't have the heart to encrust them in almonds and fry them up.

But there's hope. On July 2nd I officially graduate from Goddard College with and MFA in Writing. Baseball season wraps up this week.

There's sunshine in the forecast. My schedule's certainly going to open up after that, right?

Right?

Saturday, January 06, 2007
The Long, Warm Winter

In my heart, I know this is all going to take some time. In my mind, I can rationalize the events into an acceptable order. But in between my heart and my mind is reality. I'm talking about everything: the publication of my book, my busy schedule teaching, and the weather, because innkeeping in Vermont demands some discussion about the weather. Let's start with the book.

We sold enough copies of Name the Boy to satisfy the pre-order goals. There should have been something celebratory surrounding that event, but instead I felt dirty. I'm still afflicted with that classic authorial dichotomy: I write books, I don't sell them. It's a silly mindset, of course. I've had to sell all my other writing over the years, from magazine articles to short stories. I just wrapped up a series of articles for the Stowe Reporter about the journey I've been on with the book. So why should I feel bad about having to roll up my sleeves and sell my own book?

I'm blaming my MFA. Coming off two years of high-minded study, rubbing elbows with successful authors, elevating my craft through countless hours of reading and writing and rewriting...It pulled me away from reality, from the part of the writing world where the rubber meets the road. The past six months have been a process of fitting my degree into my life, my reality. I think I'm almost there. Though I just received a terrifying email from my publisher saying he lost the artwork for the cover of the book, everything else is ready to go. Writing in the real world takes optimism and persistence. Writing for the theoretical world takes disembodiment and spirituality. And here the twain shall meet.

Into that I've added a busy teaching schedule. I'm teaching three days a week at the Mt. Mansfield Winter Academy. MMWA is where ski racers come to train and study during the winter. I have a variety of classes, including Science Fiction, American Lit, Creative Writing, and Shakespeare. Most of the students come with a class in progress, and it's my job to keep them up to speed while they race their mornings away. It partly frustrating, partly exhilirating, and good experience for my teaching muscles. I'll also be teaching at the Community College of Vermont this spring. It's a lot of work, but I'm looking forward to the experience for the same reasons just listed. By the spring I hope to have a better idea about the role teaching will play in my future. Part of my hopes it will be a big role, but I'm writer from start to finish.

Finally, there's the weather. It's fitting that I throw the weather over everything else, because that's what the weather's doing to us right now. For innkeepers in northern Vermont ski areas, it's been horrible. Business has been okay, but as I look out the window the rain's pounding the white into mud. Like my experience with the book publisher or some of the frustrations I've encountered teaching, I have to take the long view. I'm lucky we don't live hand to mouth, that we have a plan. We'll make it through the worst of what nature throws our way by taking the long view. And when the book's finally published (sometime this month, I'm told), you'll be the first--or second, I should say--to know.

Monday, June 04, 2007
Leave me alone, I'm a family man

I did a quick head count of the innkeepers in Stowe recently, and out of nearly 60 inns, motels, lodges, and B&B's, I came up with about a half dozen places staffed by innkeepers with kids. That number is probably shrinking, too, and with good reason. Few people are willing to run an inn at the level needed to devote adequate time to your family and your business. I know that in the seven years we've done this, we've struggled at times, and only within the past couple of years have we been able to choose family over business when we needed to. The big obstacle is timing: when you're kids are available for travel and activities, you're inn is usually at its busiest.

This weekend we closed and went camping. We go every year, to the same park, and it's one of the highlights of our year as a family. We also closed for several days in April to go to Washington, D.C. It's never an easy decision to close. My wife told me we turned away enough business last weekend to half fill the inn, and it's likely we would have been completely full, because we'd pulled our inventory off the Internet a long time ago. Who knows how many potential lodgers found us, only to discover that we weren't open on the weekend they wanted to visit?

One thing is certain: You don't get time back. Once your kids have grown, their childhood is over. Many is the man or woman who wakes up in their late forties and discovered that they haven't really lived at all, they've just worked for some imaginary piece of pie in the sky. People become innkeepers for all kinds of reasons, but many of them never realize the amount of work and time it takes to become successful. And then they ask themselves, "What is success?" And if you end up hiring employees to run your inn so that you can have the family time you're craving, is that innkeeping? Or has something been lost in the pursuit of success?

These questions aren't unique to innkeeping, and that might be the biggest surprise at all. For me, having the ability to keep my business at a manageable size allows the kind of flexibility I need to have a family and a job. Is it perfect? Nope, and I don't recommend it for everyone. But when I'm sitting by the campfire getting chomped by black flies while my kids embed memories for a lifetime, I think I'm on the right track.

Friday, July 13, 2007
That Little Souvenir, of a Terrible Year

As you may know from my other blog, The Innkeeper's Husband, I'm writing a book--another book, that is. I'm following up my literary collection of short stories with a sardonic, self-effacing account of my life as an innkeeper--of course. I mean, how else do you follow up your literary debut? And as I was writing and structuring the book, I realized I'd have to revistit an unpleasant time: September 11, 2001.

When I say unpleasant, I mean it in only the most objective way. Perhaps being an innkeeper connected me a little more closely to the events of that day than the ordinary American, yet I never suffered the horrors of so many, or that so many suffer still due to the consequences which unfold even as I write. But we did absorb some cancellations, and this on the eve of our first foliage season as innkeepers, a season we desperately needed for the business to succeed. I've written about this several times, and revisiting those articles lances old boils best left untouched.

As I revisited those events, what struck me was the difficulty I had in defining myself according to the terms of that day. I found that the old internal struggle had resurrected itself within me. Was I a patriot, or was I a cynical bystander? Or, was there room for something in between? Events like that tend to polarize societies, and for good reason. But action and inaction need balance, like everything else in the universe. And it was my struggle to find balance that caught my attention. It was that search for balance that caused me so much discomfort as I wrote about that date for my book, The Innkeeper's Husband.

I never came to any conclusions, no tidy endings, no neat summations. I'm still left with an uneasy feeling as I continue to write. Maybe that kind of internal conflict makes for the best fuel for a writer. Maybe not. But I'm more convinced than ever that remembering that date, revisiting it, reliving it, is critical to our survival as a species. The object isn't to dwell on a subject; rather it's to use the benefits of time to allow a different kind of access, one that might eventually give us the kind of insight we need to put things in their proper places--if, that is, we let them.

Tuesday, August 07, 2007
Gillnetting the Hammock

In the summer of 1984, I was a roofer. I was between my sophomore and junior years of college, and I was working for Jack Madden, my friend Pete's father. Okay, so maybe I wasn't a roofer. Maybe my skill set was somewhere between laborer and comedian. But as the summer progressed, I learned more and more from Pete and Mr. Madden, until I could be trusted to lay out a course of asphalt shingles on my own.

Our big job that summer was re-roofing St. Theresa's church in Humarock, Massachusetts. St. Theresa's was a single roof structure, but large, and steeply angled. It took the right blend of courage, experience, and the suspension of disbelief to scale that roof, first ripping the two layers of shingles off that were already on there, then nailing down the new shingles. I had everything but experience going for me. More importantly, for Pete and me, was the fact that next door to the church was the McKinnon house. The McKinnons were fisherman, and Mr. McKinnon owned a nice gillnetting rig that he fished out of Scituate Harbor. That summer Mike McKinnon and his brother, Scott, were fishing with their father. And one of the many duties they had was net repair.

Net repair usually happened on rainy days, or when it was blowing too hard to fish. Sometimes Mike and Scott didn't go out for unexplained reasons, left behind to mend nets. On those days, Pete and I would call over to them from the top of St. Theresa's roof, making drinking plans for later in the day. Sometimes we'd throw shingles at them, and they'd throw rocks back at us. And sometimes Pete and I would wander over there during lunch, and watch them mend nets.

Their hands would blur between the strands of monofilament, quickly closing up any holes. The McKinnons were good-natured guys, and they laughed and traded barbs with us as they furiously worked to repair the nets that put food on their table. I could never figure out how they mended the nets--they never let me try, and I wasn't concerned with that skill. But this week, I found myself thinking about the McKinnons as I tried to mend a net of my own.

Actually, it was a hammock. One afternoon a guest came up from the pool and reported a "large hole in the hammock. Large enough to fall through." When I saw the hole, I knew I was in trouble: how do you mend a hammock? There wasn't enough rope for a proper splice, and since a hammock is essentially one long rope woven into a pattern, there was no chance of replacing a single section. That's when I remembered the McKinnons.

I went straight to my fishing tackle box and found some 36-pound nylon line that I use as backing for my fly fishing reel. I pulled off a long length of it and went down to the hammock. After cutting the ends of the broken rope evenly, I spliced as much as I could, then set upon it with the nylon line. I tried to remember how the McKinnons had done it, so fast, so easy. Soon I found a rhythm, and I discovered that if I didn't think too much about what I was doing, it went together quickly. When I finished, I looked at the newly mended hammock. It looked nothing like the lines the McKinnons had mended, but it didn't look bad. There even appeared to be some sort of pattern there.

I flipped the hammock back over and tested it. It held. I got out and yanked on the mended section: tight and fast. It just might work. Sometimes innkeeping affords me the opportunity to sample the experiences I've acquired throughout my life. And as I dozed off in the hammock that afternoon, I wondered if the McKinnons were still out there, mending lines.

Thursday, November 01, 2007
A Room With A Review

There's a website called Tripadvisor.com that allows travelers to offer "objective" reviews of the places they've stayed in. Ostensibly, this service helps others decide where to book a room when visiting a place such as Stowe. While on the surface this seems a good idea, there's really nothing objective about the idea. In fact, the site relies on the subjective experiences of its users to offer advice--advice they may not be qualified to give.

Once we fielded a complaint through AAA from someone who had stayed with us. Actually, it turned out not to be a complaint, just a matter of opinion. The person who wrote to AAA, listed among her complaints a pink toilet in her bathroom. Not a dirty toilet, or a broken toilet, but a pink toilet. She also mentioned the layout of the rooms, and the fact that many things looked old. Of course, we had the same thought you're having right now: "Soooo, is this going somewhere?" It didn't. While it's obvious that this person didn't care for pink toilets or old fashioned furniture, it said nothing about the quality or service we offered.

Though most of our reviews on Tripadvisor are positive, you can see there's room for abuse, or at least subjectivity. Where's the harm in letting people tell other people about the experience they've had? Well, there's none, except that an opinion is just that: a view or judgment about something, not necessarily based on fact or knowledge. It's the "fact or knowledge" part that gets sticky. What one person craves, another abhors, and if someone books a room at a roadside inn for eighty dollars, then doesn't like the fact that there's no turndown service, and writes about it online, there's not much you can do about it. And the opposite is true, too. Inflated reviews may paint a picture of an inn that isn't really there. I haven't even mentioned the ethical pitfalls inherent in this model, like trading free room nights for favorable reviews. Yikes.

All this innkeeping stuff leads me to a review of my own. The first real review of my book, *Name the Boy*, came out in the Stowe Reporter today, and it was a lot like the lady who was shocked to find a pink toilet in her bathroom. The reviewer seemed focused on the surface elements, and never made it to the rich subtext. And though the reviewer never said anything bad, the impression left was that this might not be a book you want to buy, it's too scary.

In Hollywood they say there's no such thing as bad publicity. But this is Stowe. I guess I'd hoped for a deeper reading of the book, but the review came off as rushed. I thanked the reviewer for the effort (after all, the paper donated nearly a square foot of type to me, which is no small feat), and told her that if she ever needed someone to review a book, I'd be happy to do it. (Hint.) What I learned today is that book reviews are like family members: you don't get to pick 'em, and once they're here, they're yours to keep.

The Innkeeper's Husband: The Blogs

Sunday, June 10, 2007
Time and Angst

There's no rush. Really there isn't. At least that's what I keep telling myself. I'm not on deadline, and nobody's contracted me to write this book, so I can make my own schedule. But it doesn't always work out that way. There is a certain amount of inertia associated with writing a book. When you get going, nothing can stop you. You're hot. You're A-Rod in April, Reggie in October. You're channeling, your body possessed by your muse, who's busy vomiting words through the tips of your fingers and onto your keyboard. And when you're not hot, you're cold. Your arms feel paralyzed. You become obsessed with cleaning your writing space. You type "the quick brown fox jumps over the lazy dog" over, and over, and over. Then you go pour yourself a drink.

I'm not describing writer's block here, because, like R.O.U.S.'s (rodents of unusual size), I don't think it exists. What's really going on is a time management problem. Just as I took on the writing of *The Innkeeper's Husband*, I found myself in the middle of dozens of other projects. I also decided to begin a novel, tentatively called Exoskeletons. Then there are the blogs, but I don't count them as negatives, because they tend to infuse my writing with energy. Same for the journal I started keeping. With me, writing success if often a matter of giving myself too much to write, because I've got so much to say it gets backed up easily.

What really cut into my time was a nasty spring cold that left me feverish and on my knees for three days last week. That delayed the opening of the pool by a week, really tossing my schedule into the dump. Plus I'm preparing for two college classes that I'm teaching in the fall. And then there's the usual host of odd duties around the inn.

So when Saturday morning rolled around and I sat down in front of The Innkeeper's Husband and nothing happened, I lost it. I turned into a monster, stomping around, growling at everyone all day. That, combined with my inability to get a reading and book signing at the Stowe Free Library, frazzled me. It's Sunday afternoon now, and I'm not sure I've recovered from all that angst. It really wrecked me. I had a good two hours this morning, and that helped. But ultimately I know that writing the book will be a matter of capitalizing on the times when the fever hits, and slogging my way through the times when nothing's happening, like this weekend.

Saturday, June 23, 2007
Structure and the Story

One of the biggest challenges I face in writing *The Innkeeper's Husband* is maintaining a strong sense of structure while keeping the story interesting. And by strong sense of structure I mean something that the reader doesn't notice. Structure can be expressed in many different ways. The most popular way is to adopt a chronological order. That's what I've done, for the most part. But there are times when it's necessary to jump around little bit, and that can lead to trouble.

This morning, I was embarking on a chapter called "Three to Five." I hope that sounds like a sentence handed down by a judge, because it's supposed to. It's also the number of years it takes to get a small B&B up to speed. If you can survive the first three to five years in this business, you'll probably make it. The theme of the chapter revolves around the time we got that advice. We'd just become innkeepers, and one savvy, long-time innkeeper leaned over to us at a business reception and delivered that line: "The first three to five years are killer. If you can make it through that, you'll be fine."

Not exactly what brand new innkeepers wanted to hear, but we took her seriously. And in that chapter, I want to relate the fears we had during the first few years, how we lost money constantly, how damn poor we were. So, as I wrote, I started drifting back toward the origins of our innkeeping dream. After three pages, it dawned on me that I might have already talked about our beginnings, and in fact I had, in an earlier chapter. That's what I mean about structure relating to the story.

I'm not writing this book from an outline; that's not the kind of writer I am. But maybe I should get a little more obvious in my structure. I can always go back and soften that during the revision. What this morning taught me was something I'd already learned as an innkeeper: you've got to have a plan, and stick to it, but not too tightly. Let the art shine through, take a little chance on yourself without losing sight of the structure. Then your readers--or your guests--will experience something they're not even aware of.

Tuesday, July 24, 2007
Hot Flashes of Obsession and How to Deal With Them

I was reading John Irving's novel *The Fourth Hand* last week, and there's a little addendum at the end, bundled into a section called "A Reader's Guide." There's a piece written by Irving called "Why I Wrote The Fourth Hand When I Wrote It." Aside from explaining nearly everything about the book and its creation, Irving offers an interesting and useful insight into the creative process. He describes how he interrupted the writing of *A Prayer for Owen Meany* to work on the screenplay for a previous novel, *The Cider House Rules*. In the essay Irving says, "It sounds strange, but my novels have benefited from my interrupting them...(during the novelist's absence, a novel that's off to a good start only stands to get better, but a struggling novel will become more difficult.)"[109]

At first, this sounded intuitive to me. But I wondered how others felt about it. Getting caught up in the writing of a novel can be like the early days of a relationship. The temptation is to turn the burners up all the way and sweat it out. But novel-writing, like a relationship (and like most things organic), follows a naturally prescribed arc that spikes in the beginning, but levels off. Writing a novel demands stamina, and Irving touches on that need to self-regulate when he explains how he's found a way to deal with it. While many of us don't have the luxury of writing an Academy Award winning screenplay in the middle of writing our next novel, the exercise remains the same.

I'm in the middle of one of those hot flashes right how with *The Innkeeper's Husband*. Everything's flowing, the narrative is coming together, and I'm at a point in the writing where I can not only see what the completed work will look like, but why it will look like that. Like Mr. Irving, I also have a built in mechanism for interrupting my creative flow when it's pouring blood in all the right places. It's called My Life. Many mornings I wake up feverish and needing to write. Too bad. At 0500, I have to go to work. When I get back around noon, the inn invades my creative space. And then there's teaching, and family, and baseball, and The Food Network. I get to write on Saturdays and Sundays, and I have to concur with what Irving said: When I return to the work, I always discover new possibilities in the storytelling.

Wednesday, August 8, 2007
Don't Ever Do This

There are no rules. Sort of. Let me tell you a story.

When I was a little boy, my father was a lobster fisherman, among other things. But he was also a mechanic, with an uncanny ability and reckless courage to fix almost anything cast in metal. I would sometimes watch him work on an engine--usually the diesel engine of his boat--and wonder how he knew what to do. Dad picked up on the curious little boy, and was always careful to emphasize safety. Just before he stuck his hand into the whirling belts of the engine, he'd look at me and say, "Don't ever do this." Then he'd plunge his hands into the land of finger-eating gears and grinding cams and hungry pistons.

What Dad meant was this: he knew all there was to know about that engine. He knew exactly where to place his hands to fix what needed

fixing, and he also knew the risks. He was deliberate and precise because he was a master of the engine. His nickname was Diesel Dan.

The same holds true in writing. When you learn the rules well
enough to forget them, you have a lot of freedom. And that's the spot I
found myself in recently in the writing of *The Innkeeper's Husband*. I decided to do something really radical: I inserted a short story, a work of
fiction, right into the middle of the whirling gears of my non-fiction account of innkeeping. I didn't do it on a whim. Rather, I felt it was the best
way to convey the point of view of the folks who come and stay with us.
So I did it.

I'm not going to lose a finger doing this, and I carefully structured the
work to lead smoothly into this fictional sideroad. But you never know.
Still, it thrilled me to know that I have this ability, that I've got this kind of
ability. And after all, who wants to read something that isn't a little risky?
But just be careful: stories, like engines, are cranky things, sometimes
possessed by gremlins. I've seen plenty of writers nicknamed "Lefty" to
know that.

Friday, October 12, 2007
Publish or Perish

Oh, how the creative have fallen. As the days shift from warm and
sunny to dark and rainy, and the leaves are stripped and left for dead on
the wet pavement, my writing output trickles.

Sometimes two or three days will go by without even a thought of
opening up one of my many writing projects. My work on *The Innkeeper's
Husband* is one of the victims.

Blame always lies with the will of the writer, and my will has been
cannibalized recently by overscheduling. It's no excuse, but it's worth
exploring, if only for the insight the writer might walk away with. First
among time thieves is teaching. I have two classes at CCV this fall, English Composition and Dimensions of Learning. Comp is a demanding

class that takes lots of preparation, and even more homework for the teacher than the students. Reading and commenting on a stack of essays from budding college writers gobbles up time the way I chow down my lunch when I get back from my morning gig at FedEx. That gig (FedEx) is the second leading time bandit. Not only do I give five hours a day there, but I'm physically spent afterwards. Third on the list is the Auberge de Stowe. It's high season around these parts of Vermont, and I think I've made several hundred beds over the past couple of weeks. Add to that all the regular duties of the paterfamilias, plus a desire to get out and hunt a little, and there's just enough time to pass out at night before the alarm clock rings.

But all good writing must overcome the obstacles of life. If I can earn a master's degree while keeping essentially the same schedule as the one described above, I can finish a book, dammit. So I'll press on, and if the blogs are a bit neglected, then imagine me busy at work, writing. Or making beds.

Friday, March 21, 2008
First Blush

One of the things I tell my writing students is that writing is a lot like a relationship. I know, some of you are recoiling at the thought, but consider this: why wouldn't writing be like a relationship? Writing is as human as talking and sex, which are both parts of a relationship. Now that I have your attention, let me explain.

New ideas are exciting. Writers have fits of passion, moments of true clarity, where they envision an entire story, experience every emotion of every character, and are swept away. This is what drives us: to communicate that feeling to everyone else, to share something so important that burns inside us we've got no choice but to write it down, and fast. New relationships are the same way. The initial passion is impossible to resist. Two people simply want everything about each other, and

332

they want to tell the world. But as the wiser among us know, the spike of passion that characterizes a new relationship diminishes. It doesn't go away completely, but it falls in temperature, until the happy couple is left with each other, and all those things they never noticed before. Relationships that are built for the long run take something else: commitment. And it's the same in writing. Ideas flood the writer, but what sticks is what's important to both artist and art.

I'm going through that with the novel I'm writing. The first twenty thousand words came pouring out of me; I was in love. But does this story have staying power? I think it does, and that's because I've got some important things to say through this work. But right now I'm in a regrouping mode. I have to go back, organize my notes a little, make sure everything makes sense. This novel and I are committed to each other, so I know we'll make it.

Coda:

And now, for something completely Goddard…

Reflection. In the Goddard tradition, it's time to think about what just happened. How have I changed? How have you changed? What's different from when we started all this reading and writing and thinking? And since all good writing starts with the truth, that's where I'll begin.

This book is the result of a contractual obligation. It's the last child of a troubled marriage, the embodiment of hope that isn't there. I know that sounds a little heavy, but I also know that a lot of people understand what I mean. When I published my first book, *Name the Boy*, I signed a two-book contract. I've always been amused at the two-book contract. It seems like too good a deal for the writer, especially the new-to-book-publishing writer. Why give someone so unproven more than one book?

I've tried looking at it from the publisher's point of view. What if the author is successful with the first book? There's a chance he or she will leave for another publisher. But what really are the odds an author will be successful, or even make money for a publisher? People in the publishing business know this, but there must be some imperative pushing them to keep signing authors.

From the author's point of view, it's a no-brainer: Would you like a two-book deal if you were an unpublished writer? (The appropriate response is, "Where do I sign?") And sign we do. Of course, we regret it immediately. It's like a chain around our spirit. Commitment, for a writer, is like a wedding ring for a rogue. The whole reason we get into the writing game is to be free from commitment, to run barefoot through our imaginations. We regret it because as soon as the first book has been published, and the reality of writing another one—to fulfill a contract, no less—sets in, we feet confined. Suddenly, we have to do something, for someone else.

That's how this book happened. *Name the Boy* came out and sold about three hundred copies, and I realized that I didn't want to go through that exercise again. That exercise was something unique to the publisher of that book. Part of the deal I signed onto was to be actively involved in the promotion and marketing of the book. In my case that meant pre-selling a certain number of copies before the publisher initiates the print run. It's a fail-safe system that limits the exposure on the publisher's side. If he's guaranteed enough book sales to cover his costs, he knows that there's a chance the book will make a little extra money, and everyone will be happy. At least that's how it's supposed to work.

The exercise taught me how much I dislike being involved in the publishing business. I'm unhappy to report that I'm not a tireless promoter of my own work. I think part of that had to do with the format of my first book. A collection of short stories is almost un-saleable, except to certain literary types. While I managed to reach my pre-sale goals and get the book published, I hated asking people for money before my book was out. It seemed backwards. So when it came time for a second book, I wasn't sure what to do. I'd begun to write a novel over the winter, but that was not even close to being finished. I had some short stories, but I didn't feel strongly enough about them to collect them. So what to do?

Discovering Edward Abbey's book was a watershed moment. And now, after completing this book, I hope it can be used as a teaching tool. I hope the writing in here provides places for readers to explore different avenues and incite new thinking about their own craft. There's certainly enough to look at. I hope you've enjoyed the ride.

Notes

1 Hemingway, Ernest. New York Times, "Hemingway is Winner of Nobel Literature Prize." Last modified 1999. Accessed October 30, 2011. http://www.nytimes.com/books/99/07/04/specials/ hemingway-nobellit.html.

2 Flannery O'Connor. *Mystery and Manners*. (New York: Farrar, Straus and Giroux, 1970), 67.

3 Edward Abbey. *Slumgullion Stew: An Edward Abbey Reader*. (New York: E.P. Dutton, Inc., 1984), ix.

4 David Quammen. *Blood Lines*. (St. Paul, Minnesota: Graywolf Press, 1988), 2.

5 Ibid, 6.

6 Ibid, 3.

7 Ibid, 14.

8 Ibid, 15.

9 Ibid, 25.

10 Ibid, 27.

11 James Joyce. *Dubliners*. (New York: The Modern Library, 1967), 9.

12 Ibid, 12.

13 Ibid, 17.

14 Ibid, 210.

15 Annie Proulx. *Heart Songs*. (New York: Simon & Schuster, 1995), 13.

16 Ibid, 73.

17 Ibid, 79.

18 Ibid, 33.

19 Ernest Hemingway. *Islands in the Stream*. (New York: Charles Scribner's Sons, 1970), 82.

20 Ibid, 85.

21 Ibid, 96.

22 Ibid, 97.

[23] John Irving. *Trying to Save Piggy Sneed*. (Arcade Publishing, New York: 1996), 217.

[24] Ibid, 322.

[25] Ibid.

[26] Ibid, 286.

[27] Carson McCullers. *The Ballad of the Sad Café*. (New York: Bantam, 1991), 25.

[28] Ibid, 115.

[29] Ibid.

[30] Avrahm Yarmolinski, ed. *The Portable Chekhov*. (New York: Penguin, 1977), 62.

[31] Ibid, 63.

[32] Ibid, 75.

[33] Ernest Hemingway. *The Garden of Eden*. (New York: Collier, 1987), 17.

[34] Ibid, ix.

[35] Matlaw, Ralph E. *Fathers and Sons, Ivan Turgenev: The Author on the Novel; Contemporary
Reactions; Essays in Criticism*. Edited and Translated by Ralph E. Matlaw. (New York:
W.W. Norton and Company, 1989), 183.

[36] Turgenev, Ivan S. *Fathers and Sons*. Translation by Constance Garnett. (New York: Walter J.
Black, 1942), 63.

[37] Ibid, 190.

[38] Ibid, 73.

[39] Ibid.

[40] Ibid, 99.

[41] Matlaw, *Fathers and Sons*, 380.

[42] Turgenev, *Fathers and Sons*, 96.

[43] Ibid, 73.

[44] Ibid, 336.

[45] Andre Dubus. *The Times Are Never So Bad*. (Boston: David R. Godine, 1983), 26.

[46] Ibid, 65.

[47] Ibid, 115.

[48] Ibid, 131.

[49] Ibid, 165.

[50] Ibid.

[51] Ibid, 180.

[52] John Irving. *Trying to Save Piggy Sneed.* (New York: Arcade Publishing, 1996), 350.

[53] John Irving. *The Imaginary Girlfriend.* (New York: Ballentine Books, 1996), 74.

[54] Josie P. Campbell. *John Irving: A Critical Companion.* (Westport, Connecticut: Greenwood Press, 1998), 2.

[55] John Irving. *The World According to Garp.* (New York: The Modern Library, 1998), 140.

[56] Ibid, 186.

[57] Campbell, *John Irving,* 12.

[58] Irving, *Imaginary Girlfriend,* 76.

[59] John Irving. "Garp Revisited." *Saturday Night.* May, 1998, 71-75.

[60] Campbell, *John Irving,* 1.

[61] Irving, *Garp,* 654.

[62] Edgar Johnson. *Charles Dickens: His Tragedy and Triumph, Volumes One & Two.* (New York: Simon and Schuster, 1952), 677.

[63] Ibid, 982.

[64] Ibid, 983.

[65] Edgar Rosenberg, ed. *Charles Dickens: Great Expectations. Authoritative Text, Backgrounds, Contexts, Criticism.* (New York: W.W. Norton & Co, 1996), 557.

[66] Ibid, 558.

[67] Ibid, 50-51.

[68] Johnson, *Charles Dickens,* 32.

[69] Ibid.

[70] Baruch Hochman and Ilja Wachs. *Dickens: The Orphan Condition.* (Cranbury, New Jersey: Associated University Press, 1999), 200.

[71] William Pollack, Ph.D. *Real Boys.* (New York: Henry Holt, 1998), 124.

[72] Irving, *Garp*, 36.

[73] Ibid, 29.

[74] Ibid, 92.

[75] Ibid, 274.

[76] Ibid, 35.

[77] Ibid, 55.

[78] Ibid, 5.

[79] Kim McKay. "Double Discourses in John Irving's *The World According to Garp.*" *Twentieth Century Literature* 38 (1982): 457-467.

[80] Charles Dickens. *Great Expectations.* Kindle Edition.

[81] Irving, *Saturday Night,* 75.

[82] Charles Dickens. *Great Expectations.* Kindle Edition.

[83] Ibid.

[84] Ibid.

[85] Ibid.

[86] Ibid.

[87] Ibid.

[88] Ibid.

[89] Ibid.

[90] Ibid.

[91] Ibid.

[92] Ruth Glancy. "Student Companion to Charles Dickens." Greenwood Publishing Group, 1999: 125-141.

[93] Irving, *Garp,* 122.

[94] Ibid, 219.

[95] Teresa M. Amabile. "Beyond Talent: John Irving and the Passionate Art of Creativity." *American Psychologist,* April, 2001, 235-238.

[96] Irving, *Sneed,* 359.

[97] Irving, *Garp,* 687.

[98] Shawn Kerivan. "The Time for the Hunt Had Come." *The Maine Sportsman,* (October, 1992).

[99] Shawn Kerivan. *A Regular Guy.* (Unpublished, 1992), 31.

[100] Richard Panek. "Packet Four Response." (April 22, 2005).

[101] Richard Panek. "Packet Two Response." (March 11, 2005).

[102] Irving, *Sneed,* 350.

[103] Flannery O'Connor. *The Complete Short Stories.* (New York: Farrar, Strauss and Giroux, 1971), viii.

[104] Hemingway, Ernest. Nobel Prize, "Ernest Hemingway--Banquet Speech." Accessed October 30, 2011. http://www.nobelprize.org/nobel_prizes/literature/laureates/1954/ hemingway-speech.html.

[105] Julia Cameron. *The Right to Write.* (New York: Jeremy P. Tarcher, 1998), 233.

[106] Natalie Goldberg. *Wild Mind.* (New York: Bantam, 1990), 2.

[107] Tom Bailey, ed. *On Writing Short Stories.* (New York: Oxford University Press, 2000), 80.

[108] Shawn Kerivan. "The Feral Father." *Backpacker Magazine.* September, 1994.

[109] John Irving. "A Reader's Guide." *The Fourth Hand.* (New York: Ballentine, 1992), 319.

www.ingramcontent.com/pod-product-compliance
Lightning Source LLC
Chambersburg PA
CBHW062157270326
41930CB00009B/1564